HUSO 2016

The Second International Conference on Human and Social Analytics

November 13 - 17, 2016

Barcelona, Spain

HUSO 2016 Editors

Els Lefever, Ghent University, Belgium

Dennis J. Folds, Georgia Tech Research Institute, USA

Printed from e-media with permission by:

Curran Associates, Inc.
57 Morehouse Lane
Red Hook, NY 12571

Some format issues inherent in the e-media version may also appear in this print version.

Printed by Curran Associates, Inc. (2016)

International Academy, Research, and Industry Association (IARIA)
412 Derby Way
Wilmington, DE 19810

Phone: (408) 893-6407
Fax: (408) 527-6351

petre@iaria.org

Additional copies of this publication are available from:

Curran Associates, Inc.
57 Morehouse Lane
Red Hook, NY 12571 USA
Phone: 845-758-0400
Fax: 845-758-2633
Email: curran@proceedings.com
Web: www.proceedings.com

Table of Contents

HUSO 2016

Foreword

The Second International Conference on Human and Social Analytics (HUSO 2016), held between November 13-17, 2016 - Barcelona, Spain continued the inaugural event bridging the concepts and the communities dealing with emotion-driven systems, sentiment analysis, personalized analytics, social human analytics, and social computing.

The recent development of social networks, numerous ad hoc interest-based formed virtual communities, and citizen-driven institutional initiatives raise a series of new challenges in considering human behavior, both on personal and collective contexts.

There is a great possibility to capture particular and general public opinions, allowing individual or collective behavioral predictions. This also raises many challenges, on capturing, interpreting and representing such behavioral aspects. While scientific communities face now new paradigms, such as designing emotion-driven systems, dynamicity of social networks, and integrating personalized data with public knowledge bases, the business world looks for marketing and financial prediction.

We take here the opportunity to warmly thank all the members of the HUSO 2016 Technical Program Committee, as well as the numerous reviewers. The creation of such a high quality conference program would not have been possible without their involvement. We also kindly thank all the authors who dedicated much of their time and efforts to contribute to HUSO 2016. We truly believe that, thanks to all these efforts, the final conference program consisted of top quality contributions.

Also, this event could not have been a reality without the support of many individuals, organizations, and sponsors. We are grateful to the members of the HUSO 2016 organizing committee for their help in handling the logistics and for their work to make this professional meeting a success.

We hope that HUSO 2016 was a successful international forum for the exchange of ideas and results between academia and industry and for the promotion of progress in the area of human and social analytics.

We are convinced that the participants found the event useful and communications very open. We also hope the attendees enjoyed the charm of Barcelona, Spain.

HUSO 2016 Chairs:

HUSO 2016 Advisory Committee

Longbing Cao, UTS Advanced Analytics Institute, Australia
Pascal Lorenz, University of Haute-Alsace, France

HUSO 2016

Committee

HUSO 2016 Advisory Committee

Longbing Cao, UTS Advanced Analytics Institute, Australia
Pascal Lorenz, University of Haute-Alsace, France

HUSO 2016 Technical Program Committee

Laura Alonso Alemany, National University of Córdoba, Argentina
Panagiotis D. Bamidis, Aristotle University of Thessaloniki, Greece
Juan Manuel Belda Lois, Universidad Politécnica de Valencia, Spain
Shreyansh Bhatt, Kno.e.sis Center - Wright State University, USA
Christian Bourret, University of Paris East - Marne la Vallée (UPEM), France
Gerd Bruder, University of Hamburg, Germany
Senaka Buthpitiya, Carnegie Mellon University, USA
M. Emre Celebi, Louisiana State University in Shreveport, USA
Wei Cheng, University of North Carolina, USA
Pietro Cipresso, Applied Technology for Neuro-Psychology Lab - Istituto Auxologico Italiano, Italy
Stefano Cresci, IIT-CNR, Italy
Sérgio Deusdado, Polytechnic Institute of Bragança, Portugal
Dennis J. Folds, Georgia Institute of Technology (Georgia Tech), Atlanta, USA
Matjaz Gams, Jozef Stefan Institute, Slovenia
Paolo Garza, Politecnico di Torino, Italy
Leontios Hadjileontiadis, Aristotle University of Thessaloniki, Greece
Yuh-Jong Hu, National Chengchi University, Taiwan
Baden Hughes, Glentworth Consulting, Australia
Clayton "C.J." Hutto, Georgia Tech Research Institute (GTRI) | Georgia Institute of Technology, USA
Abdessamad Imine, LORIA-INRIA, France
Roberto Interdonato, University of Calabria, Italy
Mehmed Kantardzic, University of Louisville, USA
Jonghwa Kim, University of Augsburg, Germany
Andreas Koch, University of Salzburg, Austria
Stefanos Kollias, National Technical University of Athens, Greece
Georgios Lappas, Technological Educational Institute of Western Macedonia, Kastoria, Greece
Els Lefever, LT3 - Ghent University, Belgium
Carson Leung, University of Manitoba, Canada
Georges Linares, LIA - Avignon University, France
Mai S. Mabrouk, Misr University for Science and Technology, Egypt
Sotiris Manitsaris, University of Thessaly, Greece / IRCAM | MINES ParisTech, France
Massimo Mecella, Sapienza Università di Roma, Italy
Hugo Miranda, University of Lisbon, Portugal
Fernanda Monteiro Eliott, Vanderbilt University, USA

Mikolaj Morzy, Institute of Computing Science - Poznan University of Technology, Poland
Farid Naït-Abdesselam, Paris Descartes University, France
Riccardo Ortale, ICAR-CNR, Italy
Carlos Enrique Palau Salvador, Universidad Politécnica de Valencia, Spain
Anabel Quan-Haase, Western University, Canada
João Manuel R. S. Tavares, Universidade do Porto, Portugal
Carsten Röcker, Fraunhofer IOSB-INA, Germany
Marcos A. Rodrigues, Sheffield Hallam University, UK
Paolo Rosso, Technical University of Valencia, Spain
Maytham Safar, Kuwait University, Kuwait
Claudio Schifanella, RAI - Centre for Research and Technological Innovation Turin, Italy
Abdullah Tansel, Baruch College, USA
Nick Taylor, Heriot-Watt University, UK
Maurizio Tesconi, IIT-CNR, Italy
Carlos Travieso González, Universidad de Las Palmas de Gran Canaria, Spain
Lorna Uden, Staffordshire University, UK
Mark van den Brand, Eindhoven University of Technology, Netherlands
Iraklis Varlamis, Harokopio University of Athens, Greece
Ben Verhoeven, CLiPS Research Center | University of Antwerp, Belgium
Chunyan Wang, Pinterest Inc., USA
Xufei Wang, LinkedIn Corporation, USA
Toyohide Watanabe, Nagoya University, Japan
Matthias Wieland, Universitaet Stuttgart, Germany
Quanzeng You, University of Rochester, USA
Erliang Zeng, University of South Dakota, USA

Copyright Information

Mining Weighted Leaders and Peripheral Workers in Organizational Social Networks based on Event Logs

Alessandro Berti

SIAV
35030 Rubano PD
Email: alessandro.berti89@gmail.com

Abstract—**Identifying important, influent individuals in a social network has been, for decades, an interesting analysis, that can lead in business contexts to a better understanding of the community structure and workers' behavior (considering, e.g., performance). In this paper, the focus is on social networks extracted from event logs, and a more powerful definition of leadership is introduced taking into account the fact that leaders may have different importance inside the organization. This concept is useful also in identifying peripheral workers, that are far from leaders. In an assessment done on the BPI Challenge 2012 event log, peripheral workers showed better performance in comparison to other workers. This discovery has been explained using Social Psychology concepts and considering several characterizations of peripheral workers.**

Keywords–Weighted Leaders; Peripheral Workers; Clustering; Social Network Analysis; Sociology.

I. INTRODUCTION

An important information about the social structure of an organization regards leadership. A leader is a person that holds a dominant or superior position within its field, and is able to exercise a high degree of control or influence over others. Much emphasis has been given by the literature to the importance of leaders in the functioning of an organization. Research on leader-member exchange [1] shows that normal workers' performance is influenced by the relation with their leader. Other studies [2][3] show that effective leaders can be generally found in the center of a social network, according to a centrality measure (see for instance [4][5]). These studies are sociometric. Sociometry [6] is a science that can be applied in business contexts, like performance management [7][8]. Blondel et al. [9] is particularly interesting because it speaks about a method to find social leaders inside an organization and how to use that information to increase the business insights (improving the community structure and the graph visualization).

In this paper, the focus has been switched from a socio-metric approach (based only on relations between individuals) to an event log approach, because it could be more powerful. In doing so, only social networks extracted from event logs [10] have been considered; they are particularly meaningful in business contexts [11]. The notion of weighted leaders will be explained (in Section 3), a simple algorithm to find them will be introduced (in Section 3) and, moreover, an improved clustering algorithm, inspired by the [9] one, will be presented (in Section 3). The concept of *peripheral workers* will then be defined (always in Section 3), showing that they usually perform better than other workers (in Section 4), exploring thanks to existing Social Psychology literature [12][13] various types of peripheral workers.

II. BACKGROUND

Social networks in business contexts [10] may be built upon event logs [14][15], which are collections of information about events happening in the organization. These include the event's timestamp; the process instance in which the event is deployed; the event's originator (i.e., the worker who does the event). A point that may need to be clarified is that, in Business Process Intelligence [16] terminology (BPI is the analysis of business processes using IT systems), an event is always instantaneous. The concept that many might be familiar with is the one of activity. To understand the difference, To understand the difference, we could think of "Cooking a pasta" as an activity built of possibly two events: a start (instantaneous) event and a completion event (in which, we declare to have already cooked the pasta).

Like in [17], a social network can be defined as a weighted graph $G = (V, E)$, where nodes represent individuals (workers), and are identified by integers (thus V, the set of nodes, is a subset of $\mathbb{N}$); edges represent relations between individuals, and are identified by couples $e = (i, j)$ (where i and j are identifiers of nodes; the set of edges E is a subset of $V \times V$); weights are associated to edges, and are the *strength* of the relationship represented by the corresponding edge (mathematically, they can be understood as functions from E to $\mathbb{R}$). Given an edge $(i, j) \in E$ the associated weight is denoted as $w((i, j)) \in \mathbb{R}$).

To effectively build the social network, a weight (between 0 and 1) to relations between individuals has to be assigned. This can be done calculating a metric between individuals. Van der Aalst et al. in [10] propose several metrics, like the Handover of Work (HoW) metric, that measures how many times the work of an individual for a process instance is followed by the work of another individual; and the Working Together (WT) metric, that measures how many times two individuals work together in process instances. In this paper, the focus will be mainly on the WT metric, as the collaborative distance between leaders and other individuals is considered (WT(p_1,p_2) is the ratio of the number of instances in which both p_1 and p_2 do events and the number of instances, contained in the log, in which p_1 do events). So, the value of the metric is high when two individuals often collaborate.

Information can be mined from a social network using a clustering algorithm, which groups individuals based on their similarity, to extract information about the community structure of the organization [18][19][20]. A clustering C of G is a family of subsets of V such that each node is assigned to exactly one cluster and a function $C : V \to \mathbb{N}$ where $C(v) = i \iff v \in S_i$ (v belongs to the cluster S_i) can be defined. There are several clustering algorithms [19][21]-[26], but unfortunately the majority of them work on undirected graphs. So, to use them on directed graphs, the graph has to be transformed into an undirected one (i.e., making edges (i, j) and (j, i) to have the same weight).

A difficult task is to evaluate the quality of the output of clustering algorithms. In the context of social networks, the most popular criteria to judge the quality of a clustering is *modularity*. Modularity is a concept, described in [21], that aims to measure group cohesion inside communities and separation between them. The higher is the modularity, the better the quality of the detected communities is. Some clustering algorithms try to maximize directly modularity (e.g., [21]). Also nodes centrality (degree centrality [27], pagerank centrality [28], betweenness centrality [5]) may be an important factor to understand which individuals are important in their group and to find overlapping communities [19][29].

Having an event log, however, means having more information than the ones contained in Social Networks extracted from the metrics: a Business Process Improvement analysis can be done [15]. An interesting analysis might regards instances completion times. Indeed, instances with an high duration may be dangerous (for example, breaking Service Level Agreements); while the ones with low duration may signal some positive things inside the organization. This concept, in Lean Manufacturing terminology, is called Lead Time [30]. Indeed, focusing on a process, the mean (M) completion time of instances, the standard deviation (SD) of completion times can be calculated, and after fixing a constant k (as example, $k = 1$) one can consider as "positive" instances the ones whose duration is below $M - k \cdot SD$, as "normal" instances the ones whose duration is between $M - k \cdot SD$ and $M + k \cdot SD$, as "negative" instances, or instances whose duration exceeds Lead Time, the ones whose duration is above $M + k \cdot SD$.

Another interesting Lean Manufacturing-inspired concept is the Flow Rate. It measures the ratio of the quantity of time in which the instance is actively worked and the instance duration. In other words, it is a measure of how many long "holes" there are between the completion of an activity and the start of the next activity. So, instances with lower Flow Rate are being worked in a more systematic way.

III. WEIGHTED LEADERS AND PERIPHERAL WORKERS

In this section, we will define the concepts of weighted leaders and peripheral workers, and we will propose a method to find weighted leaders.

A. Weighted Leaders

Blondel et al. [9] have introduced a method to discover leaders. However, the authors do not consider the fact leaders in an organization may have different weights, i.e., there are leaders which are more important than others.

Definition: A weighted leader is a couple (i, w) where i is a (leader) individual and w is the weight (comprised between 0 and 1) that measures the importance of the leader.

This is meaningful because less important leaders may have a less wide "sphere of influence" than the most important ones, and this observation can be used to improve the community structure (clustering). Indeed, a clustering algorithm is proposed, inspired to the one described in [9] and reported in Fig. 1, that takes into account weighted leaders. It is described in Fig. 2, and consists in inserting each node in the cluster of its most (weighted) near leader. This method takes into account both the (topological) distance and the power / weight of the leader. In the Assessment section, there is a comparison between this algorithm and the one presented in [9].

```
Blondel_Clustering(G, L)
Require: A weighted social network graph G = (V, E, w)
         A set of leaders L = {l_1, ..., l_n}, l_i ∈ V ∀i
Ensure: A clustering C : V → ℕ of G
  C ← ∅ ▷ Clustering, initially empty
  new_C ← ∅ ▷ Ausiliar clustering, initially empty
  i ← 0
  for all l ∈ L do
    i ← (i + 1)
    new_C(l) ← i
  end for
  while new_C ≠ C do
    C ← neq_C
    ▷ π_1 is the projection on the first component
    ▷ So, roughly speaking, I are taking the nodes
    for all n ∈ V \ π_1(C) do
      L_n ← {(k, w((n, k))) | (n, k) ∈ E} ▷ w(e) is the weight
      of the edge
      l_n ← π_1(arg max_{L_n} π_2)
      new_C(n) ← C(l_n)
    end for
  end while
  ▷ After that, isolated nodes are inserted
  for all n ∈ V \ π_1(C) do
    i ← (i + 1)
    C(n) = i
  end for
  return C
```

Figure 1. Blondel's algorithm to cluster organizational social networks, having in input the set of leaders

B. Peripheral Workers

The proximity of a worker to other workers expresses how much the given worker is profoundly embedded in the organization, and is expressed by the weight of the connections of the given worker to other workers. Having introduced the notion of (weighted) leader, there is interest in observing which workers are far from leaders.

Peripheral workers are workers that are far, in the sense of collaboration, from leaders. They can be found by calculating for each worker a quantity, that is called *leader proximity*, expressing the distance of the worker from the leaders. The algorithm to calculate leader proximity, and to discover peripheral workers, is described in Fig. 3: the minimum topological distance from a leader, considering also his weight, is found.

The peripheral workers concept is not strictly coincident with other Social Psychology concepts, but two possible categories of peripheral workers can be considered:

- *Newcomers* are workers that are new in the organization, or were previously assigned to different processes. They can feed new energy to the organization, and new ideas (see [12][31][32]). However, they can be considered marginal in the organization because a new worker usually does not suddenly collaborate with organizational leaders, and his initial collaboration network is usually strict. To enhance their position in the organization, they usually start working harder than their

Weighted_Clustering(G, L_W)
Require: A weighted social network graph $G = (V, E, w)$
A set of weighted leaders $L_W = \{(l_1, w_1), \ldots, (l_n, w_n)\}$, $l_i \in V\ \forall i$
Ensure: A clustering $C : V \rightarrow \mathbb{N}$ of G
▷ π_1 is the projection on the first component
$L \leftarrow \pi_1(L_W)$ ▷ L is the set of leaders, considered without weight
$C \leftarrow \emptyset$ ▷ Clustering, initially empty
new_C $\leftarrow \emptyset$ ▷ Ausiliar clustering, initially empty
$W_L \leftarrow L_W$ ▷ Leader proximity of workers, initially equal to the weighted leaders set
$i \leftarrow 0$
for all $l \in L$ **do**
  $i \leftarrow (i + 1)$
  new_C$(l) \leftarrow i$
end for
while *new_C* $\neq C$ **do**
  $C \leftarrow$ *neq_C*
  for all $n \in V \setminus \pi_1(C)$ **do**
    $L_n \leftarrow \{(k, w((n, k))) \mid (n, k) \in E\}$ ▷ $w(e)$ is the weight of the edge
    ▷ The following is different from the Blondel's algorithm
    $\mathbf{l_n} \leftarrow \pi_1(\arg\max_{\mathbf{L_n}} \pi_2 * \mathbf{W_L}(\pi_1))$
    new_C$(n) \leftarrow C(l_n)$
    $W_L \leftarrow W_L \cup (n, W_L(l_n) * w((n, l_n)))$
    ▷ In the leader proximity set, the worker with its leader proximity have been inserted
  end for
end while
▷ After that, isolated nodes are inserted
for all $n \in V \setminus \pi_1(C)$ **do**
  $i \leftarrow (i + 1)$
  $C(n) \leftarrow i$
end for
return C

Figure 2. The algorithm to cluster organizational social networks, having in input the set of weighted leaders

mates [33], and this suggests that peripheral workers of this category may offer better performance than other workers. Also, they may motivate old-timers to reflect on the group's work practices [34][35][36], and be a source of diversity regarding the skills and values, which can stimulate the group to consider new ideas and adopt new practices [32][37][38], and this can also contribute to better performances.

- Workers suffering phenomenons similar to *social exclusion* [39], so they are not, or are not considered by other workers, full part of the organizational processes and work force. Social exclusion usually leads to offering a lower performance level [40]. However, possible reasons could be asserted on why peripheral workers may not be full part of the organizational work force, yet offering a good performance level: they are external collaborators or consultants (so they do not always work for the organization). They might have a good working behaviour in order to convince the organization to collaborate again with them. This category contains also workers with expiring contracts that wish to be called again by the organization. A second reason is that they might not feel adequately considered by colleagues, and work hard in order to improve their position in the organization (see [41]).

Peripheral_Workers(G, L_W, t)
Require: A weighted social network graph $G = (V, E, w)$
A set of weighted leaders $L_W = \{(l_1, w_1), \ldots, (l_n, w_n)\}$, $l_i \in V\ \forall i$
A threshold t for peripheral workers
Ensure: A set of peripheral workers P
▷ π_1 is the projection on the first component
$L \leftarrow \pi_1(L_W)$ ▷ L is the set of leaders, considered without weight
$P \leftarrow \emptyset$ ▷ P is the set of peripheral workers, initially empty
$W_L \leftarrow \emptyset$ ▷ Leader proximity of workers, initially empty
*new_*$W_L \leftarrow L_W$ ▷ Ausiliar set of workers' leader proximity, initially equal to the set of weighted leaders
while *new_*$W_L \neq W_L$ **do**
  $W_L \leftarrow$ *new_*W_L
  for all $n \in V \setminus \pi_1(W_L)$ **do**
    $L_n \leftarrow \{(k, w((n, k))) \mid (n, k) \in E\}$ ▷ $w(e)$ is the weight of the edge
    $l_n \leftarrow \pi_1(\arg\max_{L_n} \pi_2 * W_L(\pi_1))$
    $W_L \leftarrow W_L \cup (n, W_L(l_n) * w((n, l_n)))$
    ▷ In the leader proximity set, the worker with its leader proximity is inserted
  end for
end while
▷ After that, isolated nodes are inserted
for all $n \in V \setminus \pi_1(W_L)$ **do**
  $W_L \leftarrow W_L \cup (n, 0)$
end for
for all $(w, v) \in W_L$ **do**
  ▷ v is the leader proximity of worker w
  if $v < T$ **then**
    $P \leftarrow P \cup \{w\}$
  end if
end for
return P

Figure 3. The algorithm to discover peripheral workers in a social network, having in input the set of weighted leaders and a threshold (for peripheral workers).

Blondel_Leaders(G)
Require: A weighted social network graph $G = (V, E, w)$
Ensure: A set of social leaders L
$L \leftarrow \emptyset$ ▷ Set of leaders, initially empty
for all $n \in V$ **do**
  $N_n \leftarrow \{k \mid (n, k) \in E\} \setminus \{C(n)\}$ ▷ Compute the set of different nodes in the neighbourhood of n
  if $N_n \neq \emptyset$ **then**
    Is_Leader $\leftarrow 1$
    for all $k \in$ *Neigborhood*(n) **do**
      ▷ 3-*cl*(k) counts the number of 3-cliques in G which k belong to
      if 3-*cl*$(k) >$ 3-*cl*(n) **then**
        Is_Leader $\leftarrow 0$
      end if
    end for
    if *Is_Leader* $= 1$ **then**
      $L \leftarrow L \cup \{n\}$
    end if
  end if
end for
return L

Figure 4. Blondel's algorithm to discover leaders in a social network

Weighted_Leaders(LOG, E)
Require: An event log LOG
A weighted social network graph $G = (V, E, w)$
Ensure: A set of weighted leaders L_W
$L_W \leftarrow \emptyset$ ▷ Set of weighted leaders, initially empty
$N \leftarrow \emptyset$ ▷ Number of instances for worker, initially empty
modularities $\leftarrow \emptyset$ ▷ Set of modularities for different number of weighted leaders
$n_{max} \leftarrow \max_w n(w)$ ▷ The greatest number of instances in LOG in which a single worker collaborated
for all $w \in V$ **do**
$N(w) \leftarrow n(w)$ ▷ Count the number of instances in LOG in which the worker w does something,
▷ and do the ratio with n_{max}
end for
order_decreasing(N)
for $i = 1, \ldots, \mid V \mid$ **do**
$L_{temp} \leftarrow$ *take_first*(N, i) ▷ Take first i elements in accordance to ordering
modularities $\leftarrow$
(i, *modularity*(*Weighted_Clustering*(G, L_{temp})))
▷ It computes the modularity of the clustering obtained using the proposed algorithm
end for
▷ π_1 is the projection on the first component
$i_{max} \leftarrow \pi_1$ (arg $\max_{modularities} \pi_2$)
$L_W \leftarrow$ *take_first*(N, i_{max})
return L_W

Figure 5. The algorithm to discover weighted leaders in a social network.

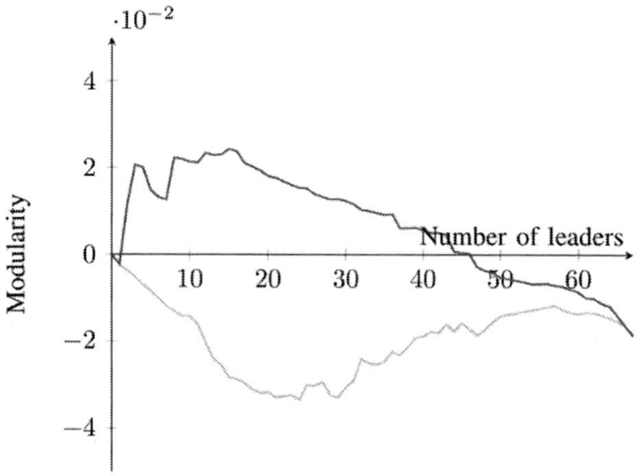

Figure 6. Modularity results of BPI Challenge 2012's Working Together based social network, using Blondel's Leaders-based clustering algorithm and the (weighted) Leaders-based clustering algorithm.

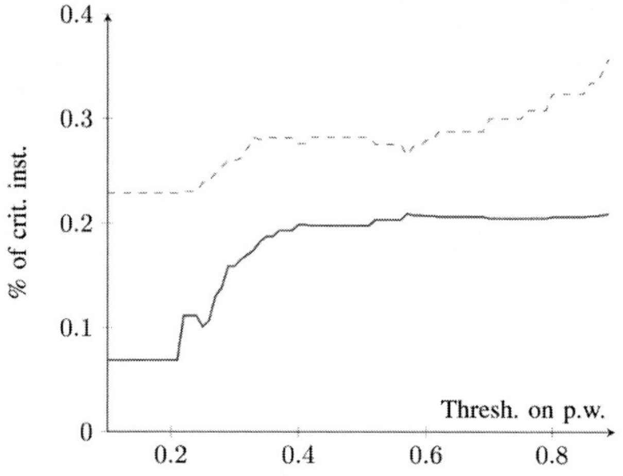

Figure 7. Mean percentage of process instances exceeding Lead Time (which is set to be $M+k{\cdot}SD$ with $k = 1.5$) for peripheral workers and other workers.

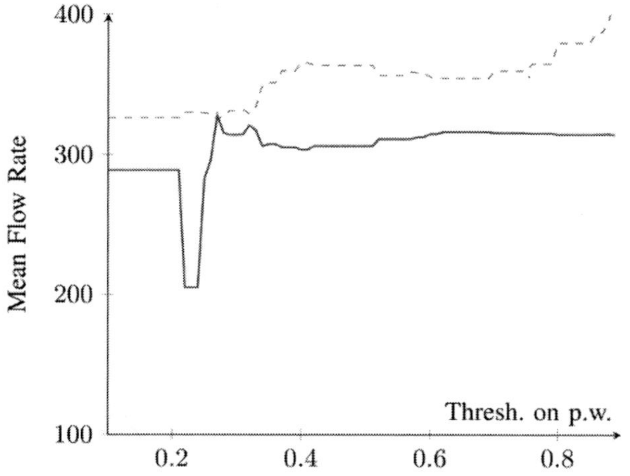

Figure 8. Mean Flow Rate of process instances exceeding Lead Time (which is set to be $M+k{\cdot}SD$ with $k = 1.5$) for peripheral workers and other workers.

An interesting theory related to this is *job embeddedness* [42]. This theory explains why workers wish to be included in an important network of relations inside the organization, as the ones most embedded in the organizational social network (i.e., having strong ties with other workers, and with leaders) have the best chance to retain the work. Or, finally, they could be members of the group that once were full members but lost their position because they failed to live up with expectations of the group (these workers were studied in [43]). This could explain their good performances as an attempt to being considered again. Basing always on [43], if they succeed in re-doing a socialization, they may resume their activities as full members.

The previous one should not be considered as conclusive categories, but are useful to categorize part of the peripheral workers, while some ones are out of these categories. In the assessment we will see that peripheral workers offer however a good performance, and this could be explained also by other reasons. Peripheral workers, given their marginality in the organization, are assigned to simpler instances. These,

TABLE I. LIST OF WORKERS IN THE BPI CHALLENGE 2012 EVENT LOG.

Worker	Number of cases worked	Leader weight	Mean Flow Rate	% of critical cases worked	Leader proximity
10861	**1786**	**1.000**	**280.696**	**23.124 %**	**1.000**
11181	**1736**	**0.972**	**343.687**	**24.654 %**	**0.972**
11169	**1714**	**0.960**	**275.473**	**17.970 %**	**0.960**
10913	**1664**	**0.932**	**315.914**	**24.700 %**	**0.932**
11119	**1662**	**0.931**	**317.680**	**24.007 %**	**0.931**
11180	**1578**	**0.884**	**284.269**	**26.869 %**	**0.884**
10909	**1555**	**0.871**	**328.306**	**26.238 %**	**0.871**
11203	**1527**	**0.855**	**318.556**	**24.100 %**	**0.855**
11189	**1424**	**0.797**	**301.353**	**21.348 %**	**0.797**
11201	**1414**	**0.792**	**295.160**	**25.672 %**	**0.792**
10982	**1344**	**0.753**	**304.367**	**21.280 %**	**0.753**
11049	**1245**	**0.697**	**290.165**	**14.056 %**	**0.697**
11259	**1094**	**0.613**	**367.576**	**17.367 %**	**0.613**
11122	**1061**	**0.594**	**401.087**	**19.039 %**	**0.594**
10899	**1033**	**0.578**	**368.085**	**13.843 %**	**0.578**
10881	1026	0.574	399.833	25.536 %	0.281
10138	1022	0.572	365.311	11.057 %	0.266
11179	1003	0.562	341.545	24.128 %	0.308
10932	1000	0.560	328.229	21.400 %	0.287
10910	986	0.552	405.910	15.822 %	0.265
11121	942	0.527	286.044	20.170 %	0.324
11000	914	0.512	251.099	27.790 %	0.338
10609	892	0.499	285.194	14.574 %	0.282
11003	861	0.482	331.269	23.229 %	0.285
10889	786	0.440	312.309	21.883 %	0.261
10972	771	0.432	327.024	13.619 %	0.313
10863	746	0.418	247.067	24.799 %	0.328
10809	744	0.417	303.471	20.699 %	0.324
11009	725	0.406	336.090	20.552 %	0.279
10929	675	0.378	294.035	20.741 %	0.302
10939	647	0.362	315.541	19.784 %	0.345
10629	640	0.358	363.460	13.438 %	0.255
11019	568	0.318	204.465	21.127 %	0.289
10912	536	0.300	280.276	15.485 %	0.245
11202	482	0.270	0.000	0.000 %	0.274
11002	467	0.261	214.214	29.550 %	0.369
10933	405	0.227	395.922	20.494 %	0.310
10789	369	0.207	416.841	17.344 %	0.261
10931	367	0.205	234.828	26.703 %	0.313
11029	365	0.204	0.000	0.000 %	0.297
11200	*341*	*0.191*	*0.000*	*0.000 %*	*0.234*
11120	*294*	*0.165*	*0.000*	*0.000 %*	*0.156*
11289	282	0.158	324.069	17.376 %	0.274
11299	278	0.156	322.202	27.698 %	0.366
10935	265	0.148	340.945	31.698 %	0.345
11300	263	0.147	649.293	6.084 %	0.244
11302	262	0.147	354.620	14.885 %	0.323
11309	229	0.128	451.385	15.721 %	0.314
10880	*226*	*0.127*	*0.000*	*0.000 %*	*0.228*
11319	204	0.114	393.516	16.667 %	0.415
10228	175	0.098	163.990	11.429 %	0.278
10862	*160*	*0.090*	*0.000*	*0.000 %*	*0.221*
10859	*136*	*0.076*	*0.000*	*0.000 %*	*0.219*
10914	135	0.076	251.794	38.519 %	0.393
10971	*130*	*0.073*	*0.000*	*0.000 %*	*0.192*
10188	*87*	*0.049*	*288.814*	*6.897 %*	*0.098*
11001	60	0.034	73.564	6.667 %	0.248
10779	*26*	*0.015*	*121.232*	*15.385 %*	*0.215*
11111	23	0.013	0.000	0.000 %	0.338
11079	16	0.009	316.709	43.750 %	0.563
11339	13	0.007	0.000	0.000 %	0.356
11304	*10*	*0.006*	*0.000*	*0.000 %*	*0.194*
10124	5	0.003	487.185	40.000 %	0.513
11269	3	0.002	42.793	33.333 %	0.333
10125	2	0.001	0.000	0.000 %	0.697
11254	2	0.001	0.000	0.000 %	0.884
10821	1	0.001	952.603	100.000 %	0.931

then, require less time and less effort to be completed. They might also be brilliant individuals, being able to work alone without requiring leaders to control them. Peripheral workers are less stressed than other workers: in the assessment, even normal workers with a similar number of worked instances perform worse than peripheral workers. Stress may be fault of leadership [44] recalling all the time workers to their duties and judging commitment. Finally, they might be more free (in work) than other workers. Freedom in a workplace may conduct to a better working behaviour and satisfaction [45].

C. Finding weighted leaders

In this section a method is proposed to discover leaders, and to assign them a weight that takes into account the social network and the event log. It is a very simple way, with some insights on how to improve it described in the "Conclusion and Future Work" section. The approach described in [9] (resumed in Fig. 4) is briefly recalled: given a node (worker), if the number of 3-cliques (a N-clique is a subset of size N of the vertices such that every two distinct vertices are adjacent) it belongs to exceeds the number of 3-cliques neighbor nodes (workers) belong to, then it is considered to be a *social* leader.

TABLE II. LIST OF WORKERS IN THE BPI CHALLENGE 2012 EVENT LOG, SORTED INCREASINGLY BY THEIR LEADER PROXIMITY.

Worker	Number of cases worked	Leader weight	Mean Flow Rate	% of critical cases worked	Leader proximity
10188	*87*	*0.049*	*288.814*	*6.897 %*	*0.098*
11120	*294*	*0.165*	*0.000*	*0.000 %*	*0.156*
10971	*130*	*0.073*	*0.000*	*0.000 %*	*0.192*
11304	*10*	*0.006*	*0.000*	*0.000 %*	*0.194*
10779	*26*	*0.015*	*121.232*	*15.385 %*	*0.215*
10859	*136*	*0.076*	*0.000*	*0.000 %*	*0.219*
10862	*160*	*0.090*	*0.000*	*0.000 %*	*0.221*
10880	*226*	*0.127*	*0.000*	*0.000 %*	*0.228*
11200	*341*	*0.191*	*0.000*	*0.000 %*	*0.234*
11300	263	0.147	649.293	6.084 %	0.244
10912	536	0.300	280.276	15.485 %	0.245
11001	60	0.034	73.564	6.667 %	0.248
10629	640	0.358	363.460	13.438 %	0.255
10789	369	0.207	416.841	17.344 %	0.261
10889	786	0.440	312.309	21.883 %	0.261
10910	986	0.552	405.910	15.822 %	0.265
10138	1022	0.572	365.311	11.057 %	0.266
11202	482	0.270	0.000	0.000 %	0.274
11289	282	0.158	324.069	17.376 %	0.274
10228	175	0.098	163.990	11.429 %	0.278
11009	725	0.406	336.090	20.552 %	0.279
10881	1026	0.574	399.833	25.536 %	0.281
10609	892	0.499	285.194	14.574 %	0.282
11003	861	0.482	331.269	23.229 %	0.285
10932	1000	0.560	328.229	21.400 %	0.287
11019	568	0.318	204.465	21.127 %	0.289

The approach proposed in this paper (described in Fig. 5) is focused on counting the number of process instances worked by the resources. The workers with the greater number of process instances are considered to be leaders. The weight is 1 for the worker with the greatest number of process instances and, for other workers that are considered to be leaders, is the ratio between their number of worked instances and the number of worked instances by the worker with the greatest number of process instances.

But how many of the workers, given they have been sorted by that number, should be taken? One should consider the number of the leaders that, according to the clustering algorithm that has been previously introduced, maximizes the quality of the obtained community structure, measured by modularity. Indeed, the number of leaders that realize the maximum represent possibly a good and synthetic covering of the social network graph.

IV. ASSESSMENT

The assessment has been done on the Business Process Intelligence Challenge 2012 event log. This event log, taken from a Dutch financial institute and regarding an application process for personal loans, has been made freely available to invite business process mining specialists to work on discovering possibly interesting business analysis, using any available approach (including Social Network Analysis).

As explained in the background, social networks extracted from event logs are being considered, so it is required to choose a metric between individuals: the Working Together metric has been chosen. Worker 112 is an automated resource, that is present in almost all instances, and it has been excluded from the analysis.

Table I resumes the obtained results, for the considered

TABLE III. LEADER PROXIMITY AND MAXIMUM PROXIMITY TO OTHER WORKERS IN THE BPI CHALLENGE 2012 EVENT LOG.

Worker	Leader proximity	Max worker proximity
10861	1.000	0.308
11181	0.972	0.327
11169	0.960	0.278
10913	0.932	0.308
10821	0.931	1.000
11119	0.931	0.300
11180	0.884	0.359
11254	0.884	1.000
10909	0.871	0.305
11203	0.855	0.315
11189	0.797	0.298
11201	0.792	0.367
10982	0.753	0.272
10125	0.697	1.000
11049	0.697	0.313
11259	0.613	0.314
11122	0.594	0.271
10899	0.578	0.302
11079	0.563	0.563
10124	0.513	0.600
11319	0.415	0.485
10914	0.393	0.444
11002	0.369	0.396
11299	0.366	0.428
11339	0.356	0.615
10939	0.345	0.345
10935	0.345	0.370
11000	0.338	0.348
11111	0.338	0.348
11269	0.333	0.333
10863	0.328	0.328
11121	0.324	0.324
10809	0.324	0.410
11302	0.323	0.378
11309	0.314	0.367
10972	0.313	0.449
10931	0.313	0.322
10933	0.310	0.363
11179	0.308	0.311
10929	0.302	0.311
11029	0.297	0.334
11019	0.289	0.310
10932	0.287	0.292
11003	0.285	0.301
10609	0.282	0.377
10881	0.281	0.289
11009	0.279	0.279
10228	0.278	0.286
11289	0.274	0.433
11202	0.274	0.282
10138	0.266	0.382
10910	0.265	0.265
10889	0.261	0.280
10789	0.261	0.377
10629	0.255	0.366
11001	0.248	0.267
10912	0.245	0.276
11300	0.244	0.274
11200	*0.234*	*0.240*
10880	*0.228*	*0.235*
10862	*0.221*	*0.250*
10859	*0.219*	*0.228*
10779	*0.215*	*0.231*
11304	*0.194*	*1.000*
10971	*0.192*	*0.192*
11120	*0.156*	*0.177*
10188	*0.098*	*0.126*

social network, using the proposed algorithms. Leaders (reported in bold) are defined using the criterion explained in Fig. 5, considering the workers having greater leader weight (this was, for completeness, reported for each worker). Then, for each worker, (worked) process instances whose duration exceeded Lead Time (which is set to be $M + k \cdot SD$, with $k = 1.5$) have been considered, calculating the mean Flow Rate, and reporting also the percentage of "critical" process instances over the number of overall worked instances. Peripheral workers (which are emphasized in italic) are the ones with lower leader proximity (in this table, the ones with measure < 0.24 are considered).

The list of leaders was found using the algorithm described in Fig. 5, with their number established trying to maximize the modularity. For $N = 15$ there is a value of modularity equal to 0.02431, which is better than the value of modularity obtained applying the algorithm described in [9] (that produces a modularity of -0.02834). So, the weighted leaders-based algorithm manages to get a better description of the community structure than the algorithm described in [9]. Also, this is not due to the chosen number of leaders: Fig. 6 (line coloured light gray represents modularity results for Blondel's Algorithm on these differently-sized lists of leaders; line with dark gray colour represents modularity results for our algorithm) shows us that, for any chosen number of leaders, the proposed algorithm works better. It provides, in addition, better modularity results than Label Propagation algorithm (that gets a 0.0000) and Multilevel algorithm (that gets a -0.0186), which are commonly used algorithms.

Using the set of (weighted) leaders, leader proximity has been calculated for all remaining workers. The considered peripheral workers are the ones with leader proximity < 0.24: this threshold was chosen for the log because it separates the ones which are peripheral workers from the other workers in Table II. However, in a different log from BPI Challenge 2012 the ideal threshold for peripheral workers is likely to be different. Peripheral workers have definitely a lower percentage of process instances exceeding Lead Time and lower mean Flow Rate.

In Fig. 7 and 8, peripheral workers are shown to perform better than other workers when the focus is on process instances whose duration exceeds Lead Time (that is set to be $M + k \cdot SD$, with $k = 1.5$): there is a lower percentage of these instances and the mean Flow Rate is inferior. This is not dependant on the threshold chosen to decide peripheral workers, as in Fig. 7 and 8.

In Table III is shown that in many times peripheral workers are also far from other workers, not only from the leaders. This confirms their substantial marginality in the organization. These workers are not clearly part of any work group in the considered organization (an hyphotesis may be that they are external collaborators), running the risk of social exclusion inside the workplace. Some insights could be given on a possible "classification" of some of the peripheral workers:

Worker **11304** enters the event log very late (Sat Feb 04 2012): this says that, relatively to the given process, he is a *newcomer*, and he may perform great to let the others know him.

Workers **10859**, **11120** and **10880** are present only at the start of the event log: this says that they are not fully part of the organization. A hypothesis could be that they are external collaborators, so they perform well to being "called again" by the organization, or they have an expiring work contract so they try to work at their best to get a renewed contract.

Workers **10188** and **10779** are not generally involved much in the organization, registering a low number of worked instances and low collaboration with others. They may perform better in order to get more involved in the process (see [41]).

For workers **11200**, **10971** and **10862**, which do not fall in the previous categories, a possible explanation can be provided: the *job embeddedness* theory; they perform good in order to improve their organizational ties and to strenghten their position in the organization.

V. Conclusion and Future Work

In this paper insights on organizational social networks extracted from event logs have been proposed, introducing the concept of weighted leader and showing how to find *peripheral workers*. Basing on these concepts, a clustering algorithm has been introduced, that is similar to the one described in [9], but is based on the concept of weighted leader. Experiments have been carried out on the freely available BPI Challenge 2012 event log, and the leaders were found based on the simple, but effective, count of the worked process instances. In this log, the proposed clustering algorithm produced the best modularity results, and peripheral workers were found to have better behaviour (relative to Flow Rate and to the percentage of cases exceeding Lead Time) than other workers.

The classification of at least some of the peripheral workers has been proposed, in some categories that come from Social Psychology literature. The analysed categories are the *newcomers* and the *social excluded workers*. In the log there is at least one peripheral worker for both the categories, and this lead to possible explanations about the good behaviour (relatively to the considered performance measures) of these workers.

For an organization, given newcomers good behaviour, it may be convenient to involve new people in (existing) processes, rather than being fixed on a static workforce [31]. Also, recurring to external collaborators and contracts that expires seems convenient in order to avoid workers to be static on a process and, in the long period, to lose motivation and performance [34][35][36].

The practical purpose of the proposed methods is to easily find, starting from an event log, high and low performing workers, doing an effective evaluation of employees. The proposed algorithms work on event logs: only few organizations have a process-awareness level such that they collect data in an event log, through Information Technology systems. These logs often are private: there is a very little number of freely available event logs and the chosen one (BPI Challenge 2012, that collects event from a Dutch financial institute) is probably one of the most meaningful.

Also, only events regarding a particular process (application process for personal loans) have been inserted in BPI Challenge 2012: this limits the social network to the people working for that particular scope. In addition to that, one does not know anything other than the information written in the event log. This has lead to a classification of peripheral workers that is plausible but must be seen like an hypothesis, that could not be confirmed given the information in the BPI Challenge 2012 log.

It must also be remarked that information obtained here regard only a process. So, the found leaders and peripheral workers might be leaders, or marginals, only in the given process, not necessarily in the organization.

An open question regards the possibility of a better criterion to discover leaders in the social network. Some ideas that are based on possible calculations on the event log are about introducing some measures, and they are briefly reported:

- A statistical measure of workload (number of things done contemporaneously), searching leaders among the workers having greater workload.
- A notion of criticality among workers, that is high when a worker does a type of activity with no or few possible replacements in the organization. Leaders often do exclusive activities, because of their role, so a good criterion to discover leaders may be calculating workers' criticality and taking the ones with the higher measure.
- Measuring responsability through the in-degree of the worker in the Handover of Work between-individuals metric [10]. Indeed, if there are many handovers, it means that many workers in the organization *need* to consult the given individual, so there is a good possibility that he is a leader.
- Measuring worktime. Leaders usually have more responsabilities, so they work longer.

Analyzing the effect of these ideas, however, is a big task, that goes beyond the purposes of this paper and, given the effectiveness of the measure that counts the number of cases, is left as future work.

References

[1] R. Basu and S. G. Green, "Leader-member exchange and transformational leadership: An empirical examination of innovative behaviors in leader-member dyads," Journal of Applied Social Psychology, vol. 27, no. 6, pp. 477–499, 1997.

[2] D. J. Brass, "Being in the right place: A structural analysis of individual influence in an organization," Administrative Science Quarterly, pp. 518–539, 1984.

[3] M. E. Burkhardt and D. J. Brass, "Changing patterns or patterns of change: The effects of a change in technology on social network structure and power," Administrative science quarterly, pp. 104–127, 1990.

[4] M. E. Newman, "A measure of betweenness centrality based on random walks," Social networks, vol. 27, no. 1, pp. 39–54, 2005.

[5] L. C. Freeman, "A set of measures of centrality based on betweenness," Sociometry, pp. 35–41, 1977.

[6] M. Rostampoor-Vajari, "What is sociometry and how we can apply it in our life?" Advances in Asian Social Science, vol. 2, no. 4, pp. 570–573, 2012.

[7] J. A. Gruman and A. M. Saks, "Performance management and employee engagement," Human Resource Management Review, vol. 21, no. 2, pp. 123–136, 2011.

[8] R. Griffin and G. Moorhead, Organizational behavior. Cengage Learning, 2011.

[9] V. Blondel, C. De Kerchove, E. Huens, and P. Van Dooren, "Social leaders in graphs," Positive Systems, pp. 231–237, 2006.

[10] W. M. Van Der Aalst, H. A. Reijers, and M. Song, "Discovering social networks from event logs," Computer Supported Cooperative Work (CSCW), vol. 14, no. 6, pp. 549–593, 2005.

[11] V. der Aalst et al., "Business process mining: An industrial application," Information Systems, vol. 32, no. 5, pp. 713–732, 2007.

[12] J. M. Levine, H.-S. Choi, and R. L. Moreland, "Newcomer innovation in work teams," Group creativity: Innovation through collaboration, pp. 202–224, 2003.

[13] M. R. Leary and R. F. Baumeister, "The nature and function of self-esteem: Sociometer theory," Advances in experimental social psychology, vol. 32, pp. 1–62, 2000.

[14] W. Van der Aalst, T. Weijters, and L. Maruster, "Workflow mining: Discovering process models from event logs," Knowledge and Data Engineering, IEEE Transactions on, vol. 16, no. 9, pp. 1128–1142, 2004.

[15] B. F. van Dongen, A. K. A. de Medeiros, H. Verbeek, A. Weijters, and W. M. Van Der Aalst, "The prom framework: A new era in process mining tool support," in Applications and Theory of Petri Nets 2005. Springer, pp. 444–454, 2005.

[16] G. Daniela, "Business process intelligence," Computers in Industry, vol. 53, no. 3, pp. 321–343, 2004.

[17] P. J. Carrington, J. Scott, and S. Wasserman, Models and methods in social network analysis. Cambridge university press, vol. 28, 2005.

[18] M. Newman and M. Girvan, "Finding and evaluating community structure in networks," PHYSICAL REVIEW E Phys Rev E, vol. 69, pp. 26–113, 2004.

[19] G. Palla, I. Derényi, I. Farkas, and T. Vicsek, "Uncovering the overlapping community structure of complex networks in nature and society," Nature, vol. 435, no. 7043, pp. 814–818, 2005.

[20] A. Lancichinetti, S. Fortunato, and J. Kertsz, "Detecting the overlapping and hierarchical community structure in complex networks," New Journal of Physics, vol. 11, no. 3, pp. 100–115, 2009.

[21] V. D. Blondel, J.-L. Guillaume, R. Lambiotte, and E. Lefebvre, "Fast unfolding of communities in large networks," Journal of Statistical Mechanics: Theory and Experiment, vol. 2008, no. 10, pp. 201–213, 2008.

[22] U. N. Raghavan, R. Albert, and S. Kumara, "Near linear time algorithm to detect community structures in large-scale networks," PHYSICAL REVIEW E Phys Rev E, vol. 76, pp. 104–120, 2007.

[23] M. Ovelgönne and A. Geyer-Schulz, "An ensemble learning strategy for graph clustering," Graph Partitioning and Graph Clustering, vol. 588, p. 187, 2012.

[24] S. Liu, Q. Kang, J. An, and M. Zhou, "A weight-incorporated similarity-based clustering ensemble method," in Networking, Sensing and Control (ICNSC), 2014 IEEE 11th International Conference on. IEEE, pp. 719–724, 2014.

[25] A. Y. Ng, M. I. Jordan, and Y. Weiss, "On spectral clustering: Analysis and an algorithm," in Advances in Neural Information Processing Systems. MIT Press, pp. 849–856, 2001.

[26] F. D. Malliaros and M. Vazirgiannis, "Clustering and community detection in directed networks: A survey," Physics Reports, vol. 533, no. 4, pp. 95–142, 2013.

[27] T. Opsahl, F. Agneessens, and J. Skvoretz, "Node centrality in weighted networks: Generalizing degree and shortest paths," Social Networks, vol. 32, no. 3, pp. 245–251, 2010.

[28] Y. Ding, E. Yan, A. Frazho, and J. Caverlee, "Pagerank for ranking authors in co-citation networks," Journal of the American Society for Information Science and Technology, vol. 60, no. 11, pp. 2229–2243, 2009.

[29] J. Baumes, M. Goldberg, and M. Magdon-Ismail, "Efficient identification of overlapping communities," in Intelligence and Security Informatics. Springer, pp. 27–36, 2005.

[30] W. J. Stevenson and M. Hojati, Operations management. McGraw-Hill/Irwin Boston, vol. 8, 2007.

[31] J. M. Levine, R. L. Moreland, and H.-S. Choi, "Group socialization and newcomer innovation," Blackwell handbook of social psychology: Group processes, vol. 3, pp. 86–106, 2001.

[32] T. Hansen and J. M. Levine, "Newcomers as change agents: Effects of newcomers' behavioral style and teams' performance optimism," Social Influence, vol. 4, no. 1, pp. 46–61, 2009.

[33] G. R. Jones, "Socialization tactics, self-efficacy, and newcomers' adjustments to organizations," Academy of Management journal, vol. 29, no. 2, pp. 262–279, 1986.

[34] D. C. Feldman, "Who's socializing whom? the impact of socializing newcomers on insiders, work groups, and organizations," Human Resource Management Review, vol. 4, no. 3, pp. 213–233, 1994.

[35] D. H. Gruenfeld and E. T. Fan, "What newcomers see and what oldtimers say: Discontinuities in knowledge exchange," Shared cognition in organizations: The management of knowledge, pp. 245–266, 1999.

[36] R. I. Sutton and M. R. Louis, "How selecting and socializing newcomers influences insiders," Human Resource Management, vol. 26, no. 3, pp. 347–361, 1987.

[37] H.-S. Choi and J. M. Levine, "Minority influence in work teams: The impact of newcomers," Journal of Experimental Social Psychology, vol. 40, no. 2, pp. 273–280, 2004.

[38] H.-S. Choi and L. Thompson, "Old wine in a new bottle: Impact of membership change on group creativity," Organizational Behavior and human decision processes, vol. 98, no. 2, pp. 121–132, 2005.

[39] N. L. Kerr and J. M. Levine, "The detection of social exclusion: Evolution and beyond." Group Dynamics: Theory, Research, and Practice, vol. 12, no. 1, p. 39, 2008.

[40] R. F. Baumeister, J. M. Twenge, and C. K. Nuss, "Effects of social exclusion on cognitive processes: anticipated aloneness reduces intelligent thought." Journal of personality and social psychology, vol. 83, no. 4, p. 817, 2002.

[41] J. K. Maner, C. N. DeWall, R. F. Baumeister, and M. Schaller, "Does social exclusion motivate interpersonal reconnection? resolving the" porcupine problem."," Journal of personality and social psychology, vol. 92, no. 1, p. 42, 2007.

[42] T. R. Mitchell, B. C. Holtom, T. W. Lee, C. J. Sablynski, and M. Erez, "Why people stay: Using job embeddedness to predict voluntary turnover," Academy of management journal, vol. 44, no. 6, pp. 1102–1121, 2001.

[43] I. R. Pinto, J. M. Marques, J. M. Levine, and D. Abrams, "Membership status and subjective group dynamics: Who triggers the black sheep effect?" Journal of personality and social psychology, vol. 99, no. 1, p. 107, 2010.

[44] L. R. Offermann and P. S. Hellmann, "Leadership behavior and subordinate stress: A 360" view." Journal of Occupational Health Psychology, vol. 1, no. 4, p. 382, 1996.

[45] A. O. Agho, C. W. Mueller, and J. L. Price, "Determinants of employee job satisfaction: An empirical test of a causal model," Human Relations, vol. 46, no. 8, pp. 1007–1027, 1993.

Tracks to Analyze Emotions around Mediator Artifacts to Improve Training and Business Creation for Unemployed People in French Universities

Christian BOURRET
Research Team DICEN IDF (Information and Communication Devices in the Digital Era)
University of Paris East Marne-la-Vallée (UPEM)
Marne-la-Vallée, France
e-mail: christian.bourret@u-pem.fr

***Abstract* - In France, with the economic crisis and the huge rate of unemployment, the role of Universities has changed in the recent years. They try to promote the creation of new economic activities to attract new people, especially coming from disadvantaged areas in great town suburbs, particularly unemployed young people. We present the experiment of Creators of Activities University Degrees (DUCA) around cooperative devices or Creators' Groups (GC). These DUCA / GC correspond to an individual project, part of a global dynamics in a collective approach. In a perspective of helping disadvantaged people to rebuild their life in a project dynamics of creation of economic activity, information and communication issues are central. We propose some tracks to analyze these cooperative devices through two Mediator Artifacts developed in the DUCA / GC areas of cooperation: the business plan of the activities' creators and the training serious game "Solutia". They help to better master the emotions and feelings of activities' creators to develop their self-confidence and their entrepreneurship skills.**

Keywords - unemployed people; economic activities creation; entrepreneurship ; disadvantadged areas; mediator artifacts.

I. INTRODUCTION / BACKGROUND

In a period of social crisis and of huge unemployment (3.58 million people in full unemployment in France in September 2016), particularly for non-graduated young people in disadvantaged areas, Paugam pointed the importance of "social links" [1] and of solidarity. In this context, in the recent years, the role of University has changed. It is no longer just only to build and transfer knowledge, but also to welcome new people and promote their vocational integration, including the creation of new economic activities. We speak of Social Responsibility of Universities (RSU). There is also the new position of "entrepreneur student" [2]. These evolutions correspond to the need of repositioning the Universities but also other organizations with public service missions, such as *Missions Locales* (ML) or Centre for Information and Orientation (CIO).

According to Azoulay [3], "there are talents in the suburbs but they need to be discovered and developed in different manners". We must give confidence to potential activities' creators and enable their talents to flourish, and also to promote "innovation in everyday life" [4] and especially social innovation.

The University of Paris East Marne-la-Vallée or UPEM, through its component University Institute of Technology (IUT) has managed since 2006 several groups of Creators of Activities University Degrees (DUCA), supported by training partnerships devices, the Creators' Groups (GC). These GC are federated in a national association: National Association of Creators' Groups (ANGC).

In this paper, we first present the researcher's position and the methodology used. Then we explain the specificity of the DUCA – GC devices, pointing particularly on their Information and Communication issues and the question of emotions. We present two emotions' Mediator Artifacts: first a training "serious game" (Solutia) and a second, the Business Plan used as the framework of the economic activity project. Finally, we give some examples of success stories of activities creation before a conclusion insisting on future works.

II. RESEARCHER'S POSITION AND METHODOLOGY

The author of this paper manages DUCAs in the IUT / UPEM and is also member of GC Coordination Committees. His analysis corresponds to a research position described by Bernard et al. [5] as "engaging communication". These researchers outline the dimensions of "engaging position" and that of projects, which is the case for DUCA-GC.

According to D'Almeida [6], organizations move "between projects and stories." The projects correspond to two types of devices: first is the organizational one, and the second she calls "symbolic narrative" part where "stories" (symbolic devices) are essential. Organizations or organizational devices build their own imaginary stories. To take an example in a presentation's leaflet of Val de Marne Creators' Group: "Creators' Groups help to switch from dream to reality." They are based on two core values: "everyone is an asset for the territory", "everyone expressing the desire to create an activity is heard".

From a methodological perspective, the author of this article belongs to the French University's interdisciplinary field of Information and Communication Sciences, in agreement with the approach proposed by Bernard [7] with the convergence of four aspects: meaning, link (relationships, interactions), knowledge and action. He positions in a research action perspective mixing theory and practice to build knowledge for action.

In this work, we meet several concepts. The first concept met is that of "device" (in French, "*dispositif*"), that we consider, according to Foucault [8], with all its socio-technical dimensions. For him, "What I'm trying to identify with that name, is first a decidedly mixed space, with speeches, institutions, architectural arrangements, regulatory decisions, laws, administrative measures, scientific statements, philosophical propositions, moral, philanthropic, in short: the words, as well as the unspoken, are mere elements of the device. The device in itself is the network that can be established between all these elements. Secondly, that I would identify in the device, is precisely the nature of the relationship that may exist between these heterogeneous elements."

In a socio-constructivist perspective, we also rely on the concept of "mediator artifact": "the tools provided by the environment do not only play a role of mediator but also of artifact in that they organize (or reorganize) cognitive functioning" [9] with all the importance of project dynamics [10] [11]. We also rely on the concepts of situations and interactions [12], defined by Zacklad as a logic of "cooperative transactions" [13].

III. THE DUCA – GC AS SOCIO-TECHNICAL DEVICES

In this section, we will show how DUCA-GC corresponds to socio-technical devices as interactions' areas with important Information and Communication Issues.

A. *DUCA and GC as interactions' areas*

According to ANGC, "The Creators Groups seek autonomy and professional integration of unemployed people, including school leavers, based on their desires to undertake as a catalyst". The main goal of the GC / DUCA devices is to restore confidence, especially for young school leavers by leveraging their creativity in a project approach from an individual project based on training (DUCA), developed in training and group work, but also with an individual coaching. So this is an individual project, part of global dynamics, in a collective approach (Creators' Groups).

Since 2006, UPEM / IUT proposed several DUCAs in partnership with different Creators Groups: Val de Marne Department (94), Val Maubuée (Torcy, 77) and, during three years, with the GC Paris 20th.

We will analyze how a new kind of training (DUCA) is based on cooperative processes and may be regarded as a "device" or an "organizational form" created by all the interactions between all the actors, to develop new opportunities for job seekers coming from disadvantaged areas, especially young school leavers. This process creates a new dynamics among all the actors, combining the individual dimension of each project with a collective dynamics.

A DUCA / GC device brings together partners including: 1) A federative structure (*Mission Locale*, Local Plan for Economic Insertion (PLIE), House of Employment (*Pôle Emploi*), other associations, etc.), 2) a University, often through an IUT, 3) a consultancy team in business creation (management shop or *boutique de gestion*, cooperative, industry and trade chamber, etc.).

B. *Importance of Information and Communication Issues*

In a perspective of helping people to rebuild their life [14] in a project dynamics, information collect and communication issues are central. Their analysis will constitute a main part of our grid to consider awareness and management of emotions and feelings as levers of creating economic activities. And so their management included in these activities' creation may help people in difficult situations to rebuild their life.

Firstly, candidates to DUCA / GC are searching in leaflets on business and crafts, books and numerous documents offered by the Local Missions and Centre for Information and Orientation (CIO), specialized websites, etc., information to better formalize their projects. They are helped in their information and documentation work by members of ML or of CIO.

The personal reconstruction of the learner / creator is based on an innovative process of creating an activity that is formalized in an oral mid-term and an end-of-year presentation. This process involves many exchanges and a strong research activity for information and documentation with the help of people resources. It is driven by Mediator Artifact such as Business Plan of each student or meetings around a training "serious game".

This paper corresponds to a complementarity of views: DUCA teachers, GC leaders, trainers, facilitators from Local Missions, members of *boutiques de gestion*, psychologists, and, of course, students-learners, and potential creators of their economic activity.

We propose some tracks to begin to try to analyze emotions and feelings of these actors, especially of young people creating activities around two Mediator Artifacts: a training serious game (Solutia) and the business plan of each activity's creator.

IV. TWO EMOTIONS' MEDIATOR ARTIFACTS

DUCA / GC devices correspond to societal innovative areas to promote interactions. Two Mediator Artifacts may act to reveal emotions and feelings and so help to improve activities creators' skills and their creativity.

A. A training "Serious Game" (Solutia) as first Mediator Artifact to develop ludic interactions

The main goal of DUCA / GC is to help increase creativity spirit and skills of creators of potential economic activity and especially young people. The DUCA-GC training teams try to invent new ways to interest the potential activities' creators in being involved and so changing their life. One specific way consists in a training game: SOLUTIA. It is actually a form of "serious game", but not developed on Internet interactions but on real exchanges in face-to-face situations between some creators (five to eight) with the help (a form of coaching) of a ML member.

This game constitutes a Mediator Artifact to develop ludic interactions to improve interest for cooperation and project dynamics. This training "serious game" may also help converge the representations and develop confidence by creating collective dynamics and some form of pride around a personal project which may be also that of a whole family and, sometimes, of a larger community.

First, this game has been thought and created by Marie Beauvais – Chevalier, member of ML of Marne-la-Vallée / Torcy, coordinator of the GC in Val Maubuée. Solutia's game corresponds to a sort of Monopoly and Game of the Goose (*Jeu de l'Oie*) for learning how to manage company's creation and its traps and opportunities.

In a second step, Solutia has been developed and marketed by a student of UPEM University with the creation of a new enterprise through a new device "Students poles for Innovation, Transfer and Entrepreneurship" (PEPITE) [15].

This business creation by a student around Solutia's serious game illustrates the important evolution of the French Universities, and especially UPEM University. UPEM University tries to develop a new spirit of entrepreneurship through various devices and especially with times of exchanges and interactions between teachers and students such as the "All Creative Day, *Tous Créatifs*" (this year on June 22 th).

B. A second Mediator Artifact: the Business Plan of the creators' projects

We have also observed the emotions and feelings of the actors of DUCA / GC Devices around another Mediator Artifact, the Business Plan of each creator of potential economic activity. The business plan is the main framework of the entire process of monitoring the development of the economic activity of the potential creator. It is a crystallizer of interactions from the beginning of the process (emergence phase) to the final presentation of the project.

The emergence phase allows the potential activity creators to better define their ideas and formalize them. It includes four steps: 1) better knowing their potentiality as project's leaders, 2) better defining the main idea of activity to develop, 3) discover the environment of the project, 4) define the suitability of their personality to the project and its environment. After this phase, the future creator formalized a file, which is the basis for presentation and defending before a jury for admission to the DUCA degree. The interview is always conducted sympathetically to give confidence to the future creator and validate his idea.

The training phase (DUCA) allows future creators to receive specific knowledge to develop skills necessary to manage any activity (company, association, etc.): management, information and communication, legal and tax information, sales management, market survey, project management, etc., and to check the feasibility of the proposed project, specifying the business plan (market survey, financing, cost calculations, etc.). The "case" is finalized and presented before a jury. Pedagogy emphasizes the collective dimension and the practical application of the teachings around creative projects.

V. INTERACTIONS ANALYSIS AROUND MEDIATOR ARTIFACTS INTEGRATING EMOTIONAL DIMENSIONS

The two presented Mediator Artifacts enable us to observe the emotions and feelings expressed in particular by young potential entrepreneurs: a phase of interactions between them in a playful position (Solutia Game) and also with interactions with the teaching team: the Business Plan. Both Mediator Artifacts converge to help to build an individual project in a collective dynamics.

Finally, our findings highlight an analysis process with the transition from the initial and spontaneous emotions of the actors, especially young creators of economic activity, to more lasting feelings, attitudes and behaviors over a long period, in relation with their personality.

We promote a dynamic dimension of integration (integrative approach) of changing emotions and feelings in the situation analysis and interactional approach proposed by Mucchielli (Situational and Interactionist Semiotics) [16] for economic activity creativity, apprehended in a grid of informational and communicational integration of actors' views. For us, it is also the challenge of development of a dynamics (process) around control of emotions and feelings on a rather long term process.

The DUCA / GC devices are also a space for converging management of project approaches [10] and quality approaches. We propose to consider this convergence through three types of processes that exists in any organization or project: the objective to compliance (control), the desire to implement changes and so the commitment to promote creativity and innovation [17]. For us, DUCA / GC devices constitute interesting areas of cooperation to observe this convergence.

The emotional skills of young creators are the central element of an emotional intelligence, in our opinion, not sufficiently taken into account. The human body is both the mediator from which the individual can sensitize his affects and constitutes a communication support of them, according to Martin-Juchat [18].

By helping to set the individual project of business creation in a collective dynamics, the two studied Mediator Artifacts may help to favor a first awareness among activity creators; they are never completely alone and there are levers, networks that they must know how to use to get the right information at the right time and in the right place (informational and communicational skills). This awareness may help activities' creators to restore their confidence and to overcome their shyness. The serious game Solutia also promotes situational skills: it allows students to discover a number of problem situations they can find in their creative activity and so help to overpass them.

The goal of the Mediator Artifacts, particularly Solutia serious game is to (re) give confidence, to raise awareness that everyone has met difficulties in his entrepreneurship's pathway and that they can be overcome. It is good to know how to go beyond emotions such as: fear of failure, withdrawal, frustration, anger, etc. Understanding and better managing emotions by relativizing them may help to recreate a positive dynamics of trust. It is also important to train the activities' creators to be aware of their emotions and feelings, so they are not paralyzed by them, and, therefore, to better manage them and to succeed in their creation of activity process.

We think that learning to better manage the emotions can become a collective goal to develop cooperation and improve skills. It is on this aspect that we propose to the other partners of the GC - DUCA to insist with a view of continuous improvement of existing devices.

Social sharing of emotions is also important for encouraging awareness of group membership [12]. This group is essential to promote the personal development of each potential creator. This integration of emotions and feelings can help to better integrate an individual project of creation of activities in a collective dynamics of exchange of experiences and feelings (Group of Creators) to better understand and support in times of doubt and (re) motivate them. We wish to analyze their mechanisms to best promote these periods of interactions and information sharing for improvement of their projects.

Our observations lead us to propose a broadening of perspectives of Situational and Interactionist Semiotics defined by Mucchielli with the integration of the experiences of the actors and their emotions and feelings [19], particularly for creators of activity.

Another approach to consider is the Sociology of Actor-Network (SAR) [20], even if the business plan and the serious game Solutia are not technical devices, but rather social and managerial devices. The idea that the collective activity ("acting elements") can be considered as a "black box" ("*boîte noire*") seems to match our approach of the business plan as the idea of "hybrid reality composed of successive translations" and the fact that the SAR "has been designed to follow the collective in their making process", which is the case of GC – DUCA devices.

We can then consider a dynamic relational semiotics approach to a certain length: global (approach by the complexity theory in a constructivist way), based on the search for meaning in the interactions' situations between all the actors (including socio-technical artifacts), and of course also including emotions, feelings, experiences of all the actors in a dynamic approach (convergence of the management of project approaches and the process approaches of quality management) to create a dynamic of change, creativity and innovation, mixing individual and collective dimensions.

VI. A Success to better Socially Integrate people By Creating New Economic Activities

Since 2006, 305 activity creators and, especially, young people, have been trained in the IUT of UPEM and 157 graduated, that is to say more than 50%, which is considered as a very positive result by the Ile-de-France Regional Council (CRIF), the main public collectivity giving funds to the GC / DUCA devices.

More globally, nearly 500 people, especially young people, have been sensitized to business creation and reality of the economic constraints of companies. Nearly 35% of the graduated students have created their business or taken over an existing activity; others have been inserted as employees in existing companies (often trade or food activities). Activities creations successes particularly concern the services sector in very different aspects. First, we have food activities such as gluten free bakeries, food to all tastes and cuisines possible, particularly Afro-Asian. Secondly, we have clothes manufacturing companies corresponding to different countries (Japan and Asia fashion, North Africa, etc.) and shops of different types of clothes. We have also organic cleaning companies, communication companies to organize special events (marriage, etc), production of video games, jewelry creations, home automation company, etc. We have also more usual activities such as: nurseries, gardening, public writers, different ways of home help, beauticians, hairdressers, sometimes with itinerant projects. But also, with the reform of school times, we have animation's projects to provide stimulating activities or sports for children after school time, etc.

A great satisfaction during the graduation ceremony for the DUCAs in December 2015 was to see some graduated of previous years come to offer jobs to those who had just come into training.

VII. Conclusion And Future Work

In this work in progress, we propose tracks to analyze emotions and feelings around two Mediator Artifacts to improve training and business creation for specific people in the French Universities.

Since 2006, with DUCA / GC devices, UPEM / IUT, in cooperation with federated partners in the GC, has trained over than 500 students in the creation of activity, including a majority of school leavers. The challenge is now finding additional funding to the specific aid the Regional Council of Ile-de-France. We hope in European subsidies.

In the cooperation areas developed around DUCA / GC devices, the position of "committed researcher" has really, for us, taken all its meaning and corresponds to a personal approach to the RSU, revisited as "social responsibility of the researcher." We have gradually become convinced that the future can be built from micro actions on the territories and on daily innovative practices.

For us, beyond the figures and examples of activities successes creations in various sectors (gardening, personal computers, clothing, cleaning, food, restaurants, personal services, etc.), the more important part is to have renewed hope through a project dynamics to allow potential creators of economic activities, especially school young leavers, to take charge of their destiny, in taking the risk of action for hope to promote a new business vision, resolutely different from "destructive innovation" discussed by Ferry [21], with the disasters of the financial and speculative capitalism. We insist on a first goal, that people dare to do the first step and also meeting the words of Mallory starting to climb to Everest Mountain (1924): "Where there is a will, there is always a way."

This approach focuses on the integration and management of emotions and feelings of all the actors of DUCA / GC devices, particularly those of the potential creators of economic activities. It also incorporates the concepts of "resilience" (ability to move again in a crisis situation), both with individual and collective aspects, of "sustainable development" of territories. Territories are then considered as built by a synergy of local projects, both individual and collective [22] in order to create a collective dynamics and give capacity for innovation and creativity [23].

REFERENCES

[1] S. Paugam., The social link / *Le lien social*, Paris: PUF, 2010.

[2] Available on : http://www.enseignementsup-recherche.gouv.fr/cid79926/statut-national-etudiant-entrepreneur.html. Retrieved 2016, June 26th.

[3] H. Azoulay, "Social Intelligence. The case of suburbs : use networks to go gout crisis / *L'intelligence sociale. Le cas des banlieues : utiliser les réseaux pour sortir de la crise*", in M.-A.Duval dir., New territories of Business Intelligence / *Les nouveaux territoires de l'Intelligence Economique*, Paris: ACFCI – IFIE Ed., pp. 119-146, 2008.

[4] N. Alter, Ordinary Innovation / *L'innovation ordinaire*, Paris: PUF, Coll. Quadrige, 2005.

[5] F. Bernard., S. Halimi-Falkowicz. and D. Courbet, "Experimentation and Environmental Communication: Instituting and Engaging Communication / *Expérimentation et communication environnementale : la communication engageante et instituante*", in D. Courbet dir., Communication and Expérimentation, Paris : Ed. Hermès Lavoisier, vol. 2, pp. 71-113, 2010.

[6] N. D'Almeida, "Organizations between projects and stories / *Les organisations entre projets et récits*", in A. Bouzon dir., Organizational Communication in debates. Fields, Concepts and Prospects / *La communication organisationnelle en débats. Champs, concepts et perspectives*, Paris : L'Harmattan, p. 145 – 158, 2006.

[7] F. Bernard, "The SIC, a Disciplinary of Openness and Decompartmentalization / *Les SIC, une discipline de l'ouverture et du décloisonnement* ", in A. Bouzon dir., op. cit., Paris : L'Harmattan, pp. 33 – 46, 2006.

[8] " The game of Michel Foucault / *Le jeu de Michel Foucault*" (interview), Ornicar ?, n° 10, July, pp. 62-93, 1977.

[9] Available on : http://www.edu-tice.org/approche-th%C3%A9orique/glossaire/concepts-5/. Retrieved 2016, June 26th.

[10] J.-P. Boutinet, Psychology of Project Conducts / *Psychologie des conduites à projet*, Paris: PUF, 1999.

[11] G. Gramaccia, "Quality, Project, Digital : three symbolic variations of Managerial Effectiveness / *Qualité, projet, numérique : trois variations symboliques de l'efficacité gestionnaire*", in C. Batazzi dir., Communication, organisation, symboles, Revue MEI, n° 29, Paris : L'Harmattan, pp. 55-67, 2008.

[12] L. Bègue and O. Desrichard dir., Treaty of Social Psychology. Science of Human Interactions / *Traité de psychologie sociale. La science des interactions humaines*, Bruxelles: De Boeck, 2013.

[13] M. Zacklad, "Economies of Conviviality in Information and Services Societies / *Les économies de la convivialité dans les sociétés de l'information et des services*", Inaugural Lecture / *Leçon inaugurale*, Paris: CNAM, 2009 June 17 th.

[14] G. Lefebvre, Identitary Reconstruction and Insertion / *Reconstruction identitaire et insertion*, Paris: L'Harmattan, 1998.

[15] Available on : http://www.enseignementsup-recherche.gouv.fr/cid79223/pepite-poles-etudiants-pour-innovation-transfert-entrepreneuriat.html. Retrieved 2016, June 26th.

[16] A. Mucchielli, Situation and Communication, Nice : Les éditions Ovadia, 2010.

[17] J.-P. Caliste and C. Bourret, "Contribution to a Typological Analysis of Processes : From Conformity to Agility / *Contribution à une analyse typologique des processus : de la conformité à l'agilité*", UTC Quality Notebooks / *Les Cahiers de la Qualité de l'UTC*, Vol 2, G. Farges and al.., Lexitis éditions, pp. 113-116, 2015.

[18] F. Martin-Juchat, The body and the media. The flesh experienced by the media and social spaces / *Le corps et les médias. La chair éprouvée par les médias et les espaces sociaux*, Bruxelles: De Boeck, 2008.

[19] D. Goleman, Working with Emotional Intelligence, Bloomsbury: London, 1998.

[20] M. Callon, " Sociology of the Network Actor / *Sociologie de l'Acteur Réseau*", in M. Akrich, M. Callon and B. Latour., Sociology of the Translation : Founding Texts / *Sociologie de la Traduction : Textes fondateurs*, Presses de l'Ecole des Mines de Paris, pp. 267-276, 2006.

[21] L. Ferry, Destructive Innovation / *L'innovation destructrice*, Paris: Plon, 2014.

[22] C. Bourret, " Elements for an Approach of Territorial Intelligence as a Synergy of Local Projects to Develop a Collective Identity / *Eléments pour une approche de l'intelligence territoriale comme synergie de projets locaux pour développer une identité collective*", International Journal of Projectics, n° 1, Bruxelles: De Boeck, pp. 79-92, 2008.

[23] M. Godet, P. Durance and M. Mousli, Unleashing innovation in the territories / *Libérer l'innovation dans les territoires*, Paris : Conseil d'Analyse Economique - La documentation Française, 2010.

Dynamic Analysis of Communication Processes using Twitter Data

Ingo J. Timm,
Jan Ole Berndt, Fabian Lorig

Business Informatics 1
Trier University
54296 Trier, Germany
Email: [itimm,berndt,lorigf]@uni-trier.de

Christof Barth,
Hans-Jürgen Bucher

Media Studies
Trier University
54296 Trier, Germany
Email: [barth,bucher]@uni-trier.de

***Abstract*—Due to the omnipresence of information technology and the increasing popularity of online social networks (OSN), communication behavior has changed. While companies benefit from, i.e., viral marketing campaigns, they are challenged by negative phenomena, like Twitterstorms. Using existing empirical approaches and theories for analyzing the dynamics of social media communication processes and for predicting the success of a campaign is challenging as the circumstances and the access to communication processes have changed. Agent-based social simulation (ABSS) provides approaches to overcome existing restrictions, e.g., privacy settings, and to develop a framework for the dynamic analysis of communication processes, e.g., for evaluating or testing OSN marketing strategies. This requires both a valid simulation model and a set of real world data serving as input for the model. In this paper, a procedure model for the creation of a simulation model is developed and the steps are demonstrated by examples.**

***Keywords*–Social Network Analysis; Conversation Detection; Networks of Communication; Data Collection and Handling; Simulation Methodology.**

I. Introduction

With the digital revolution initiated by the Internet, social media platforms have gained popularity and have become an inherent part of our private communication. Nowadays, popular OSN, e.g. Facebook, Twitter, or Google+, have more than 1 billion registered users each and the tendency is still rising. Studies report that approximately 28% of the online-time of internet users is spend in OSN [1]. Companies have observed this trend, too, identified the potential of OSN as a platform of aggregated customer contact, and have shifted the focus of many business units to OSN, e.g., customer service or marketing. This has the benefits of facilitating the determination of the customers' demands, of decreasing the efforts of client contact, and of allowing for an identification of trends at an early stage.

A. Dynamics of Communication Processes in OSN

Especially the high degree of connectivity between the users make OSN beneficial for companies, e.g., in terms of word-of-mouth marketing. Compared to the real world, users of OSN are connected with a large average number of people which results in an increased speed of information distribution. This is utilized by marketing strategies of companies to quickly reach a high level of awareness, e.g., in viral marketing campaigns [2]. The self-replicating process of gaining awareness for a certain product or brand is driven by messages or media which are spread by users and which contain information on the entity that is advertised.

However, the effects and mechanisms which are beneficial for companies in terms of viral marketing and for gaining a high level of awareness can also result in harmful consequences. Due to the fast diffusion of information in OSN, negative comments or criticism can be multiplied in an uncontrollable way and cause in a storm of protest. As these storms often occur on Twitter, they are called *Twitterstorms*. A recent example is the *#CrippledAmerica* Twitterstorm. In late 2015, Donald Trump, an American businessman who announced his candidacy for the US presidential election in 2016, mocked a disabled reporter during a political rally while promoting his book "Crippled America". Stuttering stand-up comedian Nina G took this as an opportunity to ask everyone to use the hashtag *#CrippledAmerica* for writing about experiences with disability [3]. As a result, the hashtag's focus shifted from promoting Trump's campaign and book to reports on peoples' experiences with disabilities and negative responses to his statement.

Currently, companies lack methods to direct or end Twitterstorms and thus sometimes inadvertently promote the distribution of negative statements. But the challenge is not only to avoid negative impacts. Also utilizing positive aspects of OSN communication is difficult as traditional concepts of communication can no longer be applied to analyze the dynamics of OSN. The reasons are multilateral communication behaviors as well as an increased number of interpersonal relationships in OSN. Furthermore, the lack of distribution barriers, e.g., (*"death of distance"* [4]), and the increased size of the potential addressees of messages need to be considered.

This does not only challenge companies. Also from a scientific perspective, there is a lack of empirical methods for investigating social mechanisms and dynamics of communication processes as well as for finding explanations in complex systems [5]. Due to their characteristics, compared to traditional offline communication, innovative concepts and techniques are required for analyzing communication processes in OSN [6]. Related research questions arise from the fields of media studies and communication research, as the content and effects of mass media as well as human communication are in focus. Considering standard research methods from these areas, two major challenges can be identified: On the one hand, operators of OSN restrict the access to data and users applying privacy settings to protect their personal data prevent researchers from accessing relevant information. Thus, field studies can only be conducted when the communication is openly accessible. On the other hand, anonymity and the large number of actors in OSN are factors influencing the behavior of the users. This is why empirical experiments under laboratory conditions are unfeasible, too. It can be assumed that actors will not behave the way they would behave in real OSN, when knowing they are part of an artificial network which is being observed as part of a scientific study. Consequently, alternative approaches are needed for analyzing communication dynamics in OSN, e.g., for evaluating Twitterstorm strategies in advance.

B. ABSS for Analyzing Communication Processes

Computer simulation is a commonly used technique for analyzing complex and inaccessible systems in many disciplines. Here, artificial systems are created by modeling and simulating actors and mechanisms which then can be studied using existing research methods. In contrast to real world systems, simulated systems can be fully accessed, modified, and recreated by the researchers as required. In social sciences, ABSS has been established as a special type of simulation for studying emergent social behavior [7]. By modeling the actors of the real world system as autonomous entities, individual decision-behavior can be simulated and global social phenomena emerge from local interactions of the actors.

For the use in OSN, a data basis as well as a procedure model for the creation of a simulation model are required. The data basis comprises both data about the actors (the users of the OSN), as well as the environment of the actors (the OSN itself). Especially information regarding the types of actors, their actions and goals but also the structure and the opportunities for actions provided by the OSN are needed for creating a suitable simulation model.

Many OSN provide APIs (application programming interfaces) for gathering data about their users and interactions between them. However, APIs provide a large amount of isolated data and the identification of relevant data in terms of ABSS studies is challenging. Thus, the handling of data needs to be assisted and integrated into the process of conducting simulation studies.

This paper presents a first step towards the development of a framework for analyzing communication dynamics in OSN and for testing communication strategies using an ABSS approach. This work particularly focuses on the automated collection, as well as the preparation and selection of relevant communication data from OSN for developing a simulation model as shown in Section IV. In Section V the implementation and evaluation of the approach is described. Here, the syntactical context of the communication will be in focus without further consideration of its semantics. Using the example of Twitter, isolated tweets related to the same topic are selected, individual actors and messages sent by them are derived, and communication dynamics are reconstructed. Furthermore, to evaluate this approach, communication dynamics of Twitterstorms and political discourses are analyzed. Finally, Section VI provides a concluding summary of the findings.

II. Foundations

For analyzing the dynamics of OSN communication processes, the act of communication itself but also the structure of OSNs need to be considered.

A. Communication

Human communication can be considered as a sequence of actions of individuals, where the behavior of a sender influences the behavior of a receiver [8]. It can be understood as a process, where the sender uses a set of characters to encode a message, which then is transmitted using an information medium. The receiver uses an own set of characters to decode and interpret the message and returns a feedback using the same mechanism but not necessarily the same medium [9]. However, a message does not necessarily need to be a verbal utterance but can also be nonverbal.

Each message consists of different layers of information. Without further knowledge, a message is only perceived as a set of characters. By adding syntax, the characters become a message, based on rules defining the relationship between characters. The meaning of a message is determined by its semantics. Because of this, the transfer of information can only be achieved if both the sender and receiver share the same semantics. Pragmatics reveal the intention of the message's sender.

The shifting of communication into technical media is accompanied by a loss of information. The transmission of the message is ensured, yet, the receiver does not know whether the message was interpreted correctly. On Twitter, e.g., the platform determines and restricts the communication processes between users and influences the understanding. The result of the communication can only be returned on the same technical way it has been received, by replying to a Tweet using another Tweet. Thus, we can focus on the analysis and simulation of sequences of Tweets and not take nonverbal communication into account at first. For this, it is necessary to know the structure of the network and how communication is made possible. As pragmatics and semantics need to be abstracted for the simulation model, tools for the automated evaluation of messages are needed and are provided by computer linguistics. Even though our example does not focus on the computer linguistic analysis of Tweets, it is an essential part of the model building process as the large amount of data requires an automated approach.

B. Social Networks

In terms of graph theory, the structure of a social network can be described by a set of users (nodes) and relationships between the users (edges), connecting those nodes [10]. Depending on the direction of the relationship, graphs can be unidirectional, defining the direction of the relationship, or bidirectional, connecting two nodes without providing information regarding the direction of the relationship.

For assessing the importance of a node in a graph, e.g., the most influential users of an OSN, centrality measures can be used [11]. The *degree* of centrality corresponds to the total number of edges a node has and can be used as a measure of a node's interconnectedness in a graph. Nodes having a high *degree* (compared to other nodes) are classified as hubs in terms of information diffusion. When considering directed graphs, the *indegree* (number of inbound edges) needs to be distinguished from the *outdegree* (number of outbound edges).

In contrast to this node-specific measure, the *density* is calculated for an entire network or graph. Doing so, it can be used for comparing different graphs. The *density* of a graph is defined by the ratio of the number of existing edges and the maximum number of edges in case every pair of nodes would be connected by an edge (complete graph).

For simulating communication in OSN, the structure of the network needs to be recreated. A representation of a network using a graph defines the communication channels and the described characteristics give indication of the conditions under which communication is taking place, e.g., who can send messages to whom and how their reach can be assessed.

C. Computational Linguistics

In addition to the structure, OSN consist of messages which are send between the users. For analyzing communication processes, the content of the messages is of relevance, too. It provides the researcher information about the intention as well as the context of communication. Thus, it is desirable to automatically classify the topic of individual messages and communication processes. Doing so, a first impression of the content of communication is given which facilitates the researcher's process of finding and selecting relevant communication processes. Furthermore, a basis for the abstraction of the content for the modeling process is provided. Yet, as the messages consist of natural language, analyzing the content in an automated way is challenging. *Computational linguistics* focuses on the modeling and processing of natural language and provides suitable techniques.

1) Machine Learning: One basic technology used in computational linguistics is *machine learning* which evolved from *artificial intelligence*. In contrast to other algorithms following hard-coded program instructions, *machine learning* algorithms learn from experiences gained from data or from models build from data [12]. Generally, a distinction is made between three types of learning: supervised, unsupervised, and reinforcement learning. While supervised algorithms try to learn rules from example inputs and outputs, unsupervised learning approaches need to find patterns in data on their own. Reinforcement learning takes place in dynamical environments and will not be considered any further in this paper.

2) Content and Lexical Analysis: When using machine learning algorithms for processing natural language, the text first needs to be divided into its linguistic entities. These include words as well as phrases or even entire paragraphs of a text. For separating words, whitespace characters can be used in most segmented writing systems, e.g., those consisting of Latin characters. The entities received when dividing a text are called *n-grams* and are used for creating a model of the language. In this work, n-grams are used for analyzing the mood of messages, i.e., tweets.

For assigning attributes (tags) to words, *part-of-speech tagging* (POST) is applied [13]. Given a text, POST identifies the grammatical categories of each word, e.g., noun, verb, or adjective. This is challenging, as words may appear in different parts of speech at the same time. Yet, analyzing the mostly used nouns, verbs, and adjectives in a large data set, e.g., a set of Tweets, may provide a first impression regarding the most commonly discussed topics.

When analyzing frequencies of words in a text or when indexing documents, a reduction of the words to their base form is needed. *Stemming* aims at reducing words with a similar or identical meaning, but which differ in its suffix, to its word stem. Here, each language requires own stemming algorithms. A commonly used algorithm for the English language is the *porter stemming algorithm* [14].

Summarizing it can be said that for evaluating communication processes in OSN, content and lexical analysis provide information regarding the topic of a conversation and allow for a first assessment of the Tweet.

D. Related Work

The approach presented in this paper is accompanied by related approaches and disciplines where networks of communication and discourses in OSN are analyzed.

Information propagation aims at identifying a group of users which can propagate an unspecified information, i.e., a message, to as many users as possible. Approaches exist where the topics of communication within OSN are explicitly modeled for providing a topic-aware estimation of the propagation probability [15]. Thus, information propagation provides valuable ex-post approaches for analyzing networks of communication but lacks methods for integrating individual and more complex opinion making processes.

Cogan et al. [16] used Twitter data to reconstruct complete conversations around an initial tweet which is given. This enables a more detailed evaluation of conversation topologies, as social interaction models can be compared to OSN. Yet, only isolated and minor conversations lasting up to six hours were analyzed, not larger networks of communication as they occur in Twitterstorms.

For analyzing political discourses among Twitter users, Hsu et al. [17] examined their participation in discussions. The identification of key users was based on the users' public data, e.g., Twitter ID, location, number of tweets, and *follower-followee-networks*, instead of considering the communicative behavior of the users.

Maireder [18] described discourses on Twitter using three perspectives: networking topics, networking media objects, and networking actors. By connecting these perspectives, the author aims at understanding the process of political opinion-making through Twitter using empirical approaches by hand.

These approaches consider the collection and preparation of data as isolated processes for social network analysis. An integration of data handling as a step of an entire research process for generating theories, testing hypotheses or deriving conclusions is not proposed and an adoption of data handling as part of a simulation study is not performed. Therefore, the approach presented in this paper complements existing approaches such that an agent-based simulation of communication processes in OSN is facilitated.

III. Analysis

For analyzing the dynamics of OSN communication processes, a data basis is needed. As the number of existing OSN is large and as OSN differ in structure and mechanisms, the process of data collection differs, too. In this paper, *Twitter* is used as an example platform due to the size of the OSN on the one hand, and the unrestricted access to data on the other hand. Compared to other OSNs like Google+ and Facebook, Twitter's data is not as much affected by privacy settings and can be accessed using the provided API. Still, the communication processes which can be observed on Twitter are of relevance as they affect the general public and have resulted in cross-media phenomena in the past, e.g., the harlem shake [19].

A. Twitter as a Communication Platform

Twitter was founded in 2006 and, compared to other OSN, its unique feature is the limitation of the message (*"tweet"*) length to 140 characters. Another difference is how friendships are represented. While most OSN consist of bidirectional relationships between users, meaning two users constitute the *friendship* together, a distinction between *followers* and *followees* is made on Twitter. Here, a user actively and voluntarily decides which other users to *follow* for receiving their status updates in an unidirectional way. Following another Twitter participant makes the following user become a *followee*, yet, the user being followed does not need to follow its *followees*. Thus, a connection between two users does not imply that they exchange information in both directions. In consequence, for analyzing communication dynamics, the directions of the relationships need to be considered.

Besides the user network, the hashtag (#) emphasis Twitter provides is of special interest from a media studies and communication research point of view. When publishing messages, Twitter users can make use of two operators for classifying a message. The #-symbol is used for categorizing messages and for marking keywords of a tweet. This simplifies the researcher's assignment of tweets to a certain topic. Furthermore, Twitter provides mechanisms for replying to other tweets and for addressing a tweet to a certain person. Using the @-symbol followed by the name of a user or by putting the prefix *"RT"* (retweet) at the beginning of a tweet, the identification of dialogs or conversations is supported. Due to these features, Twitter has been widely used for conducting online studies of certain subjects or events, e.g., spread of news [20], the activity of diseases [21] or political communication [22].

B. ABSS of Communication Processes in OSN

For developing a dynamic analysis framework which makes use of simulation techniques, the simulation method needs to be chosen according to the phenomena to be analyzed. A special feature of phenomena occurring in OSN, e.g., Twitterstorms, is that they are emergent [23]. Due to the local interactions of the users on a micro level, global effects occur on a macro level. Yet, they can not (entirely) be explained by the local actions. For analyzing, reproducing, and investigating such emergent phenomena, agent-based computer simulation has been established as a standard means. By modeling real world actors, in this case the users of an OSN, as autonomous software agents, individual behavior and anticipation of behavior on the micro level can be simulated resulting in emergent effects on a macro level [24]. The observation of the global phenomena in combination with the knowledge of the actions and interactions of the actors can then be used for deriving as well as examining scientific explanations regarding the mechanisms of the system. In terms of social sciences, using agent-based actor models for doing social simulation studies is referred to as ABSS [25].

For using ABSS to analyze communication dynamics in OSN, three entities need to be modeled: the users of an OSN (actors), the decisions and actions of the users (behavior), and the connections between the actors (network). While actors and their behavior can be considered as the micro level of the model, the network is a macro phenomenon and can be observed in the real world. Accordingly, an understanding of the macro level needs to be established first, as a basis for further consideration of the actor-based micro level.

During the model-building process, domain expertise is needed for modeling real world mechanisms and processes according to observations or results from discourse and content analysis over time. This information, enriched with theories from software agent technology, can then be technically formalized and used for specifying a multiagent system for simulating OSNs. As a result of this, different artificial scenarios and processes can be observed based on how stochastic events influence the mechanisms. Instead of using the real world system as an object of research, domain-specific research methods can then be applied to the artificial system. Compared to the real world system, a more cost-efficient and restriction-free access to data is provided. Furthermore, variations of the spatial or temporal dimension as well as repetitions of experiments are possible and the real world system is not exposed to any risk or needs not be existent at all. Results of the simulation experiments will be used for refining the model. This enables domain experts to draw conclusions and implications from the model regarding the real world system using specific theories, e.g., for analyzing viral marketing or for preventing Twitterstorms.

The described process results in two interconnected loops of research methodologies where a central interdisciplinary model serves as intermediator. This model is improved and refined stepwise by both disciplines, i.e., simulations and media, until a satisfying state is reached (see Figure 1). The model then can be used in the dynamic analysis framework for simulating OSN and communication processes within them.

IV. Concept

The process of performing a simulation study for analyzing dynamics of communication in OSN can be divided into three major steps (see Figure 3): the acquisition of relevant data, the conduction of the simulation experiments, and the drawing of conclusions from the results of the experiments regarding the real world. In this paper, we focus on the first step, the acquisition of relevant data.

In order to decide which data is relevant for a specific simulation study, the experiments need to be designed in advance. This includes the determination of the methodology of the simulation study as well as the definition of research hypotheses to be tested. After the experimental design has been defined in consultation with the domain experts, e.g., PR experts, relevant data needs to be collected, prepared, and selected accordingly.

A. Data Collection

When gathering OSN data using APIs, most of the data is provided in standardized data formats, e.g., JSON or XML. Due to the structure of the data format, each message or contribution (e.g., tweet or Facebook posting) is transferred as a single piece of information. Additionally, each entity is described by meta data, e.g., a unique ID, the name of the author, a timestamp when it was published, and a reference to which other message it replies.

Twitter provides REST APIs for both, reading and writing data. The access to the API is at no charge and the data can be downloaded as JSON files. Each tweet is characterized by up to 35 attributes, e.g., favorite count and geo coordinates, and up to 500 million tweets are sent per day. Two APIs are intended for the assessment of data, the *streaming* API for accessing the global stream of data and the *search* API

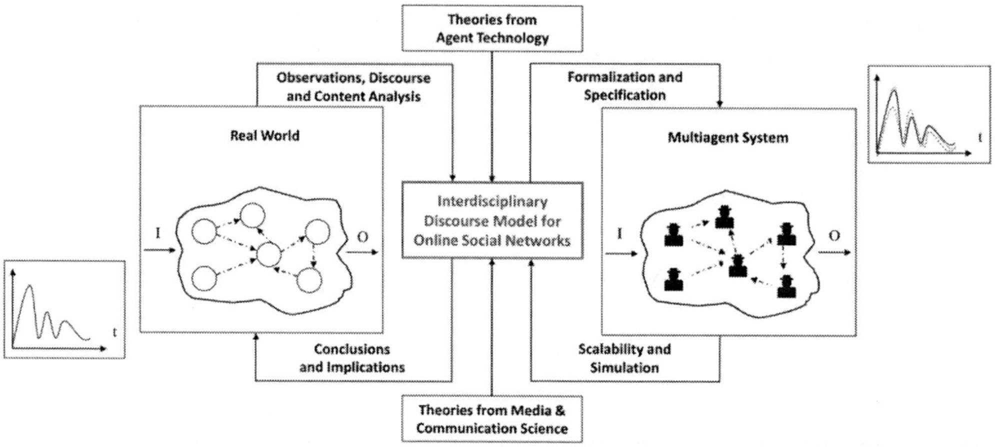

Figure 1. Integrated research method for creating an interdisciplinary model.

allowing queries against a subset of tweets from the past week. Still, both APIs need to be requested with a set of predefined keywords, i.e., hashtags, restricting the results. Here, the tradeoff is the extent of the data. The streaming API provides complete data regarding a hashtag, yet, this results in large datasets which need to be collected and stored in real-time. Technical problems during this process may result in a loss of data, as past data can not be accessed. In contrast to this, the *search* API provides relevant data only which decreases the size of the dataset. The data of the last week can be accessed, which enables a non-real-time collection of data, but the completeness as well as representativity of the provided data are questionable.

Certainly in terms of topics and events that are not discussed using a hashtag which is known in advance, e.g., a Twitterstorm, the advantages and disadvantages of the two APIs are noticeable. The keywords of the real-time streaming API need to be modified in order to capture the tweets of the storm of protest. Yet, when the Twitterstorm is recognized, the beginning has been in the past and thus can not be captured using a real-time API. The search API, in contrast, can be used to collect "popular" tweets of an event which has occurred up to one week ago. Yet, Twitter determines the popularity of a Tweet without providing any information regarding the weighting function being used. Thus, the completeness of the dataset collected using the search API can not be assessed. Consequently, according to the design of experiment, the appropriate API needs to be chosen or a combination of both APIs needs to be used for the collection of data.

B. Data Preparation & Selection

After a dataset has been collected using the API provided by the OSN, it needs to be stored for further processing. In this phase of the data handling, communication processes are identified in the set of isolated tweets, and the content of the communication is analyzed. Furthermore, the network of communication is reconstructed representing related messages and conversations.

1) Conversation Detection & Content Analysis: Topic-related communication processes, i.e., discourses, are considered as coherent dialogs between users or groups of users regarding a certain topic [26]. From a media studies and communication research perspective, the identification and analysis of these discourses within a network of communication is of high relevance. They are the foundation for reconstructing and evaluating topics and opinion-making processes over time.

For discovering discourses in a network of communication, both the conversations between users and the content of the messages need to be analyzed. A conversation is defined by the direction as well as the order of messages which were sent. First, the beginning of a discourse, i.e., the *initial tweet*, needs to be identified. The identification of this tweet in a dataset can be achieved by selecting all tweets, one after another, and checking the following two conditions: 1) Does another tweet exist in the dataset, which is a reply to the selected tweet? and 2) Is the selected tweet no reply to other tweets itself? In case both conditions are fulfilled, a tweet is considered an *initial tweet*. Still, the dataset may contain only a part of a conversation. This might occur, if the initial tweet has not been part of the collection received from the API. In this case, the initial tweet is the one which is a reply itself, yet, the tweet it replies to is not part of the dataset. By iteratively applying this procedure (see Figure 2), communication processes can be identified as shown.

After identifying communication processes between users in networks of communication, an automated analysis of the conversation is desirable due to the large amount of data. Doing so, researchers can get a first impression regarding the type and topic of the conversation. On the one hand, the tonality of tweets can be determined using sentiment analysis, providing information about the mood expressed in the tweets. In terms of discourses, an alternating tonality can be assumed, as two parties talk about the truth of a certain statement. Furthermore, communication processes can be differentiated according to differences of opinion, i.e., pro and contra. On the other hand, an automated analysis of the topic of the conversation can be performed. Content analysis provides techniques for determining commonly used terms in tweets, giving a first impression regarding the potential topic of the conversation.

The tweets are analyzed in two ways. First, the hashtags used in the tweets are identified and collected. An overview of the most commonly used hashtags of a conversation provides

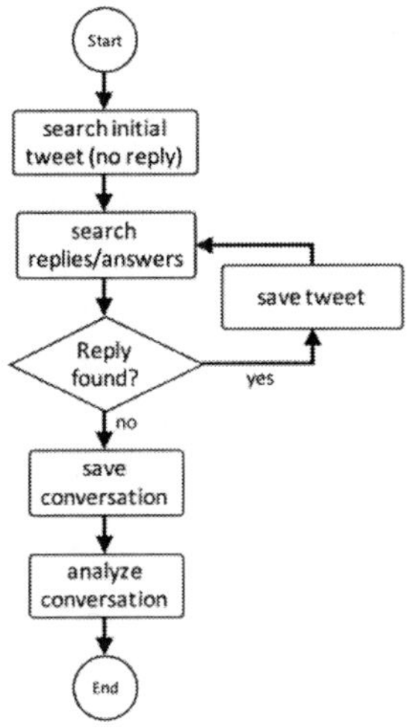

Figure 2. Conversation detection in Twitter dataset.

a first impression regarding the topic of the conversation. As a second step, a POST approach is used for analyzing nouns and adjectives. For doing so, all tweets of the conversation need to be divided into single words. Hashtags can be removed from the set of words, as they have already been evaluated individually and as hashtags often consist of made-up words or abbreviations. Thus, the decision whether a hashtag is a noun or adjective is difficult, too. POST will then be applied to the remaining words to identify nouns and adjectives which occur multiple times. The outcome enables a first assessment of the conversations' topics.

Furthermore, the tonality of a tweet is another indicator for assessing its content. Applying supervised learning algorithms for classifying tweets according to their tonality requires a three-stage approach [27]. As a first step, classification algorithms require a set of training data, which has been classified by hand. Using this data, the learning algorithm is trained and configured for the third step, the automated classification of the remaining tweets. In order to increase the accuracy of the algorithm, a preprocessing of the data should be performed. As the mood of the tweet is assessed by analyzing natural language only, artificial constructs, such as links to websites, @-mentions, and the "RT" prefix can be removed. Doing so, the disturbance of the algorithm can be reduced.

2) Network of Communication: At this point, the dataset contains a large number of individual communication processes. Yet, for analyzing the dynamics of communication, these conversations must not remain separate. Instead, the entire network obtained when merging all individual communication processes is of interest. It contains dependencies between different conversations and provides a chronological order of each conversation. In the following, this topic-specific network of users and messages sent between the users is referred to as *network of communication*.

When reconstructing networks of communication in OSN, the relationships between the users are of relevance. Generally, Twitter provides two kinds of relationships between users: communicative relationships expressed by the use of the *RT* or @ operator and social relationships which are represented by Twitter's *follower-followee-mechanism*.

Analyses of the communicative structure of past Twitterstorms have shown that a small amount of the involved OSN users operate as central nodes and drive the diffusion of the criticism (see Section V). Thus, for reconstructing networks of communication, communicative relationships seem to be most relevant. Social relationships, in contrast, do not contain any information regarding the participation and intensity of communication. Yet, the "communicative power" [26] of a user can be determined by the social interconnectedness of a user. This is relevant when analyzing scenarios that potentially can lead to Twitterstorms, i.e., prospective analysis. In terms of networks of communication, communicative power can be considered as the ability to gain a high level of awareness for a message due to the large number of users the writer is connected with. Accordingly, for reconstructing networks of communication, these types of relationships need to be extracted from the dataset.

Beginning with a large amount of separate tweets and related attributes derived from the Twitter API, a preselection regarding a defined hashtag of interest needs to be performed. At this point, additional filters can be applied for limiting the extent of data, e.g., structure, content or mood filters. Doing so, the dataset is reduced to the relevant tweets directly associated with the topic to be analyzed. Here, the assumption is made that the hashtags mentioned by the tweet imply the topics the tweet is related to, as intended by Twitter. Tweets, that are meant to be related to a topic, yet, do not mention the hashtag in particular, can not be considered as part of the study, as they are not recognized by the API. As a next step, isolated users need to be removed, as they are not part of the network of communication. Accordingly, isolated tweets need to be removed as well, as they are considered not to be of interest to other users. A tweet is classified as *isolated* when it is neither addressing a certain user nor is a retweet or reply to a previous tweet. By considering retweets, circles may occur, as some users tend to retweet their own tweets. These tweets are irrelevant for the network of communication, too.

Based on this cleaned dataset, a directed graph can be generated. In this graph, the nodes represent the users of the OSN and the edges represent the tweets of the users. For simplification purposes, just one type of edges will be used for all three types of communication: retweets, replies, and @-mentions. At that point, the calculation of centrality measures can be performed, e.g., degree or closeness centrality. When visualizing the graph, the researcher gets a first impression of the structure of the network of communication.

As the aim of this process is to create a realistic and valid simulation model, the conceptualization of the simulation model is performed parallel to the data collection and preparation. This facilitates the coordination and enables a harmonization of these two interdependent processes. For one thing, the simulation model is created according to the dataset which has been collected and thus can take account of certain characteristics of the dataset, e.g., involved actor types or specifics of the topic. For another thing, the collection and preparation of data can be adapted to the model ensuring the suitability of the dataset. Starting with a basic conceptualization of the model during the design of experiment and data collection phases, a more detailed conceptualization during the preparation and selection phase is done. This results in the creation of an applicable simulation model which matches the acquired data as it has been developed based on them.

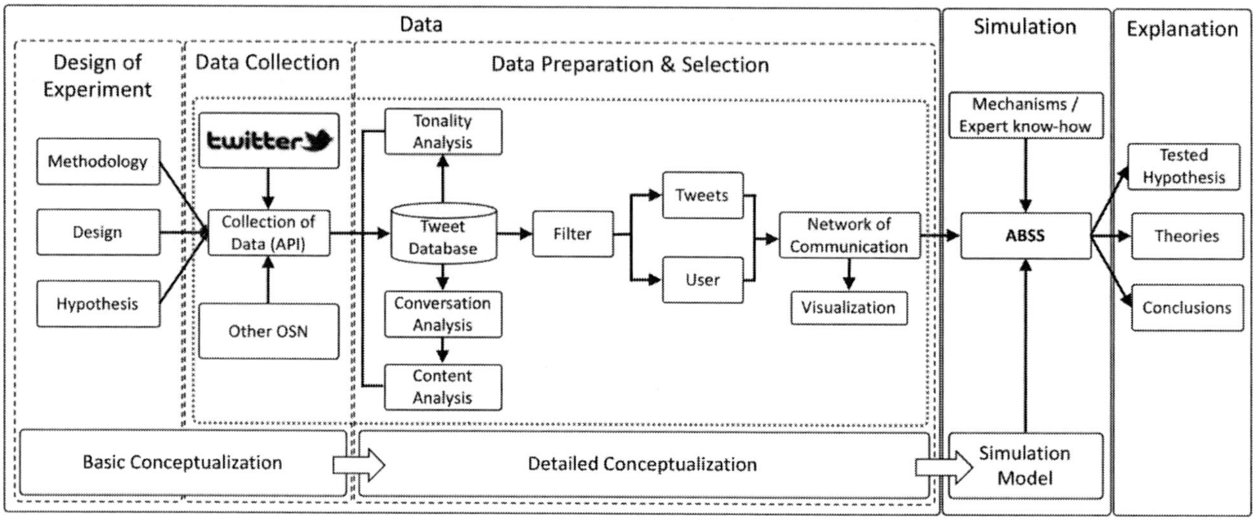

Figure 3. Procedure model for collecting, editing, and aggregating OSN data for ABSS studies.

The data collected and prepared in the previous steps can now serve as input for the simulation model that has been developed simultaneously. At this step, ABSS experiments can be conducted using the results of the previous process step. In addition, expert know-how is needed in order to validate and verify the simulation model as well as to interpret the results of the experiments. This includes proving or disproving of the hypotheses defined during the design of experiment phase as well as deriving conclusions or theories from the results.

V. Implementation and Evaluation

As a proof of concept and for evaluating the procedure model proposed in Section IV, the process of collecting and preparing data for ABSS studies is implemented. Furthermore, the feasibility of the implementation is evaluated by analyzing the datasets of two Twitterstorms.

A. *Implementation of the Framework*

For querying the Twitter API, a *PHP* script has been developed and used. The results are formatted as *JSON* objects and include all necessary information regarding the tweet itself as well as the user which has been the author of the tweet. The data is stored in a *MySQL* database which is used for the central data management.

For the preparation of the data, existing software packages can be used providing basic algorithms, e.g., machine learning or part-of-speech tagging algorithms. A number of frameworks exist, e.g., Apache Mahout or Scikit-Learn. However, due to the programming language it is implemented with and the large amount of preimplemented algorithms, the *DatumBox* framework [28] has been chosen for this implementation. *DatumBox* is a framework which provides natural language processing and classifying services written in *JAVA*. It focuses on social media monitoring as well as text analysis and quality evaluation in online communities. The learning algorithms of the *DatumBox machine learning framework* have been used for this implementation, as the framework can handle large datasets and is open-source. The implementation of the *support vector machine* uses *LIBSVM* [29], a widely used open-source implementation of SVM. Furthermore, *Apache Lucene* [30] is used as text search engine, which is open-source and used by large companies, e.g., Twitter, for real-time search.

After collecting raw communication data, this implementation allows for performing tonality analyses using the algorithms of the *DatumBox* framework and *Apache Lucene*. In order to obtain the required training data, a number of tweets needs to be classified by human beings, after they have been edited. This training data as well as SVM, n-gram, and stemming algorithms provide a classification of the tweets regarding their mood.

The conversation detection has been implemented as shown in Figure 2, followed by an analysis of the conversations' topics. The results of both analyses are then saved in the central database, too.

As a next step, for reconstructing networks of communication, the tweets of the database are filtered regarding the hashtags of interest. Additionally, the involved users are loaded from the database and a graph is created. The users serve as nodes, while each tweet is illustrated as a directed edge indicating the direction of the communication. For a reply, the edge would point from the user who replied to it to the author of the original tweet.

B. *Analysis of the #pegida Twitterstorm*

For evaluating the proposed approach, Twitter data has been collected since the beginning of 2015. For doing so, the hashtags of current topics of online news media have been used as keywords. During this period, 18 Mio. tweets containing 8 Twitterstorms have been recorded. Both *#pegida* and *#deflategate* are hashtags of considerable communication processes which took place on Twitter during this period of time.

The evaluation of the conversation analysis requires a highly discursive topic, providing conversations with a high depth. For this reason, the social media echo of the *Pegida* protests has been chosen as dataset containing 3.2 Mio. Tweets [31]. Pegida is a right wing political movement that was founded in Dresden, Germany in October 2014 and opposes the perceived "Islamisation" of the Western world. Hence, due to the formation of opposing interest groups supporting or rejecting Pegida's point of view, opinions are divided and the formation of discourses is facilitated.

Analyzing the dataset, 19 685 conversations were identified consisting of nearly 51 000 tweets. Conversations can be classified by the number of replies as well as by the depth (steps) of the conversation. Figure 4 shows the distribution of the conversations by number of replies and depth. Conversations of a depth higher than 10, meaning that two users wrote 5 messages each replying to the previous message of the other user, are not existing whereas 136 conversations have more than 10 replies.

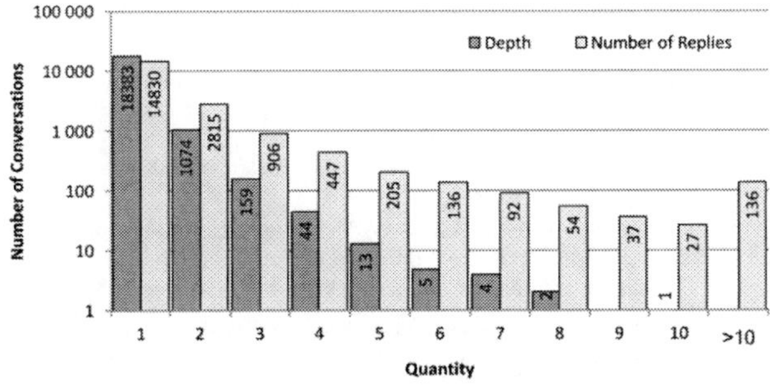

Figure 4. Distribution of conversations by number of replies and depth of conversation frm the #pediga analysis.

The structure of conversation trees can be divided into two major groups: *paths* and *stars* [32]. A *star* is defined by a low depth of the tree combined with a high number of tweets, consequently, a high amount of replies to one or a few tweets. In contrast, *paths* have a high depth while the total number of tweets is low.

Further analysis of the data showed that two types of *stars* exist in the dataset that differ in the number of involved users. The most extensive conversations of the dataset, consisting of 107 and 100 tweets, are the result of only 3 resp. 2 users. On closer examination, these conversations were classified as spam. Thus, we assume that for conversations on Twitter the ratio between the number of tweets and the number of involved users can serve as a indicator for spam. This assumption was strengthened by a manual analysis of the dataset. For most spam conversations, the ratio between users and tweets was at least 1 to 10. Accordingly, this type of star can be referred to as *spam star* and is not relevant for further analysis.

A second type of stars exists where the ratio is inverted. In this case, the number of tweets and the number of users is almost equal implying that the majority of users commented on the conversation only once. In over 90% of the conversations which were detected in the dataset, 90% of the tweets have been written by different users. Consequently, most of the tweets have not been replied to. Even though these stars represent relevant conversations, they may not be considered as discourses, as the *"back-and-forth"* character of discourses is missing.

The paths, in contrast, are what we consider to be discursive behavior. Two or more users respond to each other's Tweets and constitute a conversation. By merging both stars and paths, the network of communication can be reconstructed for further analysis. Furthermore, for the modeling of agent behavior, it appears that the communication rather than the exchange of opinions is in focus. This is triggered by an initial tweet and results in a *Fire-and-forget* behavior of the users.

C. Analysis of the #deflategate Twitterstorm

The reconstruction of the networks of communication is evaluated using the dataset of the *#deflategate* Twitterstorm. Due to the limited timespan of a Twitterstorm, the collection of a complete dataset is simplified. Furthermore, analyzing a Twitterstorm's network of communication is of interest, as central users or tweets can be identified.

The *#deflategate* storm started three days after the 49th NFL Super Bowl and was triggered by a Tweet of the journalist Chris Mortensen, claiming 11 of the 12 footballs were under-inflated [33]. As each team plays with separate footballs and as the hosting team supplies the balls, this appeared to have happened on purpose, to influence the behavior of the ball when thrown, kicked or caught. 17 621 tweets from 9 870 users have been collected during the *#deflategate* storm. Out of this, 41 tweets reply to themselves and 4 577 users are isolated and thus were removed. Consequently, the network of communication consists of 5 293 users and 6 067 tweets.

Two central nodes can be identified in the network of communication. This observation is confirmed when comparing the *degree* centrality of the nodes. While the average *degree* is 1, a user named *TomBradysEgo* (Twitter User-ID: 317170443) is having the maximum *degree* of 509. *TomBradysEgo* is a parody account on Tom Brady, the quarterback of the New England Patriots, having 235 000 followers and posting an average of 113 tweets per month. During the Twitterstorm, 39 tweets were published by the account. Due to the high *outdegree*, 97.4% of the total *degree* of the node, in combination with the low number of published tweets, it can be assumed that the user's tweets have often been retweeted. Thus, a central role of *TomBradysEgo* can be implied and the account can be classified as a hub.

Similarly, the user named *brownjenjen* (Twitter User-ID: 2453787236) has a *degree* of 485 and is an American blogger. Having only 23 000 followers, *brownjenjen* published 43 tweets during the Twitterstorm. Due to the *outdegree* of 100%, a large number of retweets can be assumed, too. As the account does not reply to other tweets and participates in different topics, it can be classified as a hub, too.

The important role the two accounts play for the Twitterstorm clarifies, when removing the two nodes and the related communication from the network of communication. Doing so, the density of the graph is reduced by 12.46% which can be compared to a reduction of the communication by the same extent. The union of the *ego-centered networks* of the two central nodes illustrates their maximal neighborhood, i.e., all nodes that can be reached from the central nodes. Here, 69.69% of the communication of the storm is linked to the two central nodes, showing their overall impact. According to this, a more detailed consideration of these two users seems promising in terms of social network analysis.

For both topics, *#pegida* and *#deflategate*, the feasibility of the approach proposed in this paper has been shown. In terms of content and discourse analysis as well as reconstruction of networks of communication, preliminary results assisting the selection of relevant data for subsequent studies were generated. Thus, when simulating emergent OSN phenomena, the different reach of agents needs to be considered. Some agents need to serve as hubs for pushing the diffusion of messages.

VI. Conclusions and Future Work

In this paper, a first step towards the development of a dynamic analysis framework for OSN communication processes is proposed. A major challenge is the collection as well as the preparation and selection of relevant data, which is addressed by the presented approach. Currently, the analysis of a set of collected data for interesting phenomena for further consideration is done by hand. Our concept aims at providing assistance functionalities, by automating the handling of data for the preparation of simulation studies.

For gaining a first overview of the dataset of isolated messages, conversations between users are detected, the content and tonality of the messages are assessed, and the network of communication is reconstructed. Using the examples of *#deflategate* and *#pegida*, the process of data collection as well as data preparation and selection has been implemented and evaluated. The network of communication has been visualized and central nodes of the communication graph have been identified automatically.

This work is only a first step towards a framework for analyzing the communication dynamics of OSN. Besides the aspect of data collection and preparation, which has been subject of this paper, the creation of the simulation model as well as the integration of data and model for conducting simulation experiments need to be considered. For building an agent-based simulation model, actor types need to be derived from social network data, too, and a consideration of communication across different networks is desirable. Furthermore, from a media studies and communication research perspective, a more detailed specification of the interactions between users and the subject of communication are needed for conducting sound ABSS studies.

Acknowledgments

We would like to acknowledge our master students Nils Dammenhayn, Stephanie Rodermund, Christopher Schulz and Nicolas Schulz for contributing to this work.

References

[1] J. Mander, "Daily time spent on social networks rises to 1.72 hours," https://www.globalwebindex.net/blog/daily-time-spent-on-social-networks-rises-to-1-72-hours, [retrieved: 09/16].

[2] J. Kirby, Connected marketing: the viral, buzz and word of mouth revolution. Amsterdam: Butterworth-Heinemann, 2010.

[3] Nina G, "Disability Community Tweet-in," https://ninagcomedian.wordpress.com/2015/12/01/donald-trump-tweet-in-for-crippledamerica/, [retrieved: 09/16].

[4] E. Tranos and P. Nijkamp, "The death of distance revisited: Cyber-place, cyber-place, physical and relational proximities," Journal of Regional Science, vol. 53, no. 5, Dec. 2013, pp. 855–873.

[5] R. Mayntz, "Mechanisms in the analysis of social macro-phenomena," Philosophy of the social sciences, vol. 34, no. 2, 2004, pp. 237–259.

[6] F. Lorig and I. J. Timm, "How to model the human factor for agent-based simulation in social media analysis?" in Proceedings of the 2014 ADS Symposium (part of SpringSim multiconference). SCS, 2014, p. 12.

[7] D. Helbing, Social self-organization: Agent-based simulations and experiments to study emergent social behavior. Springer, 2012.

[8] C. R. Berger, "Interpersonal communication," The International Encyclopedia of Communication, 2008.

[9] C. E. Shannon, "A mathematical theory of communication," ACM SIGMOBILE Mobile Computing and Communications Review, vol. 5, no. 1, 2001, pp. 3–55.

[10] F. Vega-Redondo, Complex Social Networks. Cambridge University Press Cambridge, MA, 2007.

[11] L. C. Freeman, "Centrality in social networks conceptual clarification," Social networks, vol. 1, no. 3, 1978, pp. 215–239.

[12] D. E. Goldberg and J. H. Holland, "Genetic algorithms and machine learning," Machine learning, vol. 3, no. 2, 1988, pp. 95–99.

[13] A. Voutilainen, "Part-of-speech tagging," The Oxford handbook of computational linguistics, 2003, pp. 219–232.

[14] M. F. Porter, "An algorithm for suffix stripping," Program, vol. 14, no. 3, 1980, pp. 130–137.

[15] C. Zhang, J. Sun, and K. Wang, "Information propagation in microblog networks," in Proceedings of the 2013 IEEE/ACM international conference on advances in social networks analysis and mining. ACM, 2013, pp. 190–196.

[16] P. Cogan, M. Andrews, M. Bradonjic, W. S. Kennedy, A. Sala, and G. Tucci, "Reconstruction and analysis of Twitter conversation graphs," in Proceedings of the First ACM International Workshop on Hot Topics on Interdisciplinary Social Networks Research (HotSocial 2012). ACM Press, 2012, pp. 25–31.

[17] C.-l. Hsu, S. J. Park, and H. W. Park, "Political Discourse Among KEy Twitter Users: The Case Of Sejong City In South Korea," Journal of Contemporary Eastern Asia, vol. 12, no. 1, 2013, pp. 65–79.

[18] A. Maireder, "Political Discourses on Twitter: Networking Topics, Objects and People," in Twitter and Society. Peter Lang, 2013.

[19] J. Bollen, H. Mao, and A. Pepe, "Modeling public mood and emotion: Twitter sentiment and socio-economic phenomena," in Proceedings of the Fifth International AAAI Conference on Weblogs and Social Media, 2011, pp. 450–453.

[20] K. Lerman and R. Ghosh, "Information contagion: An empirical study of the spread of news on digg and twitter social networks," ICWSM, vol. 10, 2010, pp. 90–97.

[21] A. Signorini, A. M. Segre, and P. M. Polgreen, "The use of twitter to track levels of disease activity and public concern in the us during the influenza a h1n1 pandemic," PloS one, vol. 6, no. 5, 2011, p. e19467.

[22] A. Maireder and S. Schlögl, "24 hours of an# outcry: The networked publics of a socio-political debate," European Journal of Communication, 2014, pp. 1–16.

[23] J. Goldstein, "Emergence as a construct: History and issues," Emergence, vol. 1, no. 1, 1999, pp. 49–72.

[24] J. O. Berndt and O. Herzog, "Anticipatory behavior of software agents in self-organizing negotiations," in Anticipation Across Disciplines. Springer, 2016, pp. 231–253.

[25] P. Davidsson, "Agent based social simulation: A computer science view," Journal of Artificial Societies and Social Simulation, vol. 5, no. 1, 2002.

[26] J. Habermas, Between facts and norms: contributions to a discourse theory of law and democracy, ser. Studies in contemporary German social thought. Cambridge, Mass: MIT Press, 1996.

[27] S. Abney, Semisupervised learning for computational linguistics. CRC Press, 2007.

[28] DatumBox Framework, http://www.datumbox.com, [retrieved: 09/16].

[29] LIBSVM, http://www.csie.ntu.edu.tw/~cjlin/libsvm, [retrieved: 09/16].

[30] Apache Lucene, http://lucene.apache.org/core, [retrieved: 09/16].

[31] E. Crecsi, "How Germans documented Pegida's far-right protests on social media," http://www.theguardian.com/world/2015/jan/06/how-germans-documented-pegidas-far-right-protests-on-social-media, [retrieved: 09/16].

[32] P. Cogan, M. Andrews, M. Bradonjic, W. S. Kennedy, A. Sala, and G. Tucci, "Reconstruction and analysis of twitter conversation graphs," in Proceedings of the HotSocial ACM International Workshop. ACM, 2012, pp. 25–31.

[33] A. Jaafari, "The goodell, the bad, and the ugly: The minimal level of integrity in the NFL's disciplinarian of players," Social Science Research Network (SSRN), 2016.

The Many Aspects of Fine-Grained Sentiment Analysis An Overview of the Task and its Main Challenges

Orphée De Clercq

LT[3], Language and Translation Technology Team
Ghent University
Ghent, Belgium
Email: orphee.declercq@ugent.be

Abstract—**In this survey paper, the task of aspect-based sentiment analysis is defined in close detail. We explain how this fine-grained task actually comprises several subtasks and focus on the domain of customer reviews. We reveal which datasets have been made publicly available and describe the state of the art on the subtasks of aspect term extraction, aspect term classification and aspect polarity classification. We conclude this survey by listing some of the main challenges the domain is still facing, which illustrate that this task is far from being solved.**

Keywords–sentiment analysis; user-generated content; natural language processing.

I. INTRODUCTION

With the arrival of Web 2.0 technologies, online communication has become commonplace. These allow site visitors to add content, called *user-generated content* [1]. Examples include forums and message boards, blogs, review sites, e-commerce platforms, but also social networking sites such as Facebook or Twitter. Not only are these a new means of interpersonal and community-level communication, they have also become an important resource for gathering subjective information.

When we need to make a decision about the purchase of a car or cell phone, a travel destination to go to, or a good restaurant to visit, we are typically interested in what other people think. Before Web 2.0, we asked for opinions from friends and family. With the explosive growth of user-generated content on the Web in the past few years, however, it has become possible to go online and find recommendations or check the experience of other customers, e.g., for a particular restaurant to have lunch at. Instead of relying on anecdotal evidence from friends, we have access to a handy overview of the main aspects of that restaurant enabling us to answer that one crucial question: 'Will I like it?'

The same applies from the perspective of companies, governments and organizations. To know the sentiments of the general public towards its brand, products, policies, etc. an organization no longer needs to resort to opinion polls or surveys. Most of that information is already available online, in the form of user-generated content. In previous studies, user-generated content has been used by companies to track how their brand is perceived by consumers [2], for market prediction [3] or to determine the sentiment of financial bloggers towards companies and their stocks [4]; by individuals who need advice on purchasing the right product or service [5] and by nonprofit organizations, e.g., for the detection of suicidal messages [6].

As the amount of online information has grown exponentially, so has the interest in new text mining techniques to handle and analyze this growing amount of subjective text. One of the main research topics is sentiment analysis, also known as opinion mining. The objective of sentiment analysis is the extraction of subjective information from text, rather than factual information. Originally, it focused on the task of automatically classifying an entire document or sentence as positive, negative or neutral. This more coarse-grained level of analysis, however, does not allow to discover what people like and dislike exactly [7].

Often, users are not only interested in people's general sentiments about a certain product, but also in their opinions about specific features, i.e., parts or attributes of that product. One way to do this is by applying aspect-based sentiment analysis (ABSA). Aspect-based (or feature-based) sentiment analysis systems [8] focus on the detection of all sentiment expressions within a given document and the concepts and aspects (or features) to which they refer. Such systems do not only try to distinguish the positive from the negative utterances, but also strive to detect the target of the opinion, which comes down to a very fine-grained sentiment analysis task and "almost all real-life sentiment analysis systems in industry are based on this level of analysis" [7, p10].

In this paper, we first define the task of aspect-based sentiment analysis in detail, with a special focus on the analysis of customer reviews. In Section 2, we explain which datasets have been made available in the framework of SemEval, a well-known workshop in the Natural Language Processing (NLP) community. Next, we move on to discuss the state of the art when applying supervised machine learning techniques to the various subtasks. In Section 4, we explain which challenges still need to be tackled in the near future after which we conclude this survey (Section 5).

II. DEFINITION

Several surveys of the field of sentiment analysis are available, such as [9] or [10]. However, the books [7], [11] are more recent and extensive summaries of this rapidly evolving field. Liu offers a comprehensive definition of what an *opinion* is:

> "An opinion is a quintuple, $(e_i, a_{ij}, s_{ijkl}, h_k, t_l)$, where e_i is the name of an entity, a_{ij} is an aspect

Figure 1. Review from a particular restaurant in Barcelona that was posted on TripAdvisor.

of e_i, s_{ijkl} is the sentiment on aspect a_{ij} of entity e_i, h_k is the opinion holder, and t_l is the time when the opinion is expressed by h_k. The sentiment s_{ijkl} is positive, negative, or neutral, or expressed with different strength/intensity levels." [11, pp19-20]

Following this definition, sentiment analysis thus consists of automatically deriving these opinion quintuples from texts and it comprises various subtasks. We will now explain each of these tasks based on an example review presented in Fig. 1.

1) **Entity extraction and categorization**: Extract all entity expressions in a document collection, and categorize or group synonymous entity expressions into entity clusters (or categories). In our example, the collection consists of restaurant reviews and the entity presented here is 'Uma', belonging to the category *Restaurants*.

2) **Aspect extraction and categorization**: Extract all aspect expressions of the entities, and categorize these aspect expressions into clusters. These aspects can be both explicit and implicit. In our example, we can find out which aspects of this restaurant are mentioned while reading through the review. The explicit aspects are 'food', 'place' and 'service'. Implicitly, the final sentence says something about the restaurant in general. If we classify all these aspect expressions into categories, these could be: *Food*, *Ambience*, *Service*, and *Restaurant* respectively.

3) **Opinion holder extraction and categorization**: Extract opinion holders –h_k– for opinions from text or structured data and categorize them. In our example, this can easily be derived from the metadata accompanying the review, i.e., we know who wrote the review. Because of privacy concerns the username was anonymized to 'Reviewer X'.

4) **Time extraction and standardization**: Extract the times when opinions are given and standardize different time formats, t_l. This information can also be easily derived from the time stamp attached to the review: the review was written on 31 May 2016.

5) **Aspect sentiment classification**: Determine whether an opinion on an aspect a_{ij} is positive, negative or neutral, or assign a numeric sentiment rating to the aspect, s_{ijkl}. We can read that the food and service were evaluated as positive, as well as the restaurant in general. Though the reviewer did note that the place is small -which might hint at a negative sentiment- this is countered in the next part, which clearly indicates that there is a positive ambience.

The quintuples that can be derived from our example are: `(Uma, Food, positive, Reviewer X, May-31-2016)`, `(Uma, Ambience, positive, Reviewer X, May-31-2016)`, `(Uma, Service, positive, Reviewer X, May-31-2016)` and `(Uma, Restaurant, positive, Reviewer X, May-31-2016)`.

This framework has been called many names, such as feature-based, topic-based, entity-based or target-based sentiment analysis, but is currently most-known under the name of aspect-based sentiment analysis. It should be noted that any real-life application will have to be able to process many reviews at once and thus a very important final step is to aggregate all aspects and sentiments over an entire document collection.

The focus of this survey is on customer reviews, in this genre one can derive the entity, opinion holder and time as such from the metadata, which is why the main focus will be on the second and fifth subtask. Actually, this second task consists of two subsequent steps: aspect term extraction and aspect term categorization. In this respect, we follow the task decomposition as suggested by the organizers of three Semantic Evaluation tasks on aspect-based sentiment analysis [8], [12], [13].

III. Datasets

When it comes to customer reviews and aspect-based sentiment analysis, systems have been developed for a variety of domains, such as movie reviews [14], reviews for electronic products, e.g., digital cameras [15] or netbook computers [16], and restaurant reviews [16], [17]. As always when research is performed on individual datasets, true advancements in the field cannot be properly evaluated.

Though several benchmark datasets had already been made publicly available, such as the product reviews dataset of Hu and Liu [15] or the restaurant reviews dataset of [17], it was not until the International Workshop on Semantic Evaluation devoted attention to the task that this problem was tackled. Parts of the previously-mentioned English datasets were extracted an re-annotated for SemEval2014 Task 4 [8] and SemEval 2015 Task 12 [12]. Last year, seven other languages were also included in a third run of the task, i.e., SemEval 2016 Task 5 [13]. Table 1 presents an overview of all the annotated data that is available in different languages and domains so far.

TABLE I. Overview of the Benchmark SemEval datasets

Domain	*Subdomain*	*Language*	*#Sentences*
Electronics	Camera	Chinese	8040
	Laptops	English	3308
	Phones	Chinese	9521
	Phones	Dutch	1697
Hotels		Arabic	6029
Restaurants		Dutch	2297
		English	2676
		French	2429
		Russian	4699
		Spanish	2951
		Turkish	1248
Telecom		Turkish	3310

Noteworthy is that all this data has been annotated using the same annotation guidelines [18]. Basically, the annotation process consists of three incremental steps. First, all explicit and implicit targets -the word or words referring to a specific entity or aspect- are annotated. Next, these targets are assigned to domain-specific clusters of aspect categories, and in the final step the sentiment expressed towards every aspect is indicated.

Three main polarities are distinguished: positive, negative and neutral.

These shared tasks can be perceived as online data competitions: during a specific time frame training data is released allowing NLP teams from all over the world to work on the same problem. In a final stage, unseen test data is released, usually for one to three days and each team can submit their system's output. This output is then evaluated for all teams in the same manner, which facilitates meaningful comparisons of different techniques.

IV. State of the Art

In this section, we discuss the state of the art, our main focus is on supervised machine learning techniques performed on English data. For more information on unsupervised and hybrid techniques we refer to the survey [19] and for an overview of the current approaches to languages other than English, we refer to the workshop proceedings of SemEval 2016 Task 5 [20].

A. Aspect Term Extraction

For the task of aspect term extraction (ATE), the most popular and successful approaches are based on frequency and supervised learning [8], [11]. Hu and Liu [15] introduced the task of aspect-based sentiment analysis and constructed the first strong baseline for aspect term extraction by identifying all nouns and noun phrases based on part-of-speech tags and counting frequencies. They only kept the frequent nouns and noun phrases using a frequency threshold. In subsequent research, this method was improved by incorporating pruning mechanisms based on pointwise mutual information, meronymy discriminators (e.g., for the camera class these would be 'camera has', 'camera comes with', etc.) and exploiting the WordNet hierarchy [21]. Another improvement was to only include those noun phrases that occur in sentiment-bearing sentences or in certain syntactic patterns [22] or to use the C-value measure, which allows to also extract multi-word aspects [23]. A combination of this frequency baseline with continuous vector space representations of words [24] has also proven effective in the work of Pavlopoulos and Androutsopoulos [25].

Using supervised learning, the most dominant method is to approach the ATE task as a sequential labeling task [11]. Following the IOB2 notation for Named Entity Recognition [26] the aspect term in the annotated training data is labeled with 'B' indicating the beginning of an aspect term, 'I' indicating the inside of an aspect term and 'O' indicating the outside of an aspect term. The two systems achieving the best performance for this subtask in SemEval 2015 Task 12 used this approach. In [27] (which was actually based on preliminary work [28]), a classifier was trained using Conditional Random Fields (CRF), and in [29] a designated Named Entity Recognition system was used. Both systems implemented typical named entity features, such as word bigrams, trigrams, token shape, capitalization, name lists, etc. For SemEval 2016, subsequent work by Toh and Su [30] found that using the output of a Recurrent Neural Network (RNN) as additional features is beneficial for the labeling tasks. More specifically the Bidirectional Elman-type RNN model [31] captures long-range dependencies.

B. Aspect Term Categorization

The next task is to group aspect terms into categories, known as aspect term categorization. The majority of existing research combines similar aspect terms into aspect groups without starting out from a predefined set of aspect categories. The most common approaches are to aggregate synonyms or near-synonyms using WordNet [32], statistics from corpora [33], [34], or semi-supervised learning, or to cluster aspect terms using (latent) topic models [16], [35]. In other research domain-specific taxonomies have been used to aggregate related terms or hierarchical relations between aspect terms [36]. More recently, a multi-granular aspect aggregation method was introduced in the work of [37] by first calculating the semantic relatedness between two frequent aspect terms and then performing hierarchical agglomerative clustering to create an aspect term hierarchy.

All the above-mentioned approaches assume that the list of aspect categories is unknown and has to be aggregated from scratch. In this respect, the task definition as proposed in the aspect-based SemEval tasks differs in that several predefined and domain-specific categories have to be predicted, thus transforming the aggregation task into a multiclass classification task. The two systems achieving the best results on this individual subtask in SemEval 2015 Task 12 both used classification to this purpose, respectively individual binary classifiers trained on each possible category, which are afterwards entered in a sigmoidal feedforward network [27] and a single Maximum Entropy classifier [38], respectively. When it comes to the features that were exploited by these systems especially lexical features in the form of bag-of-words (such as word unigrams and bigrams [27] or word and lemma unigrams [38]) have proven successful. The best system [27] also incorporated lexical-semantic features in the form of clusters learned from a large corpus of reference data, whereas the second-best [38] applied filtering heuristics on the classification output and thus solely relied on lexical information for the classification. As is the case for many NLP problems, the added value of deep learning is becoming more apparent for this task as well. For SemEval 2016 Toh and Su [30] found that when their sigmoidal feedforward network is enhanced with the probability output of a Deep Convolutional Neural Network (CNN) [39] as additional features, the performance increases. Moreover, ablation experiments revealed that these CNN features contribute the most to performance.

C. Aspect Term Polarity Classification

The final task is aspect term polarity classification. In the context of aspect-based sentiment analysis, the sentiment polarity has to be determined for each mentioned aspect term of a target entity. Existing sentiment analysis systems can be divided into lexicon-based and machine learning approaches. Lexicon-based methods (see [40] for an overview) determine the semantic orientation of a piece of text based on the words occurring in that text. Crucial in this respect, are sentiment or subjectivity lexicons allowing to define the semantic orientation of words. Lexicons comprise various sentiment or opinion words together with their strength and overall polarity. The word *wonderful*, for example, indicates a positive sentiment, whereas the word *terrible* has a negative connotation. Many subjectivity lexicons were constructed in the past, mainly for English, such as the well-known MPQA lexicon [41] or

SentiWordNet [42], but also for other languages, such as the Pattern [43] and Duoman [44] lexicons for Dutch.

Machine learning approaches to sentiment analysis make use of classification algorithms, such as Naïve Bayes or Support Vector Machines trained on a labeled dataset [10]. This dataset can be extracted from existing resources, such as reviews labeled with star ratings [45] or manual annotations [46]. Crucial in this respect is the engineering of a set of effective features [11]. Current state-of-the-art approaches model a variety of contextual, lexical and syntactic features [47], allowing them to capture context and the relations between the individual words. Though deep learning techniques have also been applied to this subtask, mainly in the form of word embeddings [24], for SemEval 2016 the best performing system relied solely on (advanced) linguistic features [48].

According to Liu [11], the key issue is to determine the scope of each sentiment expression within aspect-based sentiment analysis. The main approach is to use parsing to determine the dependency relations and other relevant information, as done in [49] where a dependency parser was used to generate a set of aspect dependent features, or in [50] where each feature is weighted based on the position of the feature relative to the target aspect in the parse tree. With respect to the SemEval tasks it has been shown that general purpose systems used to classify at the sentence level are very effective, which even seems to hold when testing on out-of-domain data [12] or on other languages [13]. However, we do believe that this is inherent to the customer reviews used for the SemEval tasks, these reviews do not contain many conflicting sentiments within one sentence. This brings us to one of the challenges in the field, i.e., domain adaptation, on which we will elaborate in the next section.

V. Challenges

Though research on sentiment analysis has flourished in the past decade, the problem is far from being solved. Excellent books and surveys have been published which also devote much attention to the various challenges that lie ahead, see [7] and [51] for recent and extensive overviews. In this section, we discuss some of the main challenges.

The focus on consumer reviews in this survey and in most of the research performed on aspect-based sentiment analysis already hints at one challenge, namely **domain adaptation**. Consumer reviews are very product-oriented and the aspect expressions that have to be extracted almost exclusively consist of nouns or noun phrases. Moreover, when someone writes a review the text will almost always include an opinion. In reality, however, large chunks of non-opinionated text co-occur with opinionated text and also verbal expressions or a variety of words can be used to refer to certain aspects. Think for example of political tweets or discussion forums. Nevertheless, it cannot be ignored that domain-knowledge is crucial for aspect-based sentiment analysis. The importance of lexical features in the classification tasks is obvious and if you have the time to compile a different lexicon for each domain you will be able to solve about 60% of the cases [7].

Even when not focussing on reviews, most of the text that is processed in the field of sentiment analysis is **user-generated content** (UGC), which is very different from standard text. Though this UGC is often highly expressive because many emoticons and techniques, such as flooding (the repetition of various characters the place emphasis, *loooool*) can be used, it is also full of misspellings, grammatical errors, abbreviations, etc., which hinder automatic text processing because the tools used for this are originally trained on standard text [52]. Especially if we consider the importance of lexical features, deviations from the standard can already have a large impact. In this respect promising research has been performed by Van Hee et. al. [53], they investigate to what extent the performance of a sentiment classifier can be further improved by applying a complex normalisation system as a preprocessing step. This normalisation system automatically translates noisy into standard text and the results reveal that this approach is beneficial, especially when testing on unseen data.

One can definitely say that UGC also allows for more **creative language use**, such as sarcasm, irony, humour and metaphor. These are all very difficult to interpret for natural language processing systems. In this respect, we see more research emerging. In 2015, for example, a SemEval shared task was organized on detecting sentiment in tweets rich in metaphor and irony [54]. The tweets provided for this task, however, were almost all ironic and negative and thus did not represent a realistic distribution of sarcastic messages in a random Twitter stream. It will be interesting to see how research in this direction is performed. Interesting in this respect is also the idea to construct a knowledge base including stereotypes and commonly used similes. According to Schouten and Frasincar [19] this evolution to more concept-centric approaches combined with machine learning will give rise to much better algorithms, not only for discovering irony but also for sentiment analysis in general.

As [55] phrases it: "sentiment analysis requires a **deep understanding** of the explicit and implicit, regular and irregular, and syntactic and semantic language rules." Extracting and classifying explicit sentiment might seem straightforward, however, in reality words are hardly ever used in isolation and whenever sentence composition comes into play both form and context can alter the intended sentiment dramatically. in this respect research is emerging on the impact of those small negation and modification words, which reveals that these are crucial to include [56]. Implicit sentiment is even more complex, much can be read between the lines and even factual statements can evoke different opinions when used in different domains [57]. Moreover, in aspect-based sentiment analysis for example a certain aspect can be referred to with a pronoun or other synonymous phrases, which brings us to the task of coreference resolution. Though many survey studies have claimed that the recognition of coreference is crucial for successful aspect-based sentiment analysis [11], [58] not much research has been performed in this direction. When it comes to this deep understanding, the field is in high expectations of the surge of deep learning techniques. It will be interesting to see whether these new techniques are apt to the task.

VI. Conclusion

In this survey, the focus has been on aspect-based sentiment analysis of consumer reviews. We have defined the task in close detail and have explained the state of the art for the subtasks of aspect term extraction, aspect term classification and aspect term polarity classification. We have discussed some of the main challenges the field still needs to overcome, such as domain adaptation, processing user-generated and creative language, solving some of the more NLP-hard problems. An interesting evolution to follow in this respect, will be the move towards deep learning in the field of Natural Language Processing.

REFERENCES

[1] M.-F. Moens, J. Li, and T.-S. Chua, Eds., Mining user generated content. Chapman and Hall/CRC, 2014.

[2] J. Zabin and A. Jefferies, "Social media monitoring and analysis: Generating consumer insights from online conversation," Aberdeen Group Benchmark Report, Aberdeen Group, Tech. Rep., 2008.

[3] T. O. Sprenger, A. Tumasjan, P. G. Sandner, and I. M. Welpe, "Tweets and trades: The information content of stock microblogs," European Financial Management, vol. 20, no. 5, 2014, pp. 926–957.

[4] N. O'Hare, M. Davy, A. Bermingham, P. Ferguson, P. Sheridan, C. Gurrin, and A. F. Smeaton, "Topic-dependent sentiment analysis of financial blogs," in Proceedings of the 1st International Conference on Information and Knowledge Management Workshop on Topic-sentiment Analysis for Mass Opinion (TSA-2009), 2009, pp. 9–16.

[5] M. Dabrowski, T. Acton, P. Jarzebowski, and S. O'Riain, "Improving customer decisions using product reviews - CROM - Car Review Opinion Miner," in Proceedings of the 6th International Conference on Web Information Systems and Technologies (WEBIST-2010), 2010, pp. 354–357.

[6] B. Desmet, "Finding the online cry for help: automatic text classification for suicide prevention," PhD, Ghent University, 2014.

[7] B. Liu, Sentiment Analysis - Mining Opinions, Sentiments, and Emotions. Cambridge University Press, 2015.

[8] M. Pontiki, D. Galanis, J. Pavlopoulos, H. Papageorgiou, I. Androutsopoulos, and S. Manandhar, "Semeval-2014 task 4: Aspect based sentiment analysis," in Proceedings of the 8th International Workshop on Semantic Evaluation (SemEval-2014), 2014, pp. 27–35.

[9] J. G. Shanahan, Y. Qu, and J. Wiebe, Eds., Computing Attitude and Affect in Text: Theory and Applications, ser. the Information Retrieval Series. Springer, 2006, no. 20.

[10] B. Pang and L. Lee, "Opinion mining and sentiment analysis," Foundations and Trends in Information Retrieval., vol. 2, no. 1-2, 2008, pp. 1–135.

[11] B. Liu, "Sentiment analysis and opinion mining," Synthesis Lectures on Human Language Technologies, vol. 5, no. 1, 2012, pp. 1–167.

[12] M. Pontiki, D. Galanis, H. Papageorgiou, S. Manandhar, and I. Androutsopoulos, "Semeval-2015 task 12: Aspect based sentiment analysis," in Proceedings of the 9th International Workshop on Semantic Evaluation (SemEval-2015), 2015, pp. 486–495.

[13] M. Pontiki, D. Galanis, H. Papageorgiou, I. Androutsopoulos, S. Manandhar, M. AL-Smadi, M. Al-Ayyoub, Y. Zhao, B. Qin, O. De Clercq, V. Hoste, M. Apidianaki, X. Tannier, N. Loukachevitch, E. Kotelnikov, N. Bel, S. M. Jiménez-Zafra, and G. Eryiğit, "Semeval-2016 task 5: Aspect based sentiment analysis," in Proceedings of the 10th International Workshop on Semantic Evaluation (SemEval-2016), 2016, pp. 19–30.

[14] T. T. Thet, J.-C. Na, and C. S. Khoo, "Aspect-based sentiment analysis of movie reviews on discussion boards," Journal of Information Science, vol. 36, no. 6, 2010, pp. 823–848.

[15] M. Hu and B. Liu, "Mining and summarizing customer reviews," in Proceedings of the 10th International Conference on Knowledge Discovery and Data Mining (KDD-2004), 2004, pp. 168–177.

[16] S. Brody and N. Elhadad, "An unsupervised aspect-sentiment model for online reviews," in Proceedings of the 11th Annual Conference of the North American Chapter of the Association for Computational Linguistics (NAACL-2010), 2010, pp. 804–812.

[17] G. Ganu, N. Elhadad, and A. Marian, "Beyond the stars: improving rating predictions using review text content," in Proceedings of the 12th International Workshop on the Web and Databases (WebDB-2009), 2009, pp. 1–6.

[18] "SemEval 2016 Task 5 Aspect Based Sentiment Analysis (ABSA-16) Annotation Guidelines," 2016, URL: http://goo.gl/wOf1dX [accessed: 2016-10-02].

[19] K. Schouten and F. Frasincar, "Survey on aspect-level sentiment analysis," IEEE Transactions on Knowledge and Data Engineering, vol. 28, no. 3, 2016, pp. 813–830.

[20] S. Bethard, M. Carpuat, D. Cer, D. Jurgens, P. Nakov, and T. Zesch, Eds., Proceedings of the 10th International Workshop on Semantic Evaluation (SemEval-2016). Association for Computational Linguistics, 2016.

[21] A.-M. Popescu and O. Etzioni, "Extracting product features and opinions from reviews," in Proceedings of the 2005 Conference on Human Language Technology and Empirical Methods in Natural Language Processing (EMNLP-2005), 2005, pp. 339–346.

[22] S. Blair-Goldensohn, T. Neylon, K. Hannan, G. A. Reis, R. Mcdonald, and J. Reynar, "Building a sentiment summarizer for local service reviews," in Proceedings of the WWW-2008 workshop on NLP in the Information Explosion Era (NLPIX-2008), 2008, pp. 1–10.

[23] J. Zhu, H. Wang, B. K. Tsou, and M. Zhu, "Multi-aspect opinion polling from textual reviews," in Proceedings of the 18th Association for Computing Machinery Conference on Information and Knowledge Management (CIKM-2009), 2009, pp. 1799–1802.

[24] T. Mikolov, I. Sutskever, K. Chen, G. S. Corrado, and J. Dean, "Distributed representations of words and phrases and their compositionality," in Advances in Neural Information Processing Systems, 2013, pp. 3111–3119.

[25] J. Pavlopoulos and I. Androutsopoulos, "Aspect term extraction for sentiment analysis: New datasets, new evaluation measures and an improved unsupervised method," in Proceedings of the 5th Workshop on Language Analysis for Social Media (LASM-2014), 2014, pp. 44–52.

[26] E. Tjong Kim Sang, "Introduction to the CoNLL-2002 shared task: Language-independent named entity recognition," in Proceedings of the 6th Conference on Natural Language Learning (COLING-2002), 2002, pp. 155–158.

[27] Z. Toh and J. Su, "NLANGP: Supervised machine learning system for aspect category classification and opinion target extraction," in Proceedings of the 9th International Workshop on Semantic Evaluation (SemEval-2015), June 2015, pp. 496–501.

[28] Z. Toh and W. Wang, "DLIREC: Aspect term extraction and term polarity classification system," in Proceedings of the 8th International Workshop on Semantic Evaluation (SemEval-2014), 2014, pp. 235–240.

[29] I. n. San Vicente, X. Saralegi, and R. Agerri, "EliXa: A Modular and Flexible ABSA Platform," in Proceedings of the 9th International Workshop on Semantic Evaluation (SemEval-2015), 2015, pp. 748–752.

[30] Z. Toh and J. Su, "NLANGP at SemEval-2016 Task 5: Improving Aspect Based Sentiment Analysis using Neural Network Features," in Proceedings of the 10th International Workshop on Semantic Evaluation (SemEval-2016), 2016, pp. 282–288.

[31] P. Liu, S. Joty, and H. Meng, "Fine-grained opinion mining with recurrent neural networks and word embeddings." in Proceedings of the 2015 Conference on Empirical Methods in Natural Language Processing (EMNLP-2015), 2015, pp. 1433–1443.

[32] Y. Liu and S. Lin, "Log-linear models for word alignment," in Proceedings of the 43rd Annual Meeting of the Association for Computational Linguistics (ACL-2005), 2005, pp. 459–466.

[33] H.-H. Chen, M.-S. Lin, and Y.-C. Wei, "Novel association measures using web search with double checking," in Proceedings of the 21st International Conference on Computational Linguistics and the 44th Annual Meeting of the Association for Computational Linguistics (COLING - ACL-2006), 2006, pp. 1009–1016.

[34] D. Lin and X. Wu, "Phrase clustering for discriminative learning," in Proceedings of the Joint Conference of the 47th Annual Meeting of the Association for Computational Linguistics and the 4th International Joint Conference on Natural Language Processing of the Asian Federation of Natural Language Processing (ACL-2009), 2009, pp. 1030–1038.

[35] I. Titov and R. McDonald, "A joint model of text and aspect ratings for sentiment summarization," in Proceedings of the 46th Annual Meeting of the Association for Computational Linguistics (ACL-2008), 2008, pp. 308–316.

[36] N. Kobayashi, K. Inui, and Y. Matsumoto, "Extracting aspect-evaluation and aspect-of relations in opinion mining," in Proceedings of the 2007 Joint Conference on Empirical Methods in Natural Language Processing

and Computational Natural Language Learning (EMNLP - CoNLL-2007, 2007, pp. 1065–1074.

[37] I. Pavlopoulos, "Aspect based sentiment analysis," PhD, Department of Informatics, Athens University of Economics and Business, 2014.

[38] J. Saias, "Sentiue: Target and aspect based sentiment analysis in SemEval-2015 Task 12," in Proceedings of the 9th International Workshop on Semantic Evaluation (SemEval-2015), June 2015, pp. 767–771.

[39] A. Severyn and A. Moschitti, "UNITN: Training Deep Convolutional Neural Network for Twitter Sentiment Classification." in Proceedings of the 9th International Workshop on Semantic Evaluation (SemEval-2015), 2015, pp. 464–469.

[40] M. Taboada, J. Brooke, M. Tofiloski, K. Voll, and M. Stede, "Lexicon-based methods for sentiment analysis," Computational Linguistics, vol. 37, no. 2, 2011, pp. 267–307.

[41] T. Wilson, J. Wiebe, and P. Hoffmann, "Recognizing contextual polarity in phrase-level sentiment analysis," in Proceedings of the 2005 Conference Empirical Methods in Natural Language Processing (EMNLP-2005), 2005, pp. 347–354.

[42] S. Baccianella, A. Esuli, and F. Sebastiani, "Sentiwordnet 3.0: An enhanced lexical resource for sentiment analysis and opinion mining," in Proceedings of the 7th International Conference on Language Resources and Evaluation (LREC-2010), 2010, pp. 2200–2204.

[43] T. De Smedt and W. Daelemans, "Vreselijk mooi! Terribly beautiful: a subjectivity lexicon for Dutch adjectives," in Proceedings of the 8th International Conference on Language Resources and Evaluation (LREC-2012), 2012, pp. 3568–3572.

[44] V. Jijkoun and K. Hofmann, "Generating a non-English subjectivity lexicon: Relations that matter," in Proceedings of the 12th Conference of the European Chapter of the Association for Computational Linguistics (EACL-2009), 2009, pp. 398–405.

[45] B. Pang, L. Lee, and S. Vaithyanathan, "Thumbs up?: Sentiment classification using machine learning techniques," in Proceedings of the 2002 Conference on Empirical Methods in Natural Language Processing (EMNLP-2002), 2002, pp. 79–86.

[46] J. Wiebe, T. Wilson, and C. Cardie, "Annotating expressions of opinions and emotions in language," Computer Intelligence, vol. 39, no. 2, 2005, pp. 165–210.

[47] L. D. Caro and M. Grella, "Sentiment analysis via dependency parsing," Computer Standards & Interfaces, vol. 35, no. 5, 2013, pp. 442–453.

[48] C. Brun, J. Perez, and C. Roux, "XRCE at SemEval-2016 Task 5: Feedbacked Ensemble Modeling on Syntactico-Semantic Knowledge for Aspect Based Sentiment Analysis," in Proceedings of the 10th International Workshop on Semantic Evaluation (SemEval-2016), 2016, pp. 277–281.

[49] L. Jiang, M. Yu, M. Zhou, X. Liu, and T. Zhao, "Target-dependent twitter sentiment classification," in Proceedings of the 49th Annual Meeting of the Association for Computational Linguistics (ACL-2011), 2011, pp. 151–160.

[50] E. Boiy and M.-F. Moens, "A machine learning approach to sentiment analysis in multilingual web texts," Information Retrieval, vol. 12, no. 5, 2009, pp. 526–558.

[51] S. M. Mohammad, "Challenges in sentiment analysis," in A Practical Guide to Sentiment Analysis, D. Das, E. Cambria, and S. Bandyopadhyay, Eds. Springer, 2016.

[52] J. Eisenstein, "What to do about bad language on the internet," in Proceedings of the 2013 Conference of the North American Chapter of the Association for Computational Linguistics: Human Language Technologies, 2013, pp. 359–369.

[53] C. Van Hee, M. Van de Kauter, O. De Clercq, E. Lefever, B. Desmet, and V. Hoste, "Noise or Music? Investigating the Usefulness of Normalisation for Robust Sentiment Analysis on Social Media Data," Expert Systems with Applications, submitted.

[54] A. Ghosh, G. Li, T. Veale, P. Rosso, E. Shutova, J. Barnden, and A. Reyes, "Semeval-2015 task 11: Sentiment analysis of figurative language in twitter," in Proceedings of the 9th International Workshop on Semantic Evaluation (SemEval 2015), 2015, pp. 470–478.

[55] E. Cambria, B. Schuller, Y. Xia, and C. Havasi, "New avenues in opinion mining and sentiment analysis," IEEE Intelligent Systems, vol. 28, no. 2, 2013, pp. 15–21.

[56] S. Kiritchenko and S. Mohammad, "The effect of negators, modals, and degree adverbs on sentiment composition," in Proceedings of the 7th Workshop on Computational Approaches to Subjectivity, Sentiment and Social Media Analysis, 2016, pp. 43–52.

[57] M. Van de Kauter, D. Breesch, and V. Hoste, "Fine-grained analysis of explicit and implicit sentiment in financial news articles," Expert Systems with applications, vol. 42, no. 11, 2015, pp. 4999–5010.

[58] R. Feldman, "Techniques and applications for sentiment analysis," Communications of the ACM, vol. 56, no. 4, 2013, pp. 82–89.

Towards a Framework for the Automatic Detection of Crisis Emotions on Social Media: a Corpus Analysis of the Tweets Posted after the Crash of Germanwings Flight 9525

Veronique Hoste
and Cynthia Van Hee

LT3 Language and Translation Technology Team
Ghent University
Ghent, Belgium
Email: firstname.lastname@ugent.be

Karolien Poels

Department of Communication Studies
University of Antwerp
Antwerp, Belgium
Email: karolien.poels@uantwerpen.be

***Abstract*—Social media, and in particular Twitter, are increasingly being utilized during crises. It has been shown that tweets offer valuable real-time information for decision-making. Given the vast amount of data available on the Web, there is a need for intelligent ways to select and retrieve the desired information. Analyzing sentiment and emotions in online text is one option for distinguishing relevant from irrelevant information. In this study, we investigate to what extent automatic sentiment analysis techniques can be used for detecting crisis emotions on Twitter. Therefore, a corpus of tweets posted after the crash of Germanwings Flight 9525 was built and labeled with polarity and emotion information. Preliminary results show better classification results for the negative sentiment class compared to the positive class. An analysis of the more fine-grained emotion classification reveals that sympathy and anger are the most frequently expressed emotions in our corpus. To further enhance the performance of emotion classification in online crisis communication, it is crucial to accurately detect i) the object of the crisis emotion and ii) the characteristics of the sender.**

Keywords–emotion detection; social media; natural language processing; organizational crisis; crisis communication.

I. Introduction

The use of social media has thrived over the past few years. As a consequence, the ways in which people communicate during crisis situations have changed. Especially the microblogging service Twitter has become a very popular web application for seeking and defusing crisis-related information [1], [2], [3]. Furthermore, it is an ideal way for crisis managers to demonstrate their compassion, concern, and empathy to stakeholders in case of an organizational crisis. An organizational crisis can be described as "the perception of an unpredictable event that threatens important expectancies of stakeholders and can seriously impact an organization's performance and generate negative outcomes" [4]. An event is partially defined as a crisis by the perceptions of stakeholders [4]. Bryson [5] defines a stakeholder as "a person or a group that is influenced by or has an influence on an organization". Crises interfere with some stakeholder expectancies, which results in people becoming angry and upset. As a consequence, the organization is perceived less positively and its reputation is damaged. It is critical for organizations and public relations practitioners working in the field of crisis communication to have knowledge about how to shape the appropriate strategies in response to crises. Coombs' [6], [7] Situational Crisis Communication Theory (SCCT) is a dominant theory on crisis response strategies. It takes an audience-centred approach in order to understand stakeholders' reactions in crisis situations by examining their attribution of crisis responsibility [8]. Attribution theory posits that people will make judgements about the causes of events, especially those that are unexpected and generate negative outcomes [6]. Since crises are (mostly) unforeseen and negative, they are just the type of event that will produce attributions. If stakeholders think an organization should have been able to control a crisis or has made serious mistakes, they will blame the organization for the crisis. Furthermore, greater attributions of responsibility result in stronger feelings of anger and more negative visions on people and organizations [9], something that should be carefully monitored.

All of this shows that understanding people's reactions and emotions during a crisis is crucial for organizations. In this paper, we explore how sentiment analysis can be used to understand how publics consume crisis information. To this end, a state-of-the-art sentiment analysis system was applied to a Twitter dataset, which we collected after the crash of a Germanwings aircraft in the French Alps in 2015. While sentiment analysis systems classifies the tweets according to their polarity (positive, negative or neutral), they do not give insights into the more fine-grained emotions expressed in texts. In order to better understand the types of emotions expressed in our corpus, we further labeled the data with the crisis-related emotion categories as proposed by Jin et al. [9] and report our findings.

The remainder of this paper is organized as follows: Section II presents a literature overview on the analysis of sentiment and emotions in crisis communication. In Section III, we describe the experiments on sentiment classification and emotion detection whereas Section IV discusses the findings of our analysis. Finally, in Section V we draw some conclusions and present prospects for future work.

II. Sentiment and Emotions in Crisis Communication

In order to handle a crisis effectively, it is crucial for crisis managers to understand how emotions are related to crisis

TABLE I. Occurrence of emotion classes in the gold standard corpus.

Emotion class	# tweets	Example tweet
Anger	25	This documentary about Andreas Lubitz is making my blood boil #GermanWingsCrash
Fear	4	Thanks to the evil #GermanWingsCrash I'm officially scared to fly, they should allow us to talk and meet our pilot incase.
Apprehension	4	If the pilot used an axe on the door, whats to stop a terrorist? What other potential weapons r laying round on flights? #GermanWingsCrash
Confusion	2	Should I be worried or reassured by the #GermanWingsCrash? It is good to know that the doors won't open from the outside...but then again...
Contempt	21	So this guy takes a picture in front of the Golden Gate Bridge..The most used bridge for suicide jumps. Dude why not then? #GermanWingsCrash
Disgust	9	The Daily Mail coverage of the #GermanWingsCrash has been repugnant. Headlines like 'how the nazis led to killer co-pilot' help no one.
Embarrassment	0	-
Guilt	0	-
Sadness	14	I feel really sad for the 150 families who are suffering as a result of the #GermanWingsCrash. Beyond tragic.
Surprise	1	Blown away. Pilot locked out of the #Germanwings cockpit?!? I thought I heard it all. #German-WingsCrash
Sympathy	26	Our thoughts and prayers go out to those who lost loved ones in the #GermanWingsCrash May God be with you in these hard times.
Other	2	I'm thinking this attn on #AndreasLubitz and the #GermanWingsCrash is overdone. It's tragic & I would rather see the focus on the victims.

responsibility and crisis communication strategies. Therefore, crisis managers should understand how crisis situations are appraised and evaluated by stakeholders [8]. It was found that stronger attributions of crisis responsibility result in feelings of anger and in some extreme cases in *schadenfreude* (i.e., getting pleasure from the pain of others) toward the organization [10]. Moreover, feelings of sympathy for the organization reduce if a crisis is not handled properly. Due to negative emotions, stakeholders can decide to break off interactions with an organization or engage in negative word of mouth about the organization.

Tweets provide useful real-time information for decision-making and communication during crises [11], [12]. However, given the vast amount of data online, this information cannot be directly used. Applying sentiment analysis is one option to make this vast amount of information manageable and usable. By using sentiment analysis, tweets expressing positive and negative emotions can be detected and analyzed against each other. Contrary to sentiment analysis, which classifies tweets as positive or negative, affect analysis or emotion recognition classifies tweets as belonging to a specific emotional state (e.g., happiness, anger) [13]. Since it is a multinomial classification problem rather than a binary classification problem, affect analysis is even more challenging than sentiment analysis [14]. Most systems for automatic analysis of emotions are based on the six basic emotions of Ekman [15], namely *anger, fear, sadness, enjoyment, disgust,* and *surprise*. Strapparava and Mihalcea [13] constructed a large data set of news headlines that were annotated with these basic emotions and developed a binary classifier for each emotion. Their experiments show that the classification performance varies strongly between the different emotion categories (F= 4.68 for *disgust* vs. F= 32.78 for *joy*). However, the Ekman scale does not account for the typical emotions expressed in organizational crises. In order to account for these crisis-related emotions, Jin et al. [9] proposed an emotion framework in which they identified three clusters of crisis emotions: i) attribution-independent emotions, which consist of anxiety, fear, apprehension, and sympathy; ii) external-attribution-dependent emotions, including disgust, contempt, anger, and sadness; and iii) internal-attribution-dependent emotions, which consist of embarrassment, guilt, and shame. Attribution-independent emotions are emotions people feel toward a crisis situation; external-attribution-dependent emotions are emotions people feel about an organization in a crisis; and internal-attribution-dependent emotions are emotions people feel for themselves as stakeholders involved in a crisis.

III. Automatic Classification of Sentiment and Emotion in Crisis-related Microposts

In this section, we report on the data and different experiments we performed on the tweets related to the crash of a Germanwings airplane in the French Alpes.

A. Dataset

On Tuesday, March 24, 2015, around 10:41 Central European Time, an Airbus A320-200 crashed in the French Alps, 100 kilometres northwest of Nice. It concerned Flight 9525, an international passenger flight from Barcelona-El Prat Airport in Spain to Düsseldorf Airport in Germany. The flight was operated by Germanwings, a low-cost airline owned by Lufthansa. First, the crash was assumed to be an accident. On March, 26, however, the French Bureau d'Enquêtes et d'Analyses pour la Sécurité de l'Aviation Civile discovered after analyzing the aircraft's flight data recorder that co-pilot Andreas Lubitz deliberately crashed the aircraft. Two pilots, four cabin crew members, and 144 passengers were on board of the aircraft. No one survived the crash. In the week after the crash, evidence was found that Lubitz suffered from a psychosomatic illness and that he was taking prescription drugs.

For this paper's study, a corpus of English tweets was collected. The Twitter search facility was used in order to find all English posts, made by any Twitter user, that contained the hashtag '#GermanWingsCrash'. Given the vast amount of tweets, a random selection was made of a maximum of 25 tweets per hour, posted between March 24, 2015 and April 6, 2015. A total of 5,490 English tweets were harvested.

B. Sentiment Classification

In order to determine the sentiment that was conveyed in the tweets, we used a machine learning approach to sentiment detection [16] to determine the polarity of the tweets. We used the system developed by Van Hee et al. [16] in the framework of the SemEval-2014 Task 9 on sentiment analysis in Twitter. First, linguistic preprocessing (including tokenization, PoS-tagging, lemmatization and dependency parsing) was performed on the datasets. Then, a number of lexical and syntactic features were implemented: n-gram features, word shape features (e.g., the number of capitalized words), lexicon features, syntactic features (e.g., Part-of-Speech information), named entity features and PMI features (PMI values indicate the association of a word with positive and negative sentiment). After performing feature selection experiments, it was discovered by Van Hee et al. [16] that features based on n-grams, sentiment lexicons, and Part-of-Speech tags were most contributive for labelling a message or an instance of that message as positive, negative, or neutral.

The system labelled 676 tweets as positive, 2,815 tweets as negative, and 1,999 tweets as neutral. Given that this corpus contains tweets referring to the crash, the large number of negative tweets is not surprising. In order to assess the quality of the automatic labelling, we manually annotated a corpus of 200 tweets with polarity information (see Table II). We observed a classification accuracy of 73.17% for the negative class, 26.92% for the positive class and 64.83% for the neutral class. The total system accuracy amounted to 63.32%. It can be concluded that the system particularly made mistakes with regard to the positive class label. This could be explained by the fact that the system has been trained with Twitter messages on a variety of general topics and not with crisis-related tweets. As a result, the training datasets delivered in the framework of the SemEval-2014 shared task contained more positive tweets (38.20%). Moreover, it can be concluded that the system performed best with regard to the negative class label. This is a significant advantage in crisis situations, in which the detection of negative emotions is highly important.

TABLE II. Polarity detection classification accuracy

Polarity	*# tweets*	*Accuracy*
Positive	26	26.92%
Negative	82	73.17%
Neutral	92	64.83%

C. Towards Emotion Detection

Research on understanding emotions in crisis-related tweets and more specifically to pinpoint those tweets which might cause organizational harm, is scarce. Consequently, no system was available yet to detect crisis-related emotional content in tweets. In order to better understand the types of emotions expressed, we took the 200 tweets which were manually labeled with polarity information and also labeled them with emotions. For this purpose, the scale of Jin et al. [9] was used, since it was specifically developed for measuring the publics' emotions in organizational crises. This crisis emotion scale consists of thirteen discrete emotions, being *anger, anxiety, apprehension, confusion, contempt, disgust, embarrassment, fear, guilt, sadness, shame, surprise,* and *sympathy*. For the annotation, we grouped a number of emotions as they were difficult to differentiate, namely anxiety and fear, and shame and embarrassment. Tweets that conveyed an emotion that did not occur in Jin et al.'s crisis emotion scale were labelled as *other*.

For the tweets expressing a positive or a negative sentiment, we tagged the emotional content as one of the classes anger, fear, apprehension, confusion, contempt, disgust, embarrassment, guilt, sadness, surprise, sympathy and other. Table I gives an overview of the occurrence of these emotion classes in our English gold standard corpus. Sympathy, anger and contempt are the emotions that were most frequently expressed in the data. No tweets conveying embarrassment or guilt were found in our gold standard corpus. For each emotion class, an example tweet is represented in the last column.

IV. Reflections

Important to note is that the current annotation scheme fails to detect the object of the expressed emotion. While the sympathy emotions are mostly expressed towards the family members of the victims, the tweets expressing anger and contempt have a completely different object, most often the co-pilot that deliberately crashed the plane (e.g., "F'ing lunatic. Kill yourself, not a load of passengers! #flight9525"). In order to make emotion detection really viable for business intelligence, a more fine-grained approach in the annotation of the external-attribution-dependent emotions should be taken into account.This way, not only emotions are labelled, but also the objects of these emotions (and maybe also the senders of these emotions), a tendency we also observe in the domain of sentiment analysis (see Pontiki et al. [17]). Important to know for crisis managers of companies such as Germanwings and Lufthansa is how people report on their organizations, something which is not being covered by the current annotation scheme.

A shallow analysis of the tweets reveals that many of them refer to the aviation sector as a whole ("sad day in aviation again", "another flight crash", "far too many planes going down", "In The Wake Of The #GermanWingsCrash Crash, Should You Trust Low-Cost Airlines?", etc.), which has a general image problem. Two main criticisms were specifically targeted towards both Germanwings and Lufthansa: i) that they did not immediately release the names of the pilots (which was done a day after the crash) and ii) that the cockpit should always have two persons present (this two-in-the-cockpit rule was very soon adopted). If this criticism would have been automatically detected, then crisis managers would have had a guiding tool for adequate crisis communications while the crisis was unfolding. This is how accurate emotion detection in the future could make a difference, ultimately reducing reputation harm for organizations.

V. Conclusion

The main goal of this study was to investigate the extent to which automatic sentiment analysis techniques can be used to detect crisis emotions on Twitter. We conclude that the sentiment analysis system performed better on negative tweets when compared to tweets expressing a positive emotion. Although during crises negative emotions are most prevalent and relevant for crisis emotions to focus upon, positive emotions should not be neglected. To have a better understanding of how stakeholders respond to crisis victims (e.g., by showing sympathy), to the organization itself –both at the beginning of a crisis, while the crisis is unfolding and after crisis communication has been made (e.g., apologies, condolences), it is also crucial to have a more fine-grained classification of specific crisis-related emotions. In order to allow for the future development of such automatic procedures, we conducted a small corpus analysis for which we manually labeled our corpus with crisis-related emotions. We found that sympathy and anger were the most frequently expressed emotions in the English gold standard corpus in the case of the Germanwings crash. We also observed that the annotation of crisis-related emotions in the tweets was insufficient to support organizational crisis communication. To further enhance the usefulness of automatic (crisis) emotion detection on social media, future studies should work on the classification of contextual information, such as the object and characteristics of the sender of the crisis emotion.

REFERENCES

[1] Y. Jin, B. F. Liu, and L. L. Austin, "Examining the role of social media in effective crisis management: the effects of crisis origin, information form, and source on publics' crisis responses," Communication Research, vol. 41, no. 1, 2011, pp. 74–94.

[2] A. Schwarz, "How publics use social media to respond to blame games in crisis communication: The Love Parade tragedy in Duisburg 2010," Public Relations Review, vol. 38, no. 3, 2012, pp. 430–437.

[3] S. R. Veil, T. Buehner, and M. J. Palenchar, "A work-in-process literature review: incorporating social media in risk and crisis communication," Journal of Contingencies and Crisis Management, vol. 19, no. 2, 2011, pp. 110–122.

[4] T. Coombs, Ongoing crisis communication : planning, managing, and responding (3 ed.). Thousand Oaks, Calif.: SAGE, 2012.

[5] J. Bryson, "What to do when stakeholders matter: Stakeholder identification analysis techniques," Public Management Review, vol. 6, no. 1, 2004, pp. 21–53.

[6] T. Coombs, "Impact of past crises on current crisis communication: Insights from Situational Crisis Communication Theory." Journal of Business Communication, vol. 41, no. 3, 2004, pp. 265–289.

[7] ——, "Protecting organization reputations during a crisis: The development and application of Situational Crisis Communication Theory," Corporate Reputation Review, vol. 10, no. 3, 2007, pp. 163–176.

[8] Y. Jin, "Making sense sensibly in crisis communication: How publics' crisis appraisal influence their negative emotions, coping strategy preferences and crisis response acceptance," Communication Research, vol. 37, no. 4, 2010, pp. 522–552.

[9] Y. Jin, B. F. Liu, D. Anagondahalli, and L. Austin, "Scale development for measuring publics' emotions in organizational crises," Public Relations Review, vol. 40, 2014, pp. 509–518.

[10] H. Kim and G. Cameron, "Emotions matter in crisis: The role of anger and sadness in the publics' response to crisis news framing and corporate crisis response," Communication Research, vol. 38, no. 6, 2011, pp. 826–855.

[11] T. Heverin and L. Zach, "Microblogging for crisis communication: examination of twitter use in response to a 2009 violent crisis in the seattle-tacoma, washington area," in Proceedings of the 7th International ISCRAM Conference, Seattle, USA, 2010, pp. 1–5.

[12] N. D. Sreenivasan, C. S. Lee, and D. H.-L. Goh, "Tweet me home: Exploring information use on twitter in crisis situations," in Proceedings of the 14th International Conference on Human-Computer Interaction, Orlando, Florida, USA, 2011, pp. 1–10.

[13] C. Strapparava and R. Mihalcea, "Learning to identify emotions in text," in Proceedings of the 2008 ACM symposium on Applied computing, 2008, pp. 1556–1560.

[14] F. Brynielsson, J.and Johansson and A. Westling, "Learning to classify emotional content in crisis-related tweets," in Proceedings of the 11th IEEE International Conference on Intelligence and Security Informatics (IEEE ISI), Seattle, Washington, USA, 2013, pp. 33–38.

[15] P. Ekman, "An argument for basic emotions," Cognition & Emotion, vol. 6, no. 3-4, 1992, pp. 169–200.

[16] C. Van Hee, M. Van de Kauter, O. De Clercq, E. Lefever, and V. Hoste, "LT3: Sentiment classification in user-generated content using a rich feature set," in Proceedings of the 8th International Workshop on Semantic Evaluation (SemEval 2014), 2014, pp. 406–410.

[17] M. Pontiki, D. Galanis, H. Papageorgiou, I. Androutsopoulos, S. Manandhar, M. AL-Smadi, M. Al-Ayyoub, Y. Zhao, B. Qin, O. De Clercq, V. Hoste, M. Apidianaki, X. Tannier, N. Loukachevitch, E. Kotelnikov, N. Bel, S. M. Jimenez-Zafra, , and G. Eryigit, "Semeval-2016 task 5: Aspect based sentiment analysis," in Proceedings of the 10th International Workshop on Semantic Evaluation, San Diego, California, USA, 2016, pp. 19–30.

Analysing Emotions in Social Media Coverage on Paris Terror Attacks: a Pilot Study

Cynthia Van Hee, Celine Verleye and Els Lefever
LT[3], Language and Translation Technology Team
Ghent University, Belgium
Groot-Brittanniëlaan 45, 9000 Ghent
Email: firstname.lastname@ugent.be

***Abstract*—Social media provide an increasingly used platform for crisis communication. Governments need to understand how publics consume and react to crisis information via social media. One option to do this is by applying emotion analysis. In this pilot study, we target the November 2015 terrorist attacks in Paris as a case study for emotion analysis and detection. We constructed a Dutch Facebook corpus manually annotated with i) Ekman's basic emotions and ii) irony use. The annotations reveal that *anger* is the most recurrent emotion, however the basic emotions do not cover all emotions in the dataset. The corpus also exhibits a fair number of ironic utterances, mostly expressing emotions like *disgust* and *anger*. The experimental results show that the detection of some emotions (e.g., *fear*) is challenging compared to others and that the classifier suffers from data sparseness.**

Keywords–Emotion detection; Social media; Natural language processing; Terrorism

I. Introduction

Social media have become primary communication tools for everyday conversations. More and more, they are also an important means of communication during crises [1], [2], allowing organisations and governments to inform the public, calm down anxiety and understand people's behaviour in such situations [3]. A recent example of this are the November 2015 Paris attacks, a series of coordinated terrorist attacks on 13 November 2015 in Paris by which 130 people lost their lives and many people were injured [4]. During the attacks, social media were extensively used by people looking for –or offering– shelter, and as a medium for spreading photos and information about missing people in the region [5]. Facebook activated the Paris Safety Check application allowing users to inform relatives about their safety and news channels provided up-to-date information and safety instructions via the platform. After the attacks, Facebook was also used by people to show their support for France and to react to the events.

As a result of their popularity, social networking sites constitute a rich source of information about the public opinion. Over the past decade, user-generated content has been investigated extensively in the field of sentiment and emotion analysis. Sentiment analysis involves machine learning techniques for determining the polarity of a text (i.e., positive or negative) [6], without taking into account specific emotions. The latter belongs to the field of emotion classification, which is a more fine-grained form of sentiment analysis that focuses on extracting emotions from text like joy, anger, and fear [7].

This paper describes a pilot study in which we apply machine learning techniques to unravel the emotions expressed on Facebook after the Paris attacks. To this end, we collected 483 Dutch Facebook reactions to news announcements covering the events. The data are retrieved from the Facebook pages of two Flemish news channels. The corpus is manually labeled for emotion-related categories including Ekman's basic six emotions [8]. Based on the annotations, we explore the feasibility of automatic emotion recognition and report our findings.

The remainder of the paper is structured as follows: in Section II, we give a brief overview of related work in the field of emotion detection. Section III describes the corpus and presents the annotation framework with some examples. Section IV elaborates on the emotion classification experiments. Finally, in Section V, we draw some conclusions and present prospects for future research.

II. Related Research

The past decade has seen an increased research interest in the field of sentiment and emotion analysis. In the framework of SemEval, the International Workshop on Semantic Evaluation[9], benchmark datasets have been made publicly available and several sentiment and emotion classification systems have been developed recently. Automatic emotion detection has been applied to different text genres including weblogs [10], emails [11], [12], news headlines [13], suicide notes [14], and tweets [3], [15]. Many systems for automatic emotion classification focus on the six basic emotions distinguished by Ekman [8], being *joy, fear, anger, disgust, sorrow* and *surprise*. Some studies, however, revealed more complicated emotions in text. For instance Plutchik [16] suggested eight bipolar primary emotions: *joy* versus *sadness*; *anger* versus *fear*; *trust* versus *disgust*; and *surprise* versus *anticipation*. Pestian et al. [17] distinguished sixteen emotion categories relevant to the domain of suicide notes. Finally, Yan & Turtle [7] composed a list of 28 emotions based on manual Twitter annotations.

Table I presents an overview of the state of the art in automatic emotion detection. Most of the work that is listed focuses on Twitter data and all but one (Yan & Turtle [7] describe a multiclass-based approach) conduct binary classification experiments per emotion category. In short, state-of-the-art emotion classifiers rely on machine learning algorithms such as LIBLINEAR, Naïve Bayes, Support Vector Machines, and k-Nearest Neighbors (k-NN). Often exploited features, i.e., information about text properties that may be relevant for emotion classification, include n-grams (i.e., sequences of n following words or characters), punctuation, Part-of-Speech

TABLE I. STATE-OF-THE-ART APPROACHES TO EMOTION DETECTION.

Reference	Corpus	# Emotion categories	Features	Results
Strapparava & Mihalcea [13]	1,25K news headlines	6	n-grams, sentiment lexicons, PMI, syntactic features	F= 0% – 32.78%
Wang et al. [18]	2.5M tweets	7	n-grams, sentiment/emotion lexicons, PoS tags	F= 13.90% – 72.10%
Roberts et al. [19]	7K tweets	7	n-grams, sentiment/emotion lexicons, PMI, punctuation, LDA	F= 60.80% – 74.00%
Mohammad et al. [20]	20K tweets	6	n-grams, sentiment/emotion lexicons	F= 18.70% – 62.40%
Yan & Turtle [7]	5.5K tweets	28	n-grams	F= 51.00% – 57.00%

tags, information from lexical resources such as WordNet-Affect [21], and topic information. The classification results vary among the emotion categories and often reveal that emotions like *joy* and *sadness* are more likely to be recognised than others [13], [18], [19].

III. CORPUS

To train and test the emotion detection classifiers, we collected a series of Facebook posts on the subject of the November 2015 Paris attacks. The corpus comprises 483 Dutch Facebook reactions to news announcements covering the attacks. The announcements date from 14 to 26 November 2015 and were posted on the Facebook page of two Flemish news channels being *Vlaamse Televisie Maatschappij (VTM)*, the main channel of commercial TV in Flanders and Brussels, and *Vlaamse Radio- en Televisieomroeporganisatie (VRT)*, the main channel of the Flemish public broadcaster. Table II presents some corpus examples covering direct reactions to the attacks (examples 1 and 2), as well as topics including house searches and safety measures implemented in Brussels (examples 3 and 4), the raid in which the alleged brain of the attacks was killed (examples 5 and 7), and communications about the threat level in the capital (example 6). After collecting the corpus, all posts were annotated for emotion and irony, the details of which are presented in the next paragraph.

A. Corpus Annotation

As mentioned earlier, the Facebook corpus was annotated for emotions and irony by trained linguists. The emotion annotation was based on Ekman's basic emotions [8]: *joy, fear, anger, disgust, sorrow* and *surprise*. We also included the label *Other* for ambiguous posts and posts expressing another emotion than one of the basic six, and *None* for posts exhibiting no emotions at all. The resulting set of manually labeled posts serves as the gold standard for the experiments. Table II presents an example for each emotion class with its corpus frequency. It should be noted that some posts received multiple labels. The sum of the second column values in the table thus reflects the total of emotion labels that were assigned for the entire corpus. Furthermore, all posts were annotated for the presence of (verbal) irony, the motivation for which is twofold: firstly we hypothesise that the subject will cause people to venture criticism, which is often 'softened' by using irony [22]. Indeed, tweets have proven rich in figurative language like irony [23], hence it wil be interesting to see if the same applies to the current dataset. Secondly, we want to investigate to what extent the presence of irony impacts the performance of the automatic emotion classifier. The next paragraph provides more details on this annotation with some ironic examples.

B. Annotation Analysis

Table II presents the different emotion classes that were annotated and provides a corpus example for each class. As described earlier, in addition to the basic emotions, we included *Other* as an annotation category. Interestingly, 278 instances were assigned this label, which means that in approximately 60% of the corpus the expressed emotion could not be matched to any of Ekman's basic six [8]. A closer inspection of the *Other* category reveals that many of these instances have a mocking or criticising tone and often express emotions like indignation and indifference (e.g., 'Yeah bla, bla, bla...', 'Guess I'm going to sleep. We'll see how it ends tomorrow *(...)*'). An analysis of the emotion distribution by gender reveals that women express more fear (14%) and sorrow (4%) as opposed to men (8% and 2%, respectively). Anger on the other hand, is the most frequent emotion expressed by men (19% vs. 16% by women). The observations seem to support the gender stereotyping of emotions [24], although further research on a larger dataset is needed.

With regards to the use of irony, we observe that approximately 20% of the corpus is labeled as ironic, which supports the findings of Ghosh et al. [23]. Here, we present two examples of ironic instances:

(1) Spijtig da fie *(sic.)* terrorist geen 60 ree waar je 50 mag! DAN zouden ze em wel hebben. **EN:** Too bad that the terrorist wasn't driving 60 where the speed limit is 50! THEN they would have caught him.

(2) Och al een geluk dat diene mens zoveel betaald *(sic.)* wordt om ons dit mee te delen! Had dat nooit zelf kunnen bedenken. **EN:** Good thing hat man is paid so much to communicate this to the public! Never could have come up with this myself.

Also, more ironic utterances are posted by men than by women (70% vs. 20%) –no author information was found for the remaining 10%. A closer look at the emotions expressed in ironic utterances reveals that the irony in the corpus often co-occurs with anger, disgust and *other* (Fig. 1).

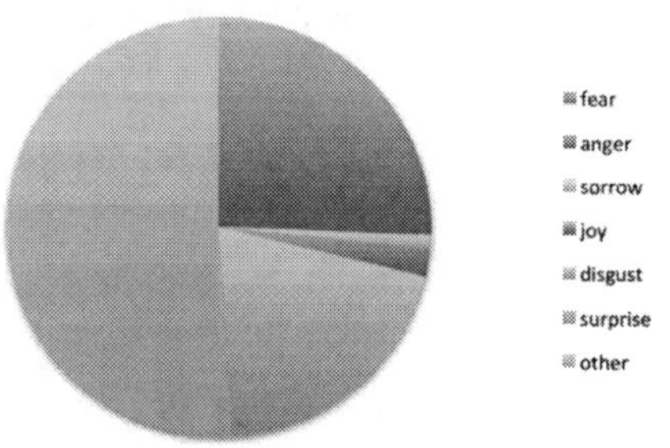

Figure 1. The distribution of ironic utterances according to the different emotion categories.

Generally, we see that the irony in these instances is mainly used for two purposes: i) expressing criticism towards the

TABLE II. CORPUS EXAMPLES.

Emotion category	# Instances	Relative freq.	Corpus example	Translation
anger	117	25.60%	1) Onnozelaars jullie maken ons van alles wijs !	1) You stupid people make us believe anything!
disgust	61	13.35%	2) Zoiets doet een beest nog niet	2) Not even an animal would do this ....
joy	62	13.57%	3) Knap van jou! jij hebt mijn verkiezingstem!	3) Excellent! You can count on my vote!
fear	52	11.38%	4) Pffff kids die bang zijn, wij zijn zenuwachtig, ... Niks om te lachen!	4) Pffff kids that are afraid, we parents that are nervous, ... Nothing to laugh about!
sorrow	10	2.19%	5) Ik treur voor zijn ouders...	5) I feel sorry for his parents...
surprise	7	1.53%	6) Snap er niks van..... Eerst zochten ze 1 terrorist en het was niveau 4, nu zoeken ze 2 terroristen en nu is het niveau 3 ?????	6) Do not get it ..... First, they were looking for one terrorist and the level was four, now they are looking for two terrorists and now the level is 3 ?????
other	278	60.83%	7) Woorden maar weinig initiatief...	7) Words, but little initiative...

Belgian government and police, and ii) lightening the subject by using irony as a form of humour, for instance by mocking with the alleged brain of the attacks. Examples of the latter tend to be more ludic than the former. However, both uses of irony share the purpose of expressing criticism towards some entity, which supports the hypothesis that irony is often used to express criticism in a less face-threatening way [22].

IV. EXPERIMENTS

We evaluated the feasibility of emotion classification in Facebook data by means of a series of binary classification experiments. For the experiments, we only considered posts in which at least one emotion category was identified by the annotators, which resulted in an experimental corpus containing 457 instances. For each emotion category –including *Other*– a binary experiment was run to predict whether the emotion is present (classification label "1") in an instance or not (label "0"). This resulted in seven binary experiments with one emotion category as the positive class, whereas the remaining emotion categories represent the negative class. Instances that were annotated with more than one emotion category (e.g., expressing both anger and fear), are subject to detection by the different corresponding classifiers.

As the classification algorithm we used LIBSVM [25] with linear kernel. As evaluation measures, we report (ten-fold cross-validated) (1) precision, (2) recall and (3) F_1-score for the positive class, calculated as follows:

$$Precision = \frac{Number\ of\ correctly\ predicted\ labels}{Total\ number\ of\ predicted\ labels} \quad (1)$$

$$Recall = \frac{Number\ of\ correctly\ predicted\ labels}{Total\ number\ of\ gold\ standard\ labels} \quad (2)$$

$$F - score = \frac{2(Precision\ *\ Recall)}{Precision\ +\ Recall} \quad (3)$$

In addition, we report accuracy figures, which simply divide the number of true predictions (both positive and negative class) by the total number of instances.

As a preprocessing step, all posts were tokenised using the LeTs Preprocess Toolkit [26]. For each classifier, the following features were exploited:

- **Bags-of-words:** token unigrams, bigrams and trigrams.
- **Sentiment features** based on two existing sentiment lexicons for Dutch [27], [28]:
    - the number of positive, negative and neutral tokens in the instance;
    - the overall polarity, i.e., the sum of the values of the identified polarity words in the instance.

Table III presents the experimental results for all binary classifiers by means of accuracy, precision, recall and F_1-score. As we approach the automatic emotion classification task as a detection taks, we only considered the positive class labels (i.e., the instances containing the emotion in question) for calculating precision and recall. In contrast, the accuracy results are measured on the complete data set (i.e., all positive and negative instances).

TABLE III. EXPERIMENTAL RESULTS PER EMOTION CLASSIFIER.

Emotion category	Accuracy	Precision	Recall	F_1-score
Anger	72.21%	42.86%	25.64%	32.09%
Joy	89.28%	76.00%	30.65%	43.68%
Fear	86.00%	25.00%	11.54%	15.79%
Disgust	89.06%	66.67%	36.07%	46.81%
Surprise	98.47%	-	-	-
Sorrow	97.81%	-	-	-
Other	71.55%	75.87%	78.06%	**76.95%**

Not considering *Other*, we see that the system performance is highest for the category *Disgust* (F_1= 46.81%), followed by *Joy* (F_1= 43.68%). The category *Other* scoring best would suggest that, albeit ambiguous, the category encompasses instances that share a number of characteristics. Another explanation for the good result would be the high relative frequency of the emotion class in the corpus compared to the other categories. The *Surprise* and *Sorrow* classifiers consistently predict the negative class, resulting in an F_1-score of zero and an accuracy equal to the proportion of negative class instances. Presumably, there are insufficient training examples in the corpus for both categories, which causes the system to fail to build a good model for recognising new instances of these classes.

A qualitative analysis of the systems' output reveals that many misclassifications could be the result of the systems exploiting only lexical information. For the *Joy* category for instance, we see a fair number of false negatives that contain negative sentiment words while expressing a positive sentiment overall (e.g., 'It's a shame I can only press the like button once!'). Inversely, false positives often include sentences with positive words while expressing an overall negative emotion (e.g., 'The government should guarantee a good policy (...)'). With respect to the category *Anger*, we see that many false positives contain flooded punctuation (e.g., 'Good job guys!!!!'), which would indicate that the system considers heavy punctuation as an indication of anger. An explanation for the poor performance of the category *Fear* would be that such emotion expressions (e.g., 'What will happen now?',

'Should we keep the kids at home tomorrow?') are much less lexicalised than expressions of anger, for instance.

A more general conclusion that can be drawn from the analysis is that many instances are ambiguous, i.e., they exhibit more than one emotion category. We see that instances containing only one emotion category are more often correctly classified than instances expressing multiple emotions. An analysis of the annotated categories shows that *Joy, Disgust* and *Other* are often the only emotion category that was identified (in 65% of the cases), whereas *Fear* and *Anger* were more often used in combination with other emotion categories (only in 37% of the cases it was the only expressed emotion). This is also reflected in Table III. We also see a fair number of ironic utterances among the wrongly classified instances, which would suggest that irony indeed affects the classification performance (cf. Section III-A).

When comparing the results to the state of the art, we see that generally, the classifiers perform less well than other systems that are trained on much larger corpora (Table I). Nevertheless, this pilot study provides valuable insights into the emotions expressed in the aftermath of a series of terrorist attacks. The main conclusions are the following:

1) Ekman's basic emotions [8] are insufficient to describe all emotions in the corpus. Expanding the list would reduce the number of ambiguous annotations and scale down the *Other* class.
2) The emotion classifiers mainly rely on lexical clues, which are often insufficient to determine the correct emotion class.
3) Many instances contained multiple emotion categories. Since a binary classification task forces the system to choose one label, it would be interesting to see whether a multiclass approach works better.
4) The results for sparse emotion categories (e.g., *Surprise*) are very low, indicating that a strong correlation exists between the occurrence of a class and the system's performance.

V. Conclusions and Future Work

In this paper, we analysed the emotions expressed online in the aftermath of the November 2015 Paris attacks. The analysis reveals that anger is one of the most salient emotions. Governments should bear this in mind when communicating with the public. Since *Other* remains the largest emotion category in the corpus, we suggest to expand the list of basic emotions. The results of the binary classification experiments show that emotion classification is not a trivial task and that the system's performance clearly suffers from data sparseness. If we discard the category *Other*, the best results are achieved for the emotion categories *Disgust* and *Joy*. This would suggest that these categories are more explicit or highly lexicalised when compared to the others. We see an inverse correlation between classification performance and the proportion of ambiguous instances (i.e., instances expressing multiple emotions) in the corpus. For instance, the proportion of ambiguous instances for the *Joy* category is 32% whereas this is 62% for *Anger*. F_1-scores for the corresponding classifiers are 43.68% and 32.09%, respectively. Another interesting observation is the good performance for the category *Other*, which was assigned to tweets that are ambiguous or that express another emotion than one of the basic six. When looking at the use of irony, we see that many ironic utterances in the corpus co-occur with the emotions anger, disgust and *other*. A closer look into the latter revealed that many of these instances contain emotions like indignation, and indifference (cf. Section III-B).

This paper presents a pilot study to emotion detection in Dutch crisis communication. To be able to generalise our findings, more experiments are needed on a larger dataset, which will be the main focus in future work. Additionally, we aim to enhance the performance of our classifiers by adding more complex features including topic models, Linguistic Inquiry and Word Count (LIWC) features and syntactic information. Another interesting direction for future work is automatic irony recognition. Since the classifier exploits sentiment lexicon features, its performance is affected by ironic utterances that contain positive sentiment words while actually conveying a negative sentiment.

References

[1] A. Schwarz, "How publics use social media to respond to blame games in crisis communication: The Love Parade tragedy in Duisburg 2010," Public Relations Review, vol. 38, no. 3, 2012, pp. 430–437, ISSN: 0363-8111.

[2] Y. Jin, A. Pang, and G. T. Cameron, "Integrated crisis mapping: Towards a publics-based, emotion-driven conceptualization in crisis communication," Sphera Publica, vol. 7, no. 1, 2007, pp. 81–96, ISSN: 1180-9210.

[3] B.-K. H. Vo and N. Collier, "Twitter emotion analysis in earthquake situations," International Journal of Computational Linguistics and Applications, vol. 4, no. 1, 2013, pp. 159–173.

[4] "November 2015 Paris attacks," 2015, URL: https://en.wikipedia.org/wiki/November_2015_Paris_attacks/ [accessed: 2016-10-03].

[5] "Quel est le rôle des réseaux sociaux dans des événements comme les attentats de Paris?" 2015, URL: http://www.la-croix.com/Actualite/France/Quel-est-le-role-des-reseaux-sociaux-dans-des-evenements-comme-les-attentats-de-Paris-2015-11-15-1380592/ [accessed: 2016-10-03].

[6] B. Pang and L. Lee, "Opinion Mining and Sentiment Analysis," Foundations and Trends in Information Retrieval, vol. 2, no. 1-2, 2008, pp. 1–135, ISSN: 1554-0669.

[7] J. S. Y. Liew and H. R. Turtle, "Exploring Fine-Grained Emotion Detection in Tweets," in Proceedings of the NAACL Student Research Workshop, June 13–15, 2016, San Diego, California, USA. Association for Computational Linguistics, Jun. 2016, pp. 73–80.

[8] P. Ekman, "An Argument for Basic Emotions," Cognition and Emotion, vol. 6, no. 3, 1992, pp. 169–200.

[9] "SemEval-2016 : Semantic Evaluation Exercises," 2016, URL: http://alt.qcri.org/semeval2016/ [accessed: 2016-10-03].

[10] R. Mihalcea and H. Liu, "A corpus-based approach to finding happiness," in Proceedings of AAAI-CAAW-06, the Spring Symposia on Computational Approaches to Analyzing Weblogs, 2006.

[11] H. Liu, H. Lieberman, and T. Selker, "A Model of Textual Affect Sensing Using Real-world Knowledge," in Proceedings of the 8th International Conference on Intelligent User Interfaces (IUI), January 12–15, 2003, Miami, Florida, USA. ACM, Jan. 2003, pp. 125–132, ISBN: 1-58113-586-6.

[12] S. M. Mohammad and T. Yang, "Tracking Sentiment in Mail: How Genders Differ on Emotional Axes," in Proceedings of the 2nd Workshop on Computational Approaches to Subjectivity and Sentiment Analysis (WASSA), June 24, 2011, Portland, Oregon, USA. Association for Computational Linguistics, Jun. 2011, pp. 70–79.

[13] C. Strapparava and R. Mihalcea, "Learning to Identify Emotions in Text," in Proceedings of the 2008 ACM Symposium on Applied Computing (SAC), March 16–20, Fortaleza, Ceará, Brazil. ACM, Mar. 2008, pp. 1556–1560, ISBN: 978-1-59593-753-7.

[14] B. Desmet and V. Hoste, "Emotion detection in suicide notes," Expert Systems with Applications, vol. 40, no. 16, 2013, pp. 6351–6358, ISSN: 0957-4174.

[15] S. M. Mohammad, "#Emotional Tweets," in *SEM 2012: The First Joint Conference on Lexical and Computational Semantics – Volume 1: Proceedings of the main conference and the shared task, and Volume 2: Proceedings of the Sixth International Workshop on Semantic Evaluation (SemEval 2012), June 7–8, Montreal, Canada. Association for Computational Linguistics, Jun. 2012, pp. 246–255.

[16] R. Plutchik, The Emotions: Facts, theories, and a new model. Random House, 1962.

[17] J. P. Pestian, P. Matykiewicz, M. Linn-Gust, B. South, O. Uzuner, J. Wiebe, K. B. Cohen, J. Hurdle, and C. Brew, "Sentiment analysis of suicide notes: A shared task," Biomedical informatics insights, vol. 5, no. Suppl. 1, 2012, p. 3.

[18] W. Wang, L. Chen, K. Thirunarayan, and A. P. Sheth, "Harnessing Twitter "Big Data" for Automatic Emotion Identification," in 2012 International Conference on Privacy, Security, Risk and Trust (PASSAT 2012), and 2012 International Confernece on Social Computing (SocialCom 2012), September 3–5, 2012, Amsterdam, Netherlands. IEEE Computer Society, Sep. 2012, pp. 587–592, ISBN: 978-0-7695-4848-7.

[19] K. Roberts, M. A. Roach, J. Johnson, J. Guthrie, and S. M. Harabagiu, "EmpaTweet: Annotating and Detecting Emotions on Twitter," in Proceedings of the 8th International Conference on Language Resources and Evaluation (LREC), May 21–27, 2012, Istanbul, Turkey. European Language Resources Association (ELRA), May 2012, pp. 3806–3813, ISBN: 978-2-9517408-7-7.

[20] S. M. Mohammad and S. Kiritchenko, "Using hashtags to capture fine emotion categories from tweets," Computational Intelligence, vol. 31, no. 2, 2015, pp. 301–326, ISSN: 0824-7935.

[21] C. Strapparava and A. Valitutti, "WordNet-Affect: An affective extension of WordNet," in Proceedings of the 4th International Conference on Language Resources and Evaluation (LREC), May 26–28, Lisbon, Portugal. ELRA, May 2004, pp. 1083–1086.

[22] P. Brown and S. C. Levinson, Politeness: Some Universals in Language Usage. Cambridge University Press, Feb. 1987, ISBN: 9780521313551.

[23] A. Ghosh and T. Veale, "Fracking Sarcasm using Neural Network," in Proceedings of the 7th Workshop on Computational Approaches to Subjectivity, Sentiment and Social Media Analysis (WASSA), June 16, 2016, San Diego, California, USA. Association for Computational Linguistics, Jun. 2016, pp. 161–169.

[24] E. A. Plant, J. S. Hyde, D. Keltner, and P. G. Devine, "The Gender Stereotyping of Emotions," Psychology of Women Quarterly, vol. 24, no. 1, 2000, pp. 81–92, ISSN: 1471-6402.

[25] C.-C. Chang and C.-J. Lin, "LIBSVM: A Library for Support Vector Machines," ACM Transactions on Intelligent Systems and Technology (TIST), vol. 2, no. 3, 2011, pp. 27:1–27:27, ISSN: 2157-6904.

[26] M. Van de Kauter, G. Coorman, E. Lefever, B. Desmet, L. Macken, and V. Hoste, "LeTs preprocess: the multilingual LT3 linguistic preprocessing toolkit," Computational Linguistics in the Netherlands Journal, vol. 3, 2013, pp. 103–120, ISSN: 2211-4009.

[27] T. De Smedt and W. Daelemans, ""Vreselijk mooi!" (Terribly Beautiful!): A Subjectivity Lexicon for Dutch Adjectives," in Proceedings of the 8th International Conference on Language Resources and Evaluation (LREC), May 21–27, 2012, Istanbul, Turkey, 2012, pp. 3568–3572.

[28] V. Jijkoun and K. Hofmann, "Generating a Non-English Subjectivity Lexicon: Relations That Matter," in Proceedings of the 12th Conference of the European Chapter of the Association for Computational Linguistics (EACL), March 30–April 3, Athens, Greece, Mar. 2009, pp. 398–405.

What Does the Bird Say?
Exploring the Link Between Personality and Language Use in Dutch Tweets

Sofie Vandenhoven and Orphée De Clercq

LT^3, Language and Translation Technology Team
Ghent University
Ghent, Belgium
Email: firstname.lastname@ugent.be

Abstract—**The aim of this paper is to ascertain whether the use of language in Dutch tweets can offer researchers insight into the personality of the user posting those tweets. A database was created, containing the tweets of twenty Belgian, Dutch-speaking Twitter users with an equal representation of both genders. All subjects filled in a personality test based on the Big Five Model of personality and two linguistic analyses were performed on the Dutch tweets. In a first analysis, a more abstract representation of the language was created by means of Part-of-Speech tagging. For the second analysis, typical sentiment and personality-charged words were derived from the tweets based on well-known lexicons. Though our database is rather limited, we were able to find some interesting correlations between certain personality traits and language use.**

Keywords–Personality; Big Five; Sentiment analysis.

I. Introduction

Social media are an important aspect of modern-day communication, which is proven by the rising number of monthly active users. This high number of users has logically drawn the attention of researchers, since people share a lot of information about themselves online: how they perceive the world, what they think of current events and how they react on other people are only a few examples. Even more, social media might also offer a deeper insight into their personality, by revealing specific character traits.

Consequently, different sorts of sociolinguistic research on social media have already been conducted: personality, gender and age [1], the use of social media among teens and young adults [2], even the motivation of older adolescents to use social network platforms [3] and also the language used on these social media [4], [5].

The focus of this paper is on personality research. The main objective, however, is not to study the explicit content of messages in order to find out what people talk about online, but to investigate what kind of language is used and whether this language use can reveal something about the personality of the person behind a social media profile. To this purpose, a dataset comprising tweets from twenty respondents -ten males and ten females- was collected. All subjects were asked to fill in a personality test and their tweets were processed using techniques from Natural Language Processing, after which correlations between specific language use and personality were investigated.

The personality model used throughout this paper is known as the Big Five Model [6]. This is one of the most well-researched measures of personality structure of the last decades [4] and it "provides an integrative descriptive model for personality research" [7, p1222]. The personality model contains five traits, marked with the anagram OCEAN or CANOE. Each trait equals a category which is labelled with one substantive. However, the category itself represents a broad range of meaning, captured within this one substantive [7]. For example, the O stands for *Openness*, which includes among others intellect and independence. The different categories are briefly listed in Table 1.

TABLE I. Overview of the Big Five Personality Traits

Trait	*Characteristic*
O for *Openness*	intellectual, polished, independent, open-minded
C for *Conscientiousness*	orderly, responsible, dependable
E for *Extraversion*	talkative, assertive, energetic
A for *Agreeableness*	good-natured, cooperative, trustful
N for *Neuroticism*	not calm, neurotic, easily upset

In the remainder of this paper, we will first discuss how the relation between personality and social media has been studied in the past (Section 2). Next, we will explain how Twitter data has been collected and processed from twenty respondents who all filled in an online personality test based on the Big Five (Section 3). In Section 4, we discuss the results, after which this paper is concluded and prospects for future research are offered in Section 5.

II. Related Work

Four main reasons make social media interesting for research. The increasing popularity of social media in the last decade has created an enormous database of personal information [8]. The content in this database, which is widely available through public profiles, is user-generated [9]. The language used on these social media, which fluctuates between spoken and written language but really is neither of them, is a new form of communication [10] and the messages often contain very personal and emotional content [11]. It is highly possible that those four elements caused or at least coincided with a surge in research regarding the Big Five and social media.

However, an often heard criticism is that online profiles might also depict a false and better image of a user, making personality research on social media useless. In the Facebook study presented in [12], no evidence was found to support this presumption. On the contrary, the results show that "people are not using their social network profiles to promote an idealized virtual identity". This would mean that the personality traits displayed online should correspond to the actual personality of the user.

There has been research on which personalities are mainly drawn to social media. Hamburger and Ben-Artzi [13] found that users of social media are in general introverted and neurotic. Moreover, they also showed a significant difference between genders: female users of social services are generally introverted and highly neurotic, whereas men are quite the opposite. Gender differences were not considered in the study by Ross [14], where almost 90% of the subjects were female. The most important conclusion drawn from this study is that *Openness* positively correlates with the general use of Facebook. A more extended study on social media use [15] concluded that it is more easily used by people scoring higher on *Openness* and *Extraversion*, whereas it is less used by people who are emotionally stable. For the network site Twitter, Hughes [16] found out that it is more appealing to users scoring higher on *Openness* and lower on *Conscientiousness* when used for social contacts. People using Twitter for information were found to be more introverted and more conscientious.

However, most of these studies take more than only linguistic features into account, or they study anything but the language used on social media. Golbeck et. al. claim to be the first to test whether all information displayed on a profile could predict one's personality. They conducted two studies, one on Facebook [4] and another on Twitter [5]. Since our paper focuses on Twitter, we will only discuss those findings. For this research not only the tweets as such were collected, but also public account data such as followers, mentions and so on. However, a linguistic analysis of the tweets formed the major part of the study. Some intuitively logical correlations between the tweets and the Big Five were discovered using the Linguistic Inquiry and Word Count tool (LIWC) [17]. They found that *Conscientiousness* was negatively correlated with words about *death* (e.g., bury, coffin, kill), meaning that the more conscientious a user is, the less he or she will refer to death. Moreover, the same trait was also negatively correlated with *negative emotions* and *sadness*. Hence, both findings suggest that highly conscientious people abandon unhappy subjects. Another finding concerning that personality trait revealed a more frequent usage of the pronoun *you*, indicating that highly conscientious people talk more about others. Also, scoring high in *Agreeableness* indicated a significant use of the pronoun *you* and those users were also less likely to talk about the LIWC categories *achievements* and *money*. When trying to predict personality, the linguistic features contributed most to the task.

In more recent years much research has been performed trying to predict personality based on language, such as [18] and [19]. Though personality prediction is beyond the scope of this paper, we believe that the dataset that was collected for this research will be of use for future research in that direction. Important to note is that most previous research has been conducted on English, whereas we want to know whether Dutch language use without any other profile information, can reveal something about someone's personality. And if this is the case, we want to find out which aspects of language are important to take into consideration.

III. DATA COLLECTION AND PROCESSING

We convinced twenty Dutch-speaking, Flemish persons to participate in our research. All participants were highly active on Twitter and tweeted mostly in Dutch. Relying on the statistics presented in Fig. 1, originally posted by the Belgian Country lead at Twitter, we made sure that half of our respondents belonged to the first age category (ages 16 to 24) and the other half to the second category (ages 25 to 34). Since there is no consensus on whether gender influences personality [13], [20], both genders were equally represented in our database: ten males and ten females.

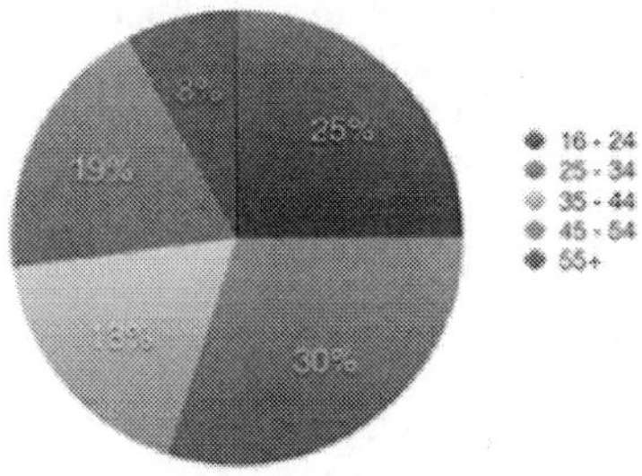

Figure 1. Twitter statistics about the Belgian twitter user profile according to age category in 2015

In order to measure the personality of our respondents, a general Big Five personality test with 46 questions was chosen. The chosen questionnaire uses a Likert-scale from 1 (strongly disagree) to 7 (strongly agree) and had to be filled in online [21]. By agreeing to participate in the research all subjects also agreed to donate their tweets, which were crawled with the Twitter API. After these tweets had been downloaded we made sure that only tweets written in Dutch were retained. In total, our dataset amounted to 8,759 female and 8,780 male tweets.

For this research we first studied whether it is possible to draw a general image of a social media user based on the personality scores that were obtained by our subjects. Next, two linguistic analyses were conducted on the tweets. For both analyses the same two steps were performed. First, a more qualitative analysis was performed by comparing the lowest and highest male and female scorers per personality trait with the outcomes of the linguistic analyses. This more intuitive analysis was followed by measuring Pearson correlations in a second step.

For the first linguistic analysis, we rely on the frequencies of the different word forms or Parts-of-Speech (PoS) used in the tweets of our test subjects, in order to derive whether personality can be connected to particular grammatical choices. To this purpose all tweets were tagged with the LeTs Preprocessing Toolkit [22], the PoS module of this tool automatically assigns morphosyntactic labels to each token. Since LeTs is normally used to process standard text material, the output of the tool was adapted in order to deal with Twitter-specific tokens such as hashtags, mentions, emoji's, etc.

The second linguistic analysis performed on the Twitter data focuses more on the occurrence of words that are known to be charged with a certain sentiment or personality on the basis of lexicons. As sentiment lexicons, we made use of the only two existing sentiment lexicons for Dutch, namely the Duoman lexicon [23] and the Pattern lexicon [24]. The Duoman lexicon comprises nouns, adjectives, verbs and adverbs that have been manually labelled by two human annotators as either positive, negative or neutral. The Pattern lexicon is a list of adjectives that were manually assigned a polarity value between -1 (negative) and +1 (positive). In order to perform the analysis all tokenized tweets were processed and all positive and negative lexicon matches retained. As personality lexicon we used LIWC [17], which was also used in previous research [4], [5]. An analysis with the LIWC results in a categorisation of all words used into lexical dimensions, accompanied by their relative percentages. Examples of those dimensions are *negemo* for negative emotions, *future* for future tenses and *cogmech* for cognitive processes. This analysis could reveal that people scoring particularly high or low on a personality trait might be recognized by the use of some lexical dimensions.

IV. RESULTS

A. General Social Media Image

The results of the online personality test filled in by our respondents, should be interpreted as follows: scoring above 50% is considered as scoring high on a particular trait and scoring lower than 50% as low. The general averages assigned to each personality trait of our twenty subjects and the average male and female scores are presented in Fig. 2 below.

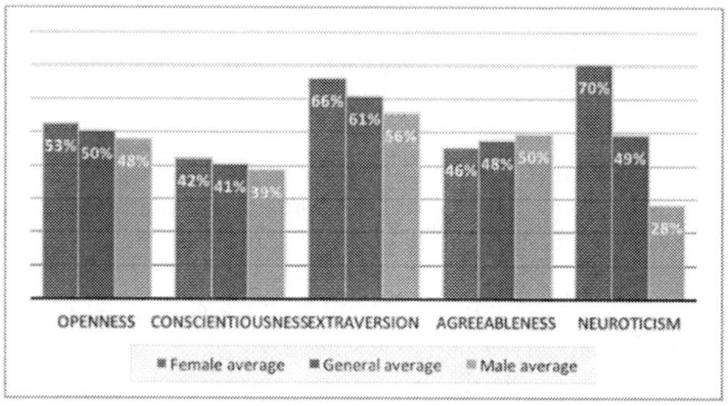

Figure 2. Bar charts representing the general, female and male averages of the Big Five scores from our twenty subjects.

As was said in previous research by [13], [14] and [15], people scoring high on *Extraversion*, *Openness* and *Neuroticism* are the individuals more easily drawn to social media in general. It has to be said that the general averages of our database are not quite convincing to either confirm or deny these results. In general, the twenty subjects do score high on *Extraversion*: 61% on average. They score neither high nor low on *Openness* with an average of 50%. The same is true for *Neuroticism*: on average, the subjects score 49%.

When zooming in on the gender differences, we see that both genders score almost the same for all traits except for *Extraversion* and *Neuroticism*. In both instances, the female subjects score higher and for the trait *Neuroticism* the average of 70% is 2.5 times higher than the male average. These findings are in line with some previous research [20] though it should be kept in mind that the database used for this research is very limited and, as a consequence, no generalizations can be made.

B. Part-of-Speech Analysis

Though our idea was to analyse the frequencies of the PoS-tags, some preliminary analyses convinced us to narrow down our research to the category of pronouns, which have also proven indicative of personality in previous research [5], [25].

In general, we found that our male and female subjects talk more about themselves and the groups they belong to, in other words, they use more first person pronouns, both singular and plural. This can easily be explained by Twitter being a microblogging website: it is very logical to talk more about one's own opinions and comments. In a next step, we checked whether there are any correlations that might indicate a relation between personality traits and the use of certain pronouns. We could not find a correlation between a high use of the pronoun *jij* (you) by people scoring high in *Agreeableness* and *Openess*, as found in [5]. The highest correlations we found were with the trait *Neuroticism*: the use of the possessive pronoun *hun* (their) is negatively correlated (-0.54), this correlation, however, is not statistically significant (p-value of 0.09). Other positive correlations between pronouns and *Neuroticism* were found with the pronouns *zij, haar and hij* (she, her and he), i.e., 0.38 and with first person possessives, 0.36. For the other personality traits no specific findings can be reported.

C. Lexicon-Based Analyses

Three different lexicon look-ups were performed: we relied on two Dutch sentiment lexicons and one well-known lexicon for personality research.

Both the Pattern [24] and Duoman [23] sentiment lexicons allowed us to have a closer look at the number of positive and negative words used by our subjects. We found that almost all respondents use more positive than negative words, with the exception of one male subject. However, no links between this finding and the personality traits of our subjects could be discovered.

When processing the data with the LIWC lexicon [17], the outcome is a table listing all LIWC categories that were found in the data, accompanied by a relative percentage. We first performed a more qualitative analysis for which a general overview of the retrieved percentages was created. The highest and lowest percentages per gender were highlighted and compared to each other.

Most of the qualitative results found in our database do make intuitive sense, such as introverted people talking more about *death* (e.g., bury, coffin, kill), *sadness* (crying, grief) and more about *negative emotions* in general (hurt, ugly, nasty). People scoring low on *Neuroticism*, and therefore calmer people, talk more about *friends* (buddy, friend, neighbour), time (end, until, season) and *certainties* (always, never), whereas they also talk more about themselves. In our database, we also discovered that highly conscientious people, talk more about their physical appearance in general: they talk about *eating, food and dieting*, about *physical states* and *grooming*. Since these findings are rather intuitive, we referred to calculating Pearson correlations in a next phase.

In Table 2, we present only the correlations of 0.5 or more that were discovered between a certain personality trait and an LIWC dimension. In our database, we found eight LIWC such categories, correlated mostly with the trait *Openness*: social processes (*social*, e.g., mate, talk, they, child), humans (*humans*, e.g., baby, adult, boy), sensory and perpetual processes (*senses*, e.g., see, touch, hear), hearing (*hear*, e.g., listening, hearing), present tenses (*present*) and communication (*comm*). For the trait *Conscientiousness*, talking about physical states (*physical*) was found to correlate positively and we also saw that people scoring higher on *Neuroticism* tend to talk more about inhibitions (*inhib*, e.g., block, constrain, stop). Nevertheless, only two of these higher correlations were actually statistically relevant, namely the positive correlation between *Openness* and the mentioning of social processes (*social*) such as mate, talk, they, child; and the positive correlation of that same personality trait with the description of sensory and perceptual processes (*senses*) such as see, touch or listen. This is surprising because our database is only built on the data of twenty people. It is thus definitely worthwhile to conduct a more elaborate study and see whether the highly correlated items will also return in an experiment with a larger database.

TABLE II. CORRELATIONS BETWEEN PERSONALITY AND LIWC DIMENSIONS

Trait	LIWC dimension	Correlation	p-value
Openness	social	**0.6193**	**0.0497**
	humans	0.5254	0.1112
	senses	**0.6242**	**0.0473**
	hear	0.5042	0.1296
	present	0.5227	0.1134
	communication	0.5284	0.1087
Conscientiousness	physical	0.5088	0.1254
Neuroticism	inhib	0.5237	0.1226

Compared to previous research [5], our findings do not support previous results: people scoring high on *Conscientiousness* in our database did not necessarily have a high negative correlation with words about *death* (death; -0.0341), a high positive correlation with *negative emotions* (negemo; 0.1080) or words about *sadness* (sad; 0.0438).

V. CONCLUSION AND FUTURE WORK

The goal of this research was to investigate whether the language used by a specific person on Twitter can reveal something about this person's personality. And if this is the case, we wanted to find out which aspects of language are important to take into consideration. In order to answer this question we first briefly discussed the Big Five and how it has been used to measure the relation between personality and social media in the past. Next, we explained how twenty respondents, ten male and ten female persons, were persuaded to participate in our research. These subjects filled in a personality test and gave their consent to have their Dutch tweets downloaded and analysed. On these tweets, two linguistic analyses were then performed: a more abstract analysis by means of Part-of-Speech tagging and a lexicon-based analysis based on two Dutch sentiment lexicons and one personality lexicon. A close analysis of all available data led to some interesting results.

Firstly, since the results of the Big Five personality test of all twenty subjects were available, our findings were compared with previous research on the link between personality and social media. We tried to answer the question whether it is possible to draw a general image of a social media or Twitter user. When it comes to the Big Five and social media in general, which was researched by [13], [14] and [15], one trait corresponds completely, namely scoring high on *Extraversion*. For the traits *Openness* and *Neuroticism*, however, our database might have been too small: the numbers fluctuate around 50%, which makes it impossible to say whether scoring high on both traits is something frequent on social media. What is remarkable is that both the social media and Twitter user are said to score high in *Openness*, which is not supported by our database: our subjects score on average 50% on this trait.

Secondly, based on the Part-of-Speech analysis of the tweets, we found that the use of pronouns in general did not seem to reveal any correlation with a particular trait; therefore, a deeper research was conducted on the use of personal and possessive pronouns. This more thorough analysis did not reveal any particular link with personality. Both male and female users do talk more about themselves and groups they belong to, in other words, they use more first person pronouns, both singular and plural.

Thirdly, based on the lexicon analyses no clear results were conveyed with two Dutch sentiment lexicons. None of the personality traits had a specifically high or low use of positive and negative words. Moreover, all but one respondent used more positive than negative words. Since that one respondent did not score particularly high or low on a trait, we can only guess about the origins of this difference. The analysis with the Dutch LIWC lexicon, however, did provide us with some interesting findings on how often certain dimensions of words are used with a particular personality trait. These were achieved after first performing an intuitive qualitative research, after which Pearson correlations were measured. In our database, we found eight LIWC dimensions to be highly correlated, six with the trait *Openness* and one each with the traits *Conscientiousness* and *Neuroticism*.

A great challenge lied in working with such a limited database. However, much to our surprise, we did discover two statistically significant correlations. The trait *Openness* is positively correlated with social terms, such as family and friends and also with sensory and perceptual processes such as see, touch or listen. This finding is a great stimulus to continue this research on a larger database: the high correlations could even be more outspoken if only they were researched on more data. In future research, it is thus definitely recommended to collect more data: this will help in defining more concretely the general image of a social media user and, of course, in discovering which language items are typical for specific Big Five personality traits. Our database definitely forms a valuable gold standard to conduct research on personality prediction in the near future.

ACKNOWLEDGMENT

The authors would like to thank all twenty Twitter users who agreed to participate in this research by filling in a personality test and donating their tweets.

REFERENCES

[1] A. Schwartz, J. Eichstaedt, M. Kern, L. Dziurzynski, S. Ramones, and M. Agrawal, "Personality, Gender, and Age in the Language of Social Media: The Open-Vocabulary Approach," PLoS ONE, vol. 8, 2013, pp. 1–16.

[2] A. Lenhart, K. Purcell, A. Smith, and K. Zickuhr, "Social Media & Mobile Internet Use among Teens and Young Adults. Millennials." 2010.

[3] V. Barker, "Older Adolescents' Motivations for Social Network Site Use: The Influence of Gender, Group Identity, and Collective Self-Esteem," Cyberpsychology & Behaviour, vol. 12, 2009, pp. 209–213.

[4] J. Golbeck, C. Robles, and K. Turner, "Predicting personality with social media," in CHI '11 Extended Abstracts on Human Factors in Computing Systems, ser. CHI EA '11. New York, NY, USA: ACM, 2011, pp. 253–262.

[5] J. Golbeck, C. Robles, M. Edmondson, and K. Turner, "Predicting personality with Twitter," in Privacy, Security, 2011 IEEE Third International Conference on Privacy, Security, Risk and Trust, and IEEE International Conference on Social Computing (SocialCom), 2011, pp. 149–156.

[6] L. Goldberg, "An alternative "description of personality": the big-five factor structure," Journal of Personality and Social Psychology, vol. 59, 1990, pp. 1216–1229.

[7] O. John and S. Srivastava, The Big-Five Trait Taxonomy: History, Measurement and Theoretical Perspectives. Guilford, 1999.

[8] A. M. Kaplan and M. Haenlein, "Users of the world, unite! the challenges and opportunities of social media," Business Horizons, vol. 53, no. 1, 2010, pp. 59 – 68.

[9] M.-F. Moens, J. Li, and T.-S. Chua, Eds., Mining user generated content. Chapman and Hall/CRC, 2014.

[10] W. G. Mangold and D. J. Faulds, "Social media: The new hybrid element of the promotion mix," Business Horizons, vol. 52, no. 4, 2009, pp. 357 – 365.

[11] B. Pang and L. Lee, "Opinion mining and sentiment analysis," Foundations and Trends in Information Retrieval., vol. 2, no. 1-2, 2008, pp. 1–135.

[12] M. Back, J. Stopfer, S. Vazire, S. Gaddis, S. Schmuckle, and B. Egloff, "Facebook Profiles Reflect Actul Personality, Not Self-Idealization," Psychological Science, vol. 21, 2010, pp. 372–374.

[13] Y. Hamburger and E. Ben-Artzi, "The relationship between extraversion and neuroticism and the different uses of the Internet," Computers in Human Behavior, vol. 16, 2000, pp. 441–449.

[14] C. Ross, E. Orr, M. Sisic, J. Arseneault, M. Simmering, and R. Orr, "Personality and motivations associated with Facebook use," Computers in Human Behavior, vol. 25, 2009, pp. 578–586.

[15] T. Correa, A. Hinsley, and H. Gil de Zúniga, "Who interacts on the Web?: The intersection of users' personality and social media use," Computers in Human Behavior, vol. 26, 2010, pp. 247–253.

[16] D. Hughes, M. Rowe, M. Batey, and A. Lee, "A tale of two sites, Twitter vs. Facebook and the personality predictors of social media usage," Computers in Human Behavior, vol. 28, 2012, pp. 561–569.

[17] J. Pennebaker, M. Francis, and R. Booth, "Linguistic Inquiry and Word Count (LIWC): LIWC2001," 2001.

[18] G. Park, H. Schwartz, J. Eichstaedt, M. Kern, M. Kosinski, D. Stillwell, L. Ungar, and M. Seligman, "Automatic personality assessment through social media language," J. Pers. Soc. Psychol., vol. 108, no. 6, 2015, pp. 9–34.

[19] G. Farnadi, G. Sitaraman, S. Sushmita, F. Celli, M. Kosinski, D. Stillwell, S. Davalos, M.-F. Moens, and M. De Cock, "Computational personality recognition in social media," User Modeling and User-Adapted Interaction, vol. 26, no. 2, 2016, pp. 109–142.

[20] M. Vianello, K. Schnabel, N. Sriram, and B. Nosek, "Gender differences in implicit and explicit personality traits," Personality and Individual differences, vol. 26, 2013, pp. 994–999.

[21] "The Big Five Project Personality Test," 2016, URL: http://www.outofservice.com/bigfive/ [accessed: 2016-10-02].

[22] M. Van de Kauter, G. Coorman, E. Lefever, B. Desmet, L. Macken, and V. Hoste, "LeTs Preprocess: The multilingual LT3 linguistic preprocessing toolkit." Computational Linguistics in the Netherlands Journal, vol. 3, 2013, pp. 103–120.

[23] V. Jijkoun and K. Hofmann, "Generating a non-English subjectivity lexicon: Relations that matter," in Proceedings of the 12th Conference of the European Chapter of the Association for Computational Linguistics (EACL-2009), 2009, pp. 398–405.

[24] T. De Smedt and W. Daelemans, "Vreselijk mooi! Terribly beautiful: a subjectivity lexicon for Dutch adjectives," in Proceedings of the 8th International Conference on Language Resources and Evaluation (LREC-2012), 2012, pp. 3568–3572.

[25] J. Pennebaker, M. Mehl, and K. Niederhoffer, " Psychological aspects of natural language use: our words, our selves," Annual review of psychology, vol. 54, 2003, pp. 547–577.

Producing Affective Language

Content Selection, Message Formulation, and Computational Modelling

Martijn Goudbeek, Nadine Braun, Charlotte Out, Emiel Krahmer
Center for Cognition and Communication
Tilburg University
Tilburg, the Netherlands
m.b.goudbeek@uvt.nl, n.braun@uvt.nl, c.out@uvt.nl, e.j.krahmer@uvt.nl

***Abstract*— We introduce a project investigating how emotional states influence language production using both experimental and corpus based approaches. Here, we illustrate our project by asking whether content selection ("deciding what to say") and linguistic realization ("deciding how to say it") are affected by the emotional state of a speaker. We do this first by assessing whether disgusted speakers are more or less prone to align with their dialogue partners than amused speakers. Second, we develop a corpus of emotionally laden soccer reports that, even though they refer to the same event, will differ depending on whether the report comes from the winning or losing team. In both cases, we focus on the production and analysis of referring expressions. Our findings will be used to build an affective natural language generation system.**

Keywords-Emotion and Cognition; Language production; Referring expressions; Natural Language Generation.

I. INTRODUCTION

Spoken language conveys a lot of information about someone's emotional state. For example, angry speakers speak with a loud and high pitched voice, while sad speakers generally speak with a soft and low voice [1][2]; the words used may also vary; even though only a limited number of words can be classified as emotional [3], word use has been shown to be indicative of speaker's feelings. For instance, suicidal poets used relatively more first person singular pronouns, more words referring to death, and fewer references to other people in their poems than non-suicidal poets [4].

The effects of emotion on speech prosody and word production are well established, but the impact of emotion on other aspects of the speech production process is understudied. Our project aims to the conjecture that emotion influences the early content selection and message formulation stages of language production. In particular, we study how language production models can be interfaced with emotion models, and will test predictions made by such a combined model in a series of studies, where we zoom in on referential communication. Based on our findings, we aim to develop a computational model that is capable of generating different linguistic realizations of the same content, as a function of emotional state.

The rest of this paper is organized as follows. Section II describes the processes involved in language production. Section III describes the relationship between emotion and language. Section IV describes the research questions we aim to address in our project "Producing Affective Language". Section V introduces two current projects, one experimental, one corpus based, that address the relationship between emotion and language production. The acknowledgment and conclusion close the article.

II. LANGUAGE PRODUCTION

Speaking is a complex cognitive activity that starts with the conceptual preparation of a message and that ends in articulation. Levelt has described the emerging consensus that speech production takes place in a number of consecutive stages, each of which produces an output representation that provides the necessary information for the next stage [5]-[7]; see also the work by Griffin and Ferreira [8]. Despite different views regarding the exact division of the processes involved (e.g., compare [5] and [6]) the two main processes preceding articulation are generally assumed to be content selection or conceptualization ("deciding what to say") and message formulation or linguistic realization ("deciding how to say it"), as illustrated in Figure 1.

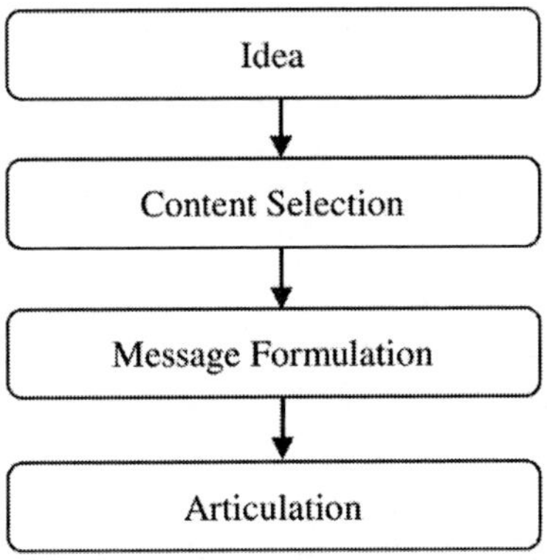

Figure 1. The stages in the speech production process.

Once a speaker has decided what to say and chosen the words to express the message, the relevant linguistic properties of these words (e.g., their gender, number, whether they are mass or count nouns) are selected and integrated [7]. In contrast to this automatic process of selecting the properties of a word, content selection and message formulation are influenced by perspective taking [6] and dialogue factors [9]. We adjust our words depending on whether we are talking to a colleague ("I study content selection") or to a family member ("I study how we decide what to say").

These psycholinguistic insights have been adopted in the field of natural language generation [10][11], although sometimes using different terminology. Generally, the results from psycholinguistic experiments have proven useful in the development of algorithms for natural language generation. For example, Levelt's *Speaking* [5] and Pechmann's work on overspecification [12] were important influences for Dale and Reiter's [13] incremental algorithm for referring expression generation [11].

Importantly, these phases of the speech production system have traditionally been understood as modules that receive and process input in an automatic and encapsulated way. However, given its basis in affective and social processes together with the accumulating evidence that many cognitive processes are cognitively permeable, it would be surprising if the language production system were entirely isolated from other affective and cognitive processes (see also [14]).

III. Emotion and Language

Beginning with Bower [15], emotional states have been linked to cognitive effects in a spreading activation approach where an individual's dominant emotional state spreads to semantic nodes related to that state, resulting in the stronger activation of conceptually related nodes [16][17]. Research in this field has provided evidence for the claim that, because they are connected to nodes that indicate a relatively safe situation, positive emotions result in global, heuristic processing [16][18], whereas negative emotions warrant more local, analytical, processing because they activate nodes that indicate a potentially dangerous situation.

In some sense, the influence of emotion on language production is obvious: when we are in a specific affective state, we express that state in words ("I'm angry"), as well as by nonverbal means (we shout and shake our fist). Almost all of this takes place at the levels of Idea and Articulation as depicted in Figure 1. However, the influence of emotion on the early stages of language production proper (content selection and message formulation) is far from trivial, and understudied as well. Our working hypothesis is that the relation between emotion and early language production is affected by specific emotional appraisals [19][20]. These are evaluations of stimuli with respect to a number of dimensions, such as novelty and pleasantness, but also attributions of agency [21], where people are either responsible for their situation and have control over the outcome (high agency) or have no control and thus no responsibility over the situation (low agency), and the possible violation of moral and social norms [22].

While there is evidence for the influence of emotion on the articulatory stage of speech production, there is surprisingly little work on the earlier stages involving content selection and message formulation. A few notable exceptions exist, of which the work of Kempe et al. [23] is a prime example. They showed that happy speakers were less likely to specify an ambiguous word such as "bat" with a property (such as baseball bat or flying bat, when both are visible) that uniquely identified the intended referent. The authors conclude that a positive mood leads to a less effortful processing style (because a positive state signals a safe situation [16][18]) that causes speakers to spend less mental energy on perspective taking [23].

IV. Research Questions

Starting from the idea that emotional appraisals inform other cognitive systems (the "affect as information" theory, see [17]), they are expected to affect the language production process as well. The main research question of this project is if and how the emotional state of language users influences the early processes involved in language production. The emotion part of this question is understood in terms of appraisal theory, and the speech production part is understood in terms of the global version of Levelt's model presented in Figure 1. Here, we will investigate content selection and message formulation by experimentally inducing in discrete emotional states such as amusement and disgust using film fragments and by analyzing the language of emotionally charged sports reporting, comparing reports of teams that won and lost their match.

Future work will be concerned with building a computational model of emotional language production. While a handful of computational models have been developed that address personality-based [24][25] and affective [26][27] text generation, this issue remains largely unexplored. This is unfortunate, given the growing interest in this topic. This kind of application could enable individually tailored reporting with appropriate emotional "shading", which is more likely to be appealing and interesting for readers than straightforward "vanilla" reports [28].

V. Current Projects

In this section, two ongoing projects are described, addressing the research questions introduced above. The first project investigates whether dialogue partners align less when in a positive emotional state (as compared to a negative one). The second project involves a newly developed corpus of soccer reports that describe the same event (a soccer match) from a positive or a negative perspective.

A. *Emotional state and Lexical Alignment*

Previous research has shown that content selection is affected by alignment processes occurring in interaction (see [9] for a recent model). Speakers tend to select the same properties as their dialogue partners when referring to objects, even if these properties were previously dispreferred [29]. Given that emotions play a central role in our social interactions and in evolution of the speech production system [6], positive emotions will likely result in a less effortful and more egocentric processing style, while negative emotions will result in a more effortful and less egocentric processing style. In addition, emotions that result in different approach or avoidance stances (such as disgust, and amusement) are also expected to influence the extent to which speakers align with their conversation partner.

We will be testing this using a non-scripted version of the interactive reference paradigm [29] in which participants engage in a dialogue and alternatingly describe objects in a director matcher task designed to elicit alignment (as can be seen in Figure 2). First, participant A has to describe the target (1). To uniquely identify the target, she can only use the dispreferred attribute (size), e.g., "the large desk", or, when she uses color redundantly, "the large green desk". By using the property size in her description, she primes participant B to use this property as well in her description (assuming that participants will align in this task). Participant B first identifies the correct object (2) by pointing at it and then describes his object (3) that is finally identified by participant A in (4). Note that in describing his target object (3) participant B can use color ("the red sofa") or size ("the large sofa") or both ("the large red sofa"), in which case one of the properties is redundant, to distinguish the target picture from the distractors. Thus, if participant B uses size more when participant A has done so previously, that would be evidence for alignment.

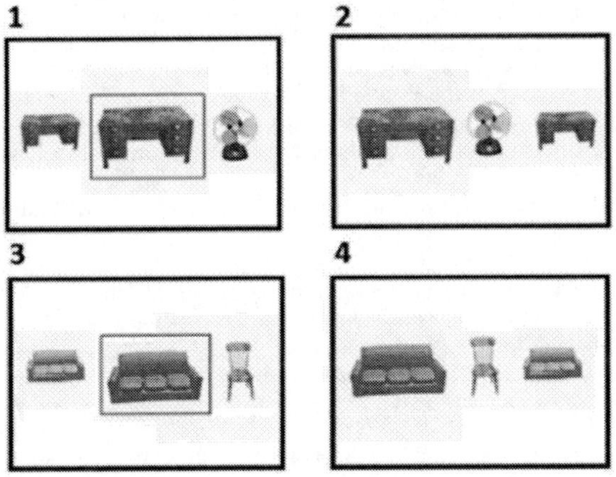

Figure 2. The four tasks that constitute a trial. In frame 1 and 3 the speaker describes the marked object, in frame 2 and 4, the listener identifies the described object.

Methodologically, the role of emotion in cognitive phenomena is often experimentally investigated by first inducing a particular emotion in participants and then asking them to perform a particular task [1]. The most used (and most effective) method has been to use validated film clips, to induce specific emotions [30][31]. In the present study, participants first view an excerpt of an amusing (e.g., the restaurant scene from "When Harry met Sally") or disgusting video (e.g., Devine eating poop in "Pink Flamingo's") and were asked to indicate their level of amusement and disgust on a seven-point scale. A preliminary manipulation check shows that participants report higher levels of amusement (*Mean* = 4.93, *Standard Deviation* = 1.34) than disgust (*Mean* = 2.50, *Standard Deviation* = 1.71) after viewing an amusing video, and, conversely, higher levels of disgust (*Mean* = 6.43, *Standard Deviation* = 1.32) than amusement (*Mean* = 2.13, *Standard Deviation* = 0.94) after viewing a disgusting video (All these differences are statistically significant; F (1, 56) = 36.70, $p < .001$ and F (1, 56) = 206.89, $p < .001$ respectively).

The proportion of attribute alignment will be used as dependent variable. As indicated, alignment at the level of content selection (i.e., deciding to say "the small chair" versus "the red chair") occurs when participant B uses the dispreferred attribute to describe the target when participant A did use the dispreferred attribute as well. If the amount of alignment indeed depends on whether the speaker is amused or disgusted, that would be evidence for the role of emotion in the conceptualization stage of speech production. Specifically, we predict that disgusted speakers, who should be less egocentric and more willing to engage in effortful processing, will align more with their partner by using the dispreferred attribute size when their partner uses the dispreferred attribute. Conversely, we predict that amused participants, who will be more egocentric and less prone to engage in effortful processing, will align less with their partner and keep using the preferred attribute color, even when their partner uses size.

B. *A multilingual corpus of affective soccer reports*

Sports reports open up a lot of room for creative language use, starting with the headlines of the match reports [32] and extending to almost every aspect of the report. For many biased ports reports, that is, sport reports that are written from the perspective of one of the competing teams, the point of view of the author of a match report is clearly definable from the beginning. So, it is easy to assume that the different possible outcomes of such a match would also produce different match reports in terms of language and communicated emotion (i.e., different conceptualizations and linguistic realizations). Take for example the following introductory sentences:

"AFC Wimbledon's five-match unbeaten league run came to an end in frustrating fashion tonight as Neal

> Ardley's men were beaten by struggling Dagenham & Redbridge." (AFC241115, EO, LOSS, MASC, 2016)
>
> Compared to:
>
> "Daggers recorded a first win in 12 league games with a 1-0 success away to AFC Wimbledon" (DR241115, EO, WIN, MASC, 2016)

Both describe the exact same match and events, with totally different emotional nuances and very different emotions shining through in the texts. For Wimbledon, all the frustration is written out in the long first sentence ("frustrating fashion", "beaten", "struggling"), while the winners limit themselves to a shorter and much more positive -possibly more objective- text ("win", "success away"). These and other differences in biased sports reporting shed light on the language conceptualization and realization process that takes place when writing in an emotional state and would be especially valuable for automatic generation of natural language [33]. Indeed, Hovy [34] describes that taking into account the speaker's emotional state, rhetorical, and communicative goals, is crucial for generating suitable texts for different readers. However, the reality of automatic text generation is that not many NLG systems are able to adapt to the mood of the recipients of the produced text [28] and to convey the mood of the author.

To find out more about the language in texts produced in negative and positive emotional states, we (manually) compiled the Multilingual Affective Soccer Corpus [33]. We collected match reports from 121 different clubs participating in the first and second league in England, Germany, and the Netherlands. A first look at our data shows that reports describing wins are, on average, longer than reports describing losses or ties (777 words versus 715 or 713 words respectively). Of course, length is but one very superficial property of a text. There are likely many other textual elements, such as word choice, grammatical constructions, and pronoun use that potentially differ between biased reports.

We plan to use text analysis tools, such as LIWC [34] to, for example, help to determine the proportions of negative and positive emotion words, such as "frustrating" in example (1) or "success" in example (2). Analyzing this corpus will contribute to the understanding of how different emotional states influence and change (written) language production. We are currently planning a detailed descriptive analysis on surface features, such as already indicated text lengths and emotion words, as well as a more in-depth analysis of, for example, referential expressions and pronouns. Analyzing pronouns possibly sheds light on the focus of the author in the respective outcome of the game. If the match results in a win, does the report focus on the own team's great performance or on the opponent's failure ("us vs. them")? Additionally, we plan to investigate whether there are linguistic features that are related to the affect present in the texts – for example, whether certain grammatical constructions occur more in positive or negative contexts.

VI. CONCLUSION

In this paper, we introduced a project investigating the relationship between emotion and language production, approaching the issue from an experimental as well as a corpus based perspective. We have briefly described the process of language production and argued for the relationship between emotion and language production. To study this relationship, we focus on two aspects of referring expression generation, namely content selection ("deciding what to say") and linguistic realization ("deciding how to say it") and use appraisal theory to generate hypotheses about the influence of specific emotions on these processes. We illustrate our approach by introducing two studies, one experimental and one corpus based, that are currently being conducted in this project. These and similar studies will shed light on the relationship between linguistic and affective processes and will serve as the basis for a computational model of affective language generation.

ACKNOWLEDGMENT

We received financial support for this work from The Netherlands Organization for Scientific Research (NWO), via Grant PR-14-87 (Producing Affective Language: Content Selection, Message Formulation and Computational Modelling), which is gratefully acknowledged.

REFERENCES

[1] K. R. Scherer, "Vocal communication of emotion : A review of research paradigms," Speech. Commun, vol. 40, pp. 227-256, 2003.

[2] J. A. Bachorowski, and M. J. Owren. "Sounds of emotion," Ann NY Acad Sci, vol. 1000, pp. 244-265, 2003.

[3] J. W. Pennebaker, M. R. Mehl, and K. G. Niederhoffer, "Psychological aspects of natural language. use: our words, our selves,". Annu. Rev. Psychol., vol. 54, pp. 547-77, 2003.

[4] S. W. Stirman and J. W. Pennebaker, "Word Use in the Poetry of Suicidal and Non-Suicidal Poets", Psychosom. Med., vol. 63, pp. 517-522, 2001.

[5] W. J. Levelt, Speaking: From Intention to Articulation, Cambridge, MA: MIT Press, 1989.

[6] W. J. Levelt, "Producing spoken language: A blueprint of the speaker", In The neurocognition of language (chapter 4), C. Brown & P. Hagoort, Eds. Oxford, UK: Oxford Press, pp. 83-122, 1999.

[7] W. J. Levelt, "Spoken word production: A theory of lexical access", P. Natl. Acad. Sci. USA, vol. 98, pp. 13464-13471, 2001.

[8] Z. M. Griffin and V. S. Ferreira, "Properties of spoken language production", In The handbook of psycholinguistics, (2nd ed.), M. J. Traxler and M. A. Gernsbacher, Eds. Amsterdam, The Netherlands: Elsevier, pp. 21-59 2006.

[9] M. Pickering and S. Garrod, "An integrated theory of language production and comprehension", Behav. Brain Sci., vol. 36, pp. 329 – 347, 2013.

[10] E. Reiter, "Has a consensus NL generation architecture appeared, and is it psycholinguistically plausible?. In Proc. of the Seventh International Workshop on Natural Language Generation, Kennebunkport, Maine: Association for Computational Linguistics, pp. 163-170, 1994.

[11] E. Krahmer, "What computational linguists can learn from psychologists (and vice versa)", Comput. Linguist., vol. 36, pp. 285-294, 2010.

[12] T. Pechmann, "Incremental speech production and referential overspecification", Linguistics, vol. 27, pp. 89-110, 1989.

[13] R. Dale and E. Reiter, "Computational interpretations of the Gricean maxims in the generation of referring expressions", Cognitive Sci., vol. 19, 233-263, 1995.

[14] G. Vigliocco and R. J. Hartsuiker, "The interplay of meaning, sound, and syntax in sentence production", Psychological Bulletin, vol. 128, pp. 442-472, 2002.

[15] G. H. Bower, "Mood and memory", American psychologist, vol. 36, pp 129-148, 1981.

[16] J. P. Forgas, "Mood and judgment: the affect infusion model (AIM)", Psychol. Bull., vol. 117, pp. 39-66, 1995.

[17] N. Schwarz and G. L. Clore, "Mood as information: 20 years later", Psychol Inq., vol. 14, pp. 296-303, 2003.

[18] B. L. Fredrickson, "The role of positive emotions in positive psychology: The broaden and build theory of positive emotions. Am. Psychol., vol. 56, pp. 218-226, 2001.

[19] N. H. Frijda, "The Emotions", Cambridge, UK: Cambridge University Press, 1986.

[20] K. R. Scherer, "The dynamic architecture of emotion: Evidence for the component process model", Cognition Emotion, vol. 23, pp. 1307-1351, 2009.

[21] C.A. Smith and P. C. Ellsworth, "Patterns of cognitive appraisal in emotion", J. Pers. Soc. Psychol., vol. 48, pp. 813-838, 1985.

[22] C. A. Hutcherson and J. J. Gross, "The moral emotions: A social–functionalist account of anger, disgust, and contempt". J. Pers. Soc. Psychol, vol. 100, pp. 719-737, 2011.

[23] V. Kempe, M. Rookes and L. Swarbrigg, "Speaker emotion can affect ambiguity production", Lang. Cognitive Proc., vol. 28, pp. 1-12, 2012.

[24] F. Mairesse and M. Walker, "PERSONAGE: Personality generation for dialogue", in Ann Meeting of the Association for Computational Linguistics, Association for Computational Linguistics, June 2007, p. 496-503.

[25] M. Walker, J. Sawyer, G. Lin and S. Wing, "Does Personality Matter? Expressive Generation for Dialogue Interaction", in Natural Interaction with Robots, Knowbots and Smartphones, vol 28, J. Mariani, S. Rosset, M. Garnier-Rizet, L Devillers, Eds. New York: Springer, pp 285-301, 2014.

[26] I. van der Sluis and C. Mellish, "Towards empirical evaluation of affective tactical NLG", in Empirical Methods in Natural Language Generation: Data-oriented Methods and Empirical Evaluation, E. Krahmer and M. Theune, Eds. Berlin: Springer, pp. 242-263, 2010.

[27] I. van Der Sluis, C. Mellish and G. Doherty, "Affective text: Generation strategies and emotion measurement issues" Proc. of the Twenty-Fourth International Florida Artificial Intelligence Research Society Conference (FLAIRS 2011), R. Charles Murray, P. M. McCarthy, Eds. The AAAI Press, May 2011, Menlo Park, California. Palm Beach, Florida., pp. 123-128.

[28] S. Mahamood and E. Reiter, E, "Generating affective natural language for parents of neonatal infants" Proc. of the 13th European Workshop on Natural Language Generation (ENLG 2011), C. Gardent and K. Striegnitz, Eds. Association for Computational Linguistics, Sept. 2011, pp. 12-21, 2011.

[29] M. Goudbeek and E. Krahmer, "Alignment in Interactive Reference Production: Content Planning, Modifier Ordering, and Referential Overspecification. Top. Cog. Sci., vol. 4, pp. 269-289, 2012.

[30] J. J. Gross and R. W. Levenson, "Emotion elicitation using films", Cognition Emotion, vol. 9, 87-108, 1995.

[31] A. Schaefer, F. Nils, X. Sanchez and P. Philippot, "Assessing the effectiveness of a large database of emotion-eliciting films: A new tool for emotion researchers", Cognition Emotion, vol. 24, pp. 1153-1172, 2010.

[32] M. K. Smith and M. B. Montgomery, "The semantics of winning and losing", Lang. Soc., vol. 18, pp. 31-57, 1989.

[33] N. Braun, M. Goudbeek and E. Krahmer, "The Multilingual Affective Soccer Corpus (MASC): Compiling a biased parallel corpus on soccer reportage in English, German and Dutch", in Proc. of the Ninth International Natural Language Generation conference (INLG 2016), Association for Computational Linguistics, Sept. 2016.

[34] E. H. Hovy, "Pragmatics and natural language generation", Artificial Intelligence, vol. 43, pp. 153-197, 1990.

[35] J. W. Pennebaker, M. E. Francis and R. J. Booth, "Linguistic inquiry and word count: LIWC 2001", Mahway: Lawrence Erlbaum Associates, 71, 2001.

Blending Quantitative, Qualitative, Geospatial, and Temporal Data: Progressing Towards the Next Generation of Human Social Analytics

C.J. Hutto
Human Systems Engineering
Georgia Tech Research Institute (GTRI)
Atlanta, GA, USA
e-mail: cjhutto@gatech.edu

Abstract—**Human social analytics in the next generation will need to embrace more multifaceted representations of human behavior with more complex models. Such models will need to integrate data of disparate forms, using disparate units of measure, collected from disparate sources, at disparate scales. Next generation social scientists will also face issues related to developing methods and tools to help facilitate the collection, processing, analyzing, and visualizing of such multifaceted social data. This paper illustrates these challenges by reporting on the development of a complex model of societal well-being (an inherently qualitative construct) which blends large scale quantitative, geospatial, and temporally referenced data of disparate forms, units, sources, and scales. We then demonstrate tools and methods intended to facilitate the progression towards next generational social analytics at large scales. We conclude by discussing several open questions with regards to social analytics, including those related to ethics and privacy concerns.**

Keywords-human centered data science; human social analytics.

I. INTRODUCTION

All sorts of human social and behavioral data are now available, and on unprecedented scales. Of course, social scientists still rely heavily on traditional sources of social and behavioral data such as in-person, telephone, or computer assisted interviews, questionnaires and survey instruments, and sources of "thick descriptions" [1] of human behavior compiled from ethnographic or anthropological observation research. However, new sources of human social behavior data are now available due to our increased use of mobile phone, GPS technology, and personal wearable technology (such as fitness trackers), as well as the digital traces of technology-mediated communications and online social interactions. These new data sources will allow researchers to conduct human social analytics for extraordinary levels of insights ranging from intra-individual scale investigations, through inter-personal and group level interactions, to organizational and even population scale research. Over the next 25 years (a generally accepted duration of a generation), social scientists and data analysts will need to modernize their ways of thinking about and interacting with human behavior data, else risk their research becoming obsolete and irrelevant.

In this paper, we address issues facing the next generation of social data scientists. We do so in the first part of the paper by presenting an example in which we progress beyond simple representations of human social behavior by constructing a complex model of individual and societal well-being. We describe the integration and analysis of data of varying forms, collected via diverse methods from a variety of sources by different groups, consisting of varied units of measure, spanning a temporal range of more than 40 years, and representing human behavioral data at disparate scales. In short, we present a case study of blending quantitative, geospatial, and temporally diverse data for the purpose of advancing human social analysis for an inherently qualitative construct using a more complex (and, we argue, more representative) model of human social behavior.

In the second half of this paper, we describe how new methods borrowed from the field of computer science can be leveraged to support next generation human social analysis of qualitative data. Computational natural language processing (NLP) and statistical machine learning (ML) techniques have the potential to be extremely useful for blending *thick data* (which is most commonly qualitative in form: e.g., descriptive text, audio, imagery, video, or similar multimedia) with the concepts of *big data* (typically more quantitative in nature). Here, we discuss three specific "tools" that embody NLP and ML techniques to support large-scale human social analysis on qualitative data. The first tool, called VADER (**V**alence **A**ware **D**ictionary and s**E**ntiment **R**easoner), provides researchers the ability to quantify both the direction (positive or negative) and magnitude of affective expressions in textual documents ranging from word-level to tome-level scales, processing millions of sentences in a matter of seconds [2]. The second tool, CASTR (**C**ommon-ground **A**cquisition for **S**ocial **T**opic **R**ecognition), produces supporting text-based information needed to establish so called *common ground*, whereby sharing mutual facts and knowledge generally facilitates faster, better understanding [3], [4]. The third tool, EAGLE-ID (**E**thnicity, **A**ge, **G**ender, **L**iteracy/**E**ducation **Id**entifier), automatically aids in characterizing demographic features of individuals based on social profile data. Finally, we discuss how digital crowdsourcing economies such as Amazon Mechanical Turk (a massive, distributed, anonymous crowd of individuals willing to perform human-intelligence micro-tasks for micro-payments) can be leveraged as a valuable resource for the next generation of social science research and practice [5].

We conclude by discussing several open questions with regards to human social analytics, including those related to ethics, data ownership and use, and personal privacy concerns.

II. Increasing Representational Complexity of Data Models for Human Social Analytics

Traditional social scientific models of human behavior are often over-simplified representations of what in actuality are very complex aspects of the world. Human social analytics in the next generation will need to embrace more multifaceted representations of human behavior with more complex models. Such models will need to integrate data of disparate forms, using disparate units of measure, collected from disparate sources, at disparate scales. In this section, we contribute an example in which we develop a complex, system-of-systems representation of societal well-being.

A. From Simple to Complex Modeling of Well-being

Individual and societal constructs of well-being are well established in traditional social science and economic literature as a person's assessment of their own general *happiness* and overall *satisfaction* with their personal life [6], [7]. Following from [8], we further posit that happiness and satisfaction are themselves complex social constructs which holistically comprise four principal constituents:

1. Affective Experiences: the longer-term experiences of pleasant affect (as well as a lack of unpleasant affect) as indicated, for example, via their general perceived happiness in life, in their marriage, and with their cohabitation companion (e.g., partner or roommates).
2. Global Life Judgements: a person's overall belief regarding how interesting they find their own life in general (e.g., whether they consider life to be dull, routine, or exciting), as well as a judgement about the general nature of humanity (whether they believe most other people to be trustworthy, fair, and helpful).
3. Cognitive Appraisals: a person's subjective self-assessment of their own current socioeconomic state relative to their life goals, as well as broader social comparisons. Determinants include financial status self-appraisals, social status self-appraisals (e.g., social rank and social class), and self-appraisals regarding their health, the relative quality of their domicile, and aspects of the city in which they reside.
4. Domain Specific Satisfaction: the degree of fulfillment or contentment with important social elements such as satisfaction with their family life, friendships, hobbies and recreational interests, job/career, and their wages.

Traditional social analytics tend to focus on a narrowly scoped subset of the above constituents. While such studies do provide useful insights, they are limited precisely because they are narrow; due to the inherent interconnectedness of these constituents, complex interactions abound. Nevertheless, they hold much greater analytical value when they are considered in conjunction with one another. The whole is greater than the sum of its parts, and aggregate-level insights may never emerge unless and until the underlying relationships are expressly represented.

To this end, we present an example in which we incorporate 130 different manifest indicators for- and correlates of- individual and societal well-being. To do so, we blend qualitative, quantitative, geospatial, and temporal data from several sources. While detailed model specification is beyond the scope of this paper, we find the model useful as a reference for discussing next generation social analytics.

B. Blending Qualitative, Quantitative, Geospatial, & Temporal Data

The data for our complex model of well-being are drawn from several public data sets comprising records from 30 different collection activities spanning 42 years (from 1972 to 2014) across nine different divisions of the United States Census Bureau [9]. This data integrates 25 manifest indicators of societal well-being, organized into latent variable constructs representing the four principal constituents described in Section II-A. An additional 17 indicators provide data providing more objective measures of individual *quality of life and standard of living*, such as highest education level attained, number of people living in a household, type of dwelling (and whether owned or rented), various employment characteristics (part time, full time, student/homemaker, unemployed, retired, etc.), and constant (i.e., annual inflation adjusted) income in dollars. Also included are data capturing information about each respondent's *demographic* details, the *general political climate* (public opinion regarding amount of taxes paid, the efficacy of the courts, and national programs related to healthcare, transportation, and public transit), established local and regional *geographic boundary data*, annually recorded data regarding the *general economic climate* of the nation (such as inflation rates, consumer price indices, prime lending rates, and annual gross domestic product (GDP) per capital growth), and data characterizing the *general security climate* (e.g., individual and community exposure to crimes, perceptions of fear, etc.).

As one might imagine, the data are operationalized in multifaceted ways, taking multiple forms, units, and scales of measurement. In all, we integrate data from nearly 60,000 respondents spanning 42 years with regard to 130 different variables of interest, where each variable puts (on average) potentially 7 unique degrees of positive or negative pressure on individual and/or societal well-being. All told, this leverages approximately 55 million data points for our model, allowing for a very rich and complex representation of well-being – much more sophisticated than many other typical, prevailing social science models.

We argue that this representation, as opposed to a simpler model (for example, one based primarily on measures of *happiness*) is a more accurate reflection of true societal well-being. To illustrate this point, consider Fig. 1, in which we visually depict how a simplistic representation of well-being (happiness scales) compare to a more complex representation of societal well-being for different geographic regions in the United States. Different insights emerge (especially in the southern regions) when affective experiences, global life judgements, cognitive appraisals, domain specific satisfaction, objective socioeconomic quality of life and standard of living data, the general political climate, general economic climate, and the general security climate are incorporated when considering societal well-being.

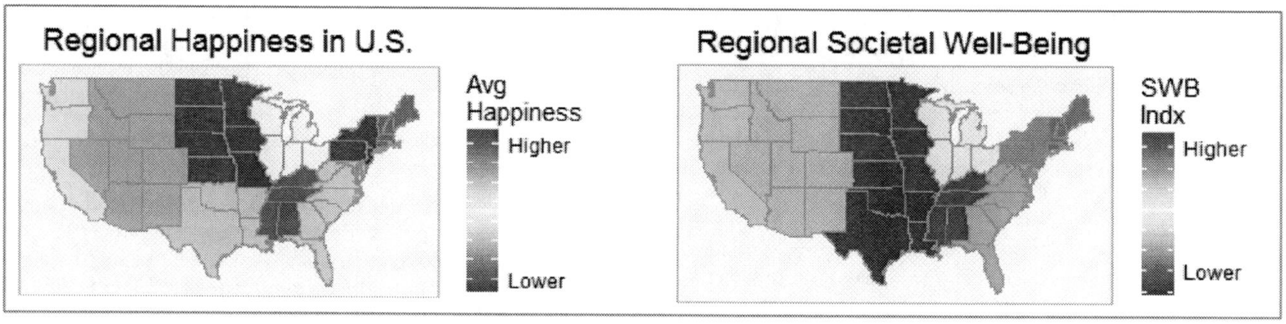

Figure 2. Comparing a simple representation of well-being (happiness scales, on left) to a more complex representation of societal well-being (on right) to derive different insights for different geographic regions in the United States.

We can also demonstrate how the model produces interesting insights in relation to political aspects of the national population, especially when considered in conjunction with temporal information. For instance, in Fig. 2 the scatterplot dots indicate national-level averages for each year of data collection (1972-2014) for each self-identified political community as measured by party affiliations (left column plots) or by ideological views (right column plots) for the simple model (top row of plots) and the complex model (bottom row). Boxes depict the middle fifty percent of the data (with mean lines) within each category, and whiskers show the range from minimum to maximum scores. The red dashed horizontal lines show overall means (across all categories). Especially interesting is how robust the results are; the general trends are qualitatively similar regardless of whether modeled with simplistic or complex representations of well-being.

C. Monte Carlo Simulations and Predictions of Well-being

The complex model, once derived as described in the previous section, may be used in Monte Carlo processes to explore the probability distributions associated with how potential changes in any subset of the input variables would impact societal well-being. The model can be extremely useful, for example, to government policy decision makers when the impacts of their decision alternatives could be vetted within a data-derived, model-driven trade space analysis tool. For example, Monte Carlo simulation modelers would be able to reliably quantify the effect that policy and funding decisions might have on societal well-being. Such considerations will enable next generation social analytics to generate better predictions, going beyond the prevailing social science policy of typically concluding a study upon reporting descriptive and inferential statistics.

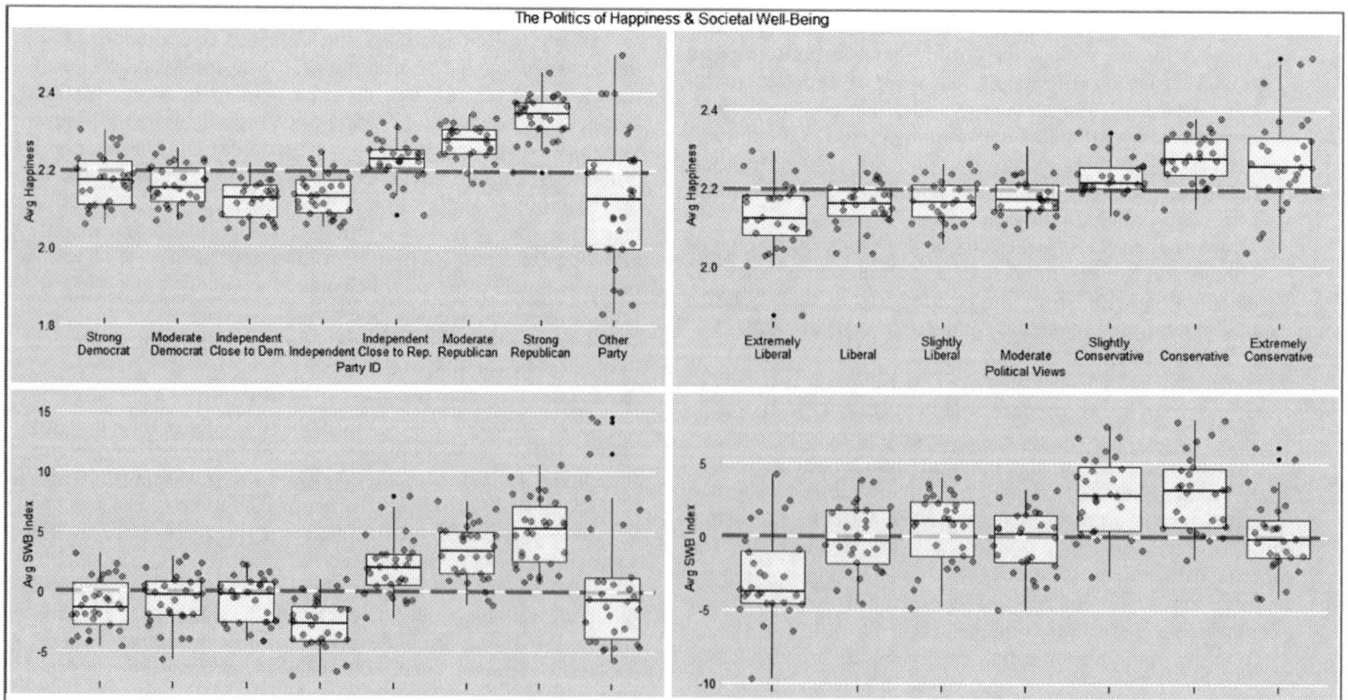

Figure 2. Aggregates of temporal data for political party and ideological views for a simplistic model of happiness versus a complex model of societal well-being

III. Methods, Techniques, and Tools for Next Generation Social Analytics of Qualitative Data

Next generation social scientists will also face issues related to developing methods and tools to help facilitate the collection, processing, analyzing, and visualizing of such multifaceted social data in near real-time. Our example model of individual and societal well-being is based on a static data set collected over many years. It is extremely valuable for generating structural equation models representing the interdependencies among the related input variables, and for paving the way for exploratory and predictive analyses.

Given the vast amount of qualitative data available in social media platforms such as Twitter, Facebook, and a host of blogging and microblogging technologies, it is possible to create "social sensors" which monitor important indicators of societal well-being, on massive scales, in near real-time. Traditional social science methods rely on labor and time intensive qualitative data analysis techniques to transform qualitative data into quantitative representations of affect (e.g., manually reading and coding individual text entries to determine if a person is expressing positive or negative affect). In contrast to most typical quantitative methods, qualitative data analysis methods do not easily scale up. Datasets are too large (consider the entire internet of social media, SMS/text messages, emails, blogs, etc.), and they are produced at extreme velocities (e.g., 500 million tweets per day, or status updates from 1.8 billion active Facebook users per day [10]). It is impossible for human researchers to even look at all the data, much less analysis it in a timely manner.

Whereas previous generations of Computer Assisted Qualitative Data AnalysiS (CAQDAS) software supported the traditional toolkit of qualitative researchers, i.e., sorting, searching, and annotating, the newest generation of tools is adding features powered by computerized natural language processing (NLP) and statistical machine learning (ML) techniques to enable automated rapid, massively large scale assessment of digital text, audio, video, and other multimedia traces of people's affective experiences as portrayed in their social media posts. The norm for next generation social analytics will be to employ such computational tools to facilitate blending of social media *thick data* (rich, descriptive qualitative data) with *big data* (i.e., data that is characterized by massive volume (amount of data), velocity (speed of data in or out), and variety (range of data types and sources)).

A. VADER: Automated Analysis of Affect in Social Media

VADER (**V**alence **A**ware **D**ictionary and s**E**ntiment **R**easoner) [2] is a computational tool for conducting automated large scale sentiment analysis [11], [12]. Sentiment analysis is useful to a wide range of problems that are of interest to next generation social analysts, practitioners, and researchers from fields such as sociology, marketing and advertising, psychology, economics, and political science. The inherent nature of microblog content - such as those observed on Twitter and Facebook - poses serious challenges to practical applications of sentiment analysis. Some of these challenges stem from the sheer rate and volume of user generated social content, combined with the contextual sparseness resulting from shortness of the text and a tendency to use abbreviated language conventions to express sentiments. VADER is a simple rule-based algorithm and model for general sentiment analysis. In previous work [2], we compared VADER's effectiveness to eleven typical state-of-practice benchmarks for automated sentiment analysis, including LIWC [13], [14], ANEW [15], the General Inquirer [16], SentiWordNet [17], and machine learning oriented techniques relying on Naive Bayes, Maximum Entropy, and Support Vector Machine (SVM) algorithms. We used a combination of qualitative and quantitative methods to produce, and then empirically validate, a *gold-standard* sentiment lexicon that is especially attuned to affective expressions in microblog-like contexts. VADER combines these lexical features with consideration for five generalizable rules that embody grammatical and syntactical conventions that humans use when expressing or emphasizing sentiment *intensity*. We found that incorporating these heuristics improves the accuracy of the sentiment analysis engine across several domain contexts (social media text, NY Times editorials, movie reviews, and product reviews). Notably, the VADER affective sentiment lexicon performs exceptionally well in the social media domain. The correlation coefficient shows that the VADER computational engine performs as well ($r = 0.881$) as individual *human* raters ($r = 0.888$) at matching ground truth (i.e., the aggregated group mean from 20 human raters for sentiment intensity of each text-based affective expression). Surprisingly, when we further inspect the classification accuracy, we see that VADER ($F1 = 0.96$) actually even outperforms individual human raters ($F1 = 0.84$) at correctly classifying the sentiment of tweets into positive, neutral, or negative classes.

B. CASTR: Aid to Automated Topic Models of Social Text

CASTR (**C**ommon-ground **A**cquisition for **S**ocial **T**opic **R**ecognition), produces the supporting text-based information needed to establish so called *common ground*, a well-known construct from psycholinguistics whereby individuals engaged in communication share mutual facts and knowledge in order to be better understood [3], [4]. CASTR is intended to aid in *computational topic modeling* [18] by automatically acquiring this background knowledge.

Computational topic modeling techniques are used to uncover the hidden, or latent, concept-based semantic structures (i.e., topics) within text documents. Topic modeling is useful for a broad collection of activities, from automatically tagging newspaper articles with their appropriate newspaper sections (e.g., sports, finance, lifestyle, etc.) to automatically clustering like-minded social media users into groups based on the similarity of their expressed interests. Unfortunately, however, these automated approaches will sometimes infer topics that match poorly to – and are less semantically meaningful than – human inferred topics [19]. The issue is compounded when mining so-called *social text*, i.e., sparse text produced explicitly for informal social consumption (e.g., via social media, instant messages, SMS/texts, personal email, and so on where people rely on one another's common knowledge, rather than extended textual documentation, to understand intended meanings). In designing and developing CASTR's algorithms, we qualitatively assess the unique characteristics of social text which present challenges to computational topic models, and which are not prevalent in other typical (non-social) text corpora like newspaper articles, scientific publications, or books. We find that a) constraints imposed by typical social media technologies, b) implicit social communication norms, and c) evolving conventions of use often confound typical computational topic modeling techniques for social text. For example, tweets are much terser than other kinds of text documents, and this sparsity is troublesome for computational topic modeling algorithms that perform posterior inference of the text. Also, tweets are often laden with a great deal of social communication "noise" (such as emoticons, emojis, hashtags, and URL links) that confuse computational models, and yet present very little trouble to humans.

CASTR leverages the concept of common ground to present a theoretically informed social and cognitive psychological framing of we refer to as the "human interpretability problem" as observed in computationally-produced topic models of text mined from social media. Additionally, CASTR employs a well-established theory from the field of Human-Centered Computing, namely Distributed Cognition (DCog) [20], [21], as a basis for mitigating the issues of developing common ground for computational topic modeling efforts. DCog is a theoretical perspective that proposes knowledge and cognition are not confined to any single individual or referent resource; instead, they are distributed across individuals, objects, artefacts, and tools in the environment, and constructed in context.

As an example of how CASTR implements the DCog inspired mitigation strategies, consider a fictitious (but representative) social media post that expresses a person's positive affective experience related to attending a musical concert at a popular venue near Atlanta, Georgia: "*Headed to Stone Mountain to see the Rolling Stones. Mick Rocks! www.rollingstones.com/band/ #StonesOnFire*". Although it is a relatively simple thing for humans to immediately understand the meaning of this social text (most Americans know who The Rolling Stones are, most people from Georgia know what Stone Mountain is, and most people understand what it means when "rock" is used as a verb in this context, even if they are not immediately sure who Mick refers to, and most people recognize the conventional use of hashtags, as well as URL links). However, the shared, socially constructed knowledge (common-ground) necessary to understand the intended meaning of the above example social text is often not readily available to computational topic models.

CASTR automatically retrieves the (previously missing) background distributed knowledge about key words, phrases, and named entities (proper nouns) within the terse text, and provides this information to the computational topic model processes. The result is a much more accurate representation of which topic(s) a particular short social media document should be belong. For example, the social text above would be appropriately grouped with music and entertainment related topics, rather than geological science related topics.

C. EAGLE-ID: Automated Demographic Profiling

EAGLE-ID (**E**thnicity, **A**ge, **G**ender, and **L**iteracy/**E**ducation **Id**entifier) automatically aids in characterizing important human social demographic features based on social media profile data. The EAGLE-ID system consists of software (currently in beta stage) which performs automatic classification of a person's ethnicity (given the person's surname), their likely age range and gender (based on their first name), and their literacy and education level based solely on information mined from the person's digital social media data (including user profile data as well as shared content). The majority of this is done via text-based computational linguistic processing (in conjunction with comparisons to data from the U.S. Census Bureau database, Social Security Administration records, and U.S. Dept. of Health and Human Services data), but it also uses computer vision for image processing on profile pictures to boost ethnicity/age/gender classification accuracy.

In addition to the obvious uses for user profiling and user modeling, the EAGLE-ID software could be useful for automatically collecting and associating demographic information with particular social media accounts, When used in conjunction with VADER and CASTR, EAGLE-ID facilitates rapid, large scale analysis of social data for use in real-time monitoring of individual and societal well-being with realistically representational complex models.

While the design and development of tools such as VADER, CASTR, and EAGLE-ID is not necessarily in the direct purview of social science, the employment and use of such tools will almost certainly be a significant part of next generation social analytics. It is already a major part of the new field of Computational Social Science. Eventually, the word "computational" will be dropped, and methods, tools, and techniques like the ones discussed in this section will be commonplace in social science research – integrated into social science education right alongside experimental study design, research ethics, and statistical analysis.

D. Crowdsourcing for Scaling-Up Qualitative Data Coding

An interesting interim step preceding fully automated artificial intelligent machine learning algorithms for conducting large scale qualitative data analyses are the emergence of digital crowdsourcing economies such as Amazon Mechanical Turk. These platforms are typically comprised of a massive, distributed, anonymous crowd of individuals willing to perform general human-intelligence micro-tasks for micro-payments, and they can be leveraged as a valuable resource for the next generation of social science research and practice. Indeed, in the past half-decade, Amazon Mechanical Turk has radically changed the way many social science scholars do research. The availability of a massive, distributed, anonymous crowd of individuals willing to perform general human-intelligence micro-tasks for micro-payments is a valuable resource for researchers and practitioners.

In other work [5], we addressed many of the challenges facing researchers using crowd-sourced platforms. Particularly, we reported on how to better ensure *high quality* qualitative data annotations for tasks of varying difficulty from a transient crowd of anonymous, non-experts. Crowdsourcing has already had a significant impact on social analytics, and we believe it will continue to play a substantial role in the next generation of social analytics.

IV. CONCLUSIONS

A. A Departure from Traditional Social Analytics

The model described in the first part of this paper (c.f., Section II) differs from traditional social science in several meaningful ways:

1. *Representational complexity*: In next generation social analytics, model complexity will increase beyond what is typical for much of social science research today. Our example integrates more than 130 indicators for- and correlates of- individual and public well-being. These data are garnered from many sources, measured in numerous different units, stored using many data types at different scales representing individuals, communities, and entire societies. Just as other disciplines such as systems engineering, economics, and computer science have embraced the notion of incorporating "big data" into their typical data models, the next generation of social analytics will need to likewise expand their scope such that social analytics like the ones we illustrate are the norm, rather than the exception.
2. *Large-N and Multiple-T*: In order to achieve useful statistical power while incorporating the expanded scope resulting from increased representational complexity, and at the same time preserving broad generalization and application capacities, next generation social analysts will need to design and conduct studies with much larger sample sizes (i.e., "Large N" studies) collected over multiple instances in time (i.e., "Multiple T", or longitudinal studies). In our example, we integrate data from nearly 60,000 respondents spanning 42 years with regard to 130 different variables of interest, where each variable puts (on average) potentially 7 unique degrees of positive or negative pressure on individual or societal well-being. All told, this leverages approximately 55 million data points for our model. Such study designs will eventually become more prevalent for social analytics.
3. *Extending exploratory and predictive analytics*: Our example model lays the foundations for predictive analysis (e.g., via Monte Carlo simulations), which would be extremely useful to government policy decision makers because the impacts of their decision alternatives could be vetted within a data-derived, model-driven trade space analysis tool. For example, we would be able to answer important questions such as: *in order to improve overall community/public well-being, should government decision makers invest tax dollars in a better public transportation system, economic development program, roads, schools, or security services*? Such considerations will enable next generation social analytics to generate better predictions, going beyond the prevailing social science policy of typically concluding a study upon reporting descriptive and inferential statistics.

B. A Vision of Next Generation Social Analytics

Combining the increase in representational complexity for social science analyses described in Section II with the methods, techniques and tools described in the Section III, a vision of how next generation social analytics will be conducted begins to emerge in which large-scale, individual and national-level, near real-time analysis of the following are common:

- social media data
- mobile and GPS technology data
- personal wearable technology data
- internet of things data

In the second part of this paper, we outlined how new tools and techniques could be leveraged to marshal in the next generation of qualitative social analytics on heretofore unprecedented scales. VADER (see Section III-A) provides researchers the ability to automatically quantify both the direction (e.g., positive or negative) and magnitude of affective expressions in textual documents ranging from word-level to tome-level scales. In a matter of seconds, VADER is capable of automatically transforming millions of rich qualitative social media documents (e.g., tweets) into quantified measures of positive and negative affect for a given Twitter user. This capability alone allows us to produce a simple representation of well-being on a national scale in near-real time [2]. When we combine it with the ability to also understand the topic towards which the affective expressions apply (see the discussion of CASTR in Section III-B), we can begin to incorporate other elements of the more complex representation of well-being previously discussed.

For example, consider when a Twitter user laments (or praises) aspects of her job, her health, her family or friends, her city/community, or her financial situation. Or consider how often she might express satisfaction (or dissatisfaction) for aspects of the general political, security, or economic climate of her community or nation. Now consider how prevalent such expressions are in aggregate for all Twitter users. Next think about how many other publically available forms of such data currently exist (other social networks like Facebook and Snapchat, place-based platform Foursquare, review platform Yelp, internet chat rooms, topical blogs, and discussion forums such as Reddit). Next generation social analytics should embrace such resources, as well as the tools needed for analyzing them at internet scale.

Typically, these social media data are time-stamped, so that temporal aspects can be incorporated (c.f., [22]). Slower changing data variables such as a person's demographic characteristics (e.g., ethnicity, age, gender, literacy and education level) can also be automatically extracted from a person's social media data (see the discussion of EAGLE-ID in Section III-C). In many cases, these data can be combined with meta-information regarding the geolocated origins of the content producers, or otherwise merged with GPS, mobile, or other location-aware wearable technologies. Additional real-time assimilation of national, regional, or local unemployment rates, crime data, housing market data, inflation, consumer price index, prime rates, and gross domestic product round out the capability to produce timely, realistically complex models of societal well-being like the one discussed in Section II.

C. Additional Issues and Items of Considertion

1) Model Complexity vs Model Interpretability

Increasing representational complexity in the way we discuss in Section II, while more characteristic of real-world human social behavior, is not devoid of its own issues; complex models are by their very nature more difficult to interpret. We offer a brief discussion of three avenues for mitigating the challenge of interpreting complex models. First, social science data analysts will need simple and intuitive interfaces for exploring the trade-space of the data. Such tools will increasing model transparency, and incorporating interactive data exploration will aid analysts in easily and quickly uncovering complex interrelationships within and among the variables of any complex model. Second, analysts need simple interfaces that allow them to rapidly build and assess Monte Carlo simulations regarding how potential changes in input variables impact selected response variables of interest. Third, advanced interactive data and information visualization tools will be critical for next generation social analytics to make sense of data at varying levels of aggregation and combination.

2) Ethical Considerations of Widespread Human Social Data Analytics

- Collection and continued monitoring – issues of personal privacy?
- Data ownership and use – do content producers exclusively own publicly available personal data?
- Consequences for types of algorithmic error – what are (or should be) the consequences?

3) Skill Sets and Education for NGSA

We must educate and train the next generation of social data analysts to be comfortable embracing representational complexity and incorporating methods, tools, and techniques like the ones discussed above. It will need to become standard parts of social science education, integrated into social science curricula right alongside research methods and experimental study design, research ethics, and statistical analysis.

ACKNOWLEDGMENT

The author thanks Elizabeth Williams, Dennis Folds, Molly Nadolski, and Tom McDermott for their work on the complex model used as a case study for the first part of this paper. The full published paper for that effort is yet to come.

REFERENCES

[1] C. Geertz, "Thick Description: Toward an Interpretive Theory of Culture," in *The interpretation of cultures: selected essays*, New York, NY: Basic Books, 1973, pp. 3–30.

[2] C. J. Hutto and E. Gilbert, "VADER: A Parsimonious Rule-based Model for Sentiment Analysis of Social Media Text," in *Proceedings of the Eighth International AAAI Conference on Weblogs and Social Media*, 2014, pp. 216–255.

[3] H. H. Clark, *Using Language*. Cambridge University Press, 1996.

[4] H. H. Clark and S. E. Brennan, "Grounding in communication," in *Perspectives on socially shared cognition*, L. B. Resnick, J. M. Levine, and S. D. Teasley, Eds. Washington DC: APA Books, 1991.

[5] T. Mitra, C. J. Hutto, and E. Gilbert, "Comparing Person- and Process-centric Strategies for Obtaining Quality Data on Amazon Mechanical Turk," in *Proceedings of the 33rd Annual ACM Conference on Human Factors in Computing Systems*, 2015, pp. 1345–1354.

[6] E. Diener, "Assessing subjective well-being: Progress and opportunities," *Soc. Indic. Res.*, vol. 31, no. 2, pp. 103–157, Feb. 1994.

[7] E. Diener, E. M. Suh, R. E. Lucas, and H. L. Smith, "Subjective well-being: Three decades of progress.," *Psychol. Bull.*, vol. 125, no. 2, pp. 276–302, 1999.

[8] D. J. Folds and V. M. Thompson, "Engineering human capital: A system of systems modeling approach," in *Proceedings of the 8th International IEEE Conference on Systems of Systems Engineering (SoSE-13)*, 2013, pp. 285–290.

[9] T. W. Smith, P. V. Marsden, M. Hout, and J. Kim, "General Social Surveys, 1972-2014 [machine-readable data file]." NORC at the University of Chicago [producer and distributor], 2014.

[10] InternetLiveStats.com, "Internet Live Stats," *Internet Live Stats - Internet Usage and Social Media Statistics*, 2016. [Online]. Available: http://www.internetlivestats.com/. [Accessed: 09-Sep-2016].

[11] B. Pang and L. Lee, "Opinion Mining and Sentiment Analysis," *Found. Trends Inf. Retr.*, vol. 2, no. 1–2, pp. 1–135, 2008.

[12] B. Liu, *Sentiment Analysis and Opinion Mining*. San Rafael, CA: Morgan & Claypool, 2012.

[13] J. W. Pennebaker, M. Francis, and R. Booth, *Linguistic Inquiry and Word Count: LIWC 2001*. Mahwah, NJ: Erlbaum Publishers, 2001.

[14] J. W. Pennebaker, C. K. Chung, M. Ireland, A. Gonzales, and R. J. Booth, *The development and psychometric properties of LIWC2007*. Austin, TX: LIWC.net, 2007.

[15] M. M. Bradley and P. J. Lang, "Affective norms for English words (ANEW): Instruction manual and affective ratings," NIMH Center for the Study of Emotion and Attention, Center for Research in Psychophysiology, University of Florida, Technical Report C-1, 1999.

[16] P. J. Stone, D. C. Dunphy, M. S. Smith, and D. M. Ogilvie, *General Inquirer: A Computer Approach to Content Analysis*. Cambridge, MA: MIT Press, 1966.

[17] S. Baccianella, A. Esuli, and F. Sebastiani, "SentiWordNet 3.0: An Enhanced Lexical Resource for Sentiment Analysis and Opinion Mining," in *Proc. of LREC*, 2010.

[18] D. Blei, A. Ng, and M. Jordan, "Latent dirichlet allocation," *J. Mach. Learn. Res.*, vol. 3, pp. 993–1022, 2003.

[19] J. Chang, J. Boyd-Graber, S. Gerrish, C. Wang, and D. Blei, "Reading Tea Leaves: How Humans Interpret Topic Models," in *Proceedings of the 23rd Annual Conference on Neural Information Processing Systems*, 2009.

[20] J. Hollan, E. Hutchins, and D. Kirsh, "Distributed Cognition: Toward a new foundation for human computer interaction research," *ACM Trans. Comput.-Hum. Interact. TOCHI*, vol. 7, no. 2, pp. 174–196, 2000.

[21] E. Hutchins, "Distributed Cognition," in *International Encyclopedia of the Social & Behavioral Sciences*, N. J. Smelser and P. B. Baltes, Eds. Oxford: Pergamon, 2001, pp. 2068–2072.

[22] C. J. Hutto, S. Yardi, and E. Gilbert, "A Longitudinal Study of Follow Predictors on Twitter," in *Proceedings of the SIGCHI Conference on Human Factors in Computing Systems*, Paris, France, 2013, pp. 821–830.

System-Level Experimentation: Social Computing and Analytics for Theory Building and Evaluation

Tom McDermott, Molly Nadolski, Dennis Folds
Georgia Institute of Technology
Atlanta, Georgia
Email: tom.mcdermott@gtri.gatech.edu

Abstract— **This paper introduces the concept of shared data experimentation platforms as a means to transform access to and sharing of social science research data. Such platforms are becoming a central component of biomedical research, and are expanding into other fields. We discuss a framework for the development of data analytic experimentation platforms in the social sciences. Social situations are inherently complex adaptive systems that a difficult to generalize without explicitly documenting both the phenomena and related context. We introduce the concept of a "campaign of experiments" that focuses on purposeful exploration of social phenomena in order to evaluate generalizable, reproducible, and repeatable theory. We also propose sociotechnical systems analysis methods to define the appropriate conceptual models of social situations, which can then be used to structure the experimentation data in a form that promotes reuse and replication. We discuss challenges and opportunities associated with an experimentation platform concept, methodologies that can support development of such platforms.**

Keywords-sociotechnical systems; complex adaptive systems; data modeling; conceptual modeling; experimentation.

I. Introduction and Problem Statement

This paper introduces the concept of shared data experimentation platforms as a means to transform access to and sharing of social science research data. Such platforms are becoming a central component of biomedical research, and are expanding into other fields as diverse as international affairs, materials research, and system design. Digital network technologies supporting cloud computing, federated data architectures, knowledge graphs, data mining and machine learning, standardized web ontologies, digital annotation, experimental workflow sharing, computer visualization, crowdsourcing, and computer gaming are creating unprecedented capability for shared study of social behaviors. Although data sharing platforms like Harvard Dataverse are available to share the detailed results of scientific studies, in this paper we discuss the idea of federated data models for experimentation – platforms that allow geographically dispersed cohorts of researchers to work together on scientific experiments around a common problem or area of study. To our knowledge such platforms have not yet entered use in the social sciences community. This paper discusses challenges and opportunities associated with an experimentation platform concept, methodologies that can support development of such platforms, and an example case where a shared experimentation platform would be useful.

Unlike many other scientific areas of study, social situations represent complex adaptive systems that are characterized by independent agents who self-organize, adapt, and learn. In complex adaptive systems, broadly applicable models of behavior are difficult to generalize. The situation under study and the context of the situation must be studied together, and generalization across multiple contexts is not always wise or possible. Adaptation often makes generalized results short-lived. Intervention in social situations focuses heavily on causal relationships, but generalizing to purely linear causal relationships is often unsuccessful. Study of such systems must eventually account for *linear causal* relationships and also *circular causal* relationships, self-organization or *adaptive causal* relationships, and *reflexivity* which acknowledges the act of studying the system can effect causal relationships [1]. Generalization of results using linear regressions is most common and appropriate, but can only be accomplished by applying assumptions with respect to the other three causal models that are often not captured with the data. These assumptions are often about which of a number of potential causes aggregate to larger populations, making explanations of causality difficult.

Because of such "shifts in causality," reduction to linear models make the generalization of effects across multiple contexts difficult. They can also limit the reproducibility and replicability of social science study [2]. Issues related to reproducibility can be reduced by use of common datasets with access to original study data, models, and tools. Study replicability requires access to the original study methods, participants, instruments, and sampling approaches. Generalization requires access to sampling methods as well as both positive and negative results, and more difficult, the original assumptions and abstractions used by the researcher to conceptualize the study. However because many of these assumptions are related to selection of causal factors, effective conceptual models that capture context in the form of broader causal factors with hypotheses related to context-specific selections can help. The ability to do this has been until recently limited by the time and effort required to collect and analyze data, a condition which is changing rapidly.

Designing data analytic and computational models that accurately reflect performance measures at different layers of society, and the aggregation of measures from one layer to the next, is the primary conceptualization problem in social analysis and policy practice. Behavioral aspects of complex sociotechnical systems can be influenced at any layer of the system, but initiatives that try to analyze and improve factors at one level do not necessarily translate into positive influence at other layers. Moreover, the timeframes for measuring effects can vary greatly across different factors and societal layers [3][4]. Lack of common methods and tools to define model abstraction and aggregation of data create further barriers to generalization, which tie back to the original conceptualization of the study and related selection of constructs and dependent variables.

Issues and concerns with use of data analytic methods in social experiments reflect the complex adaptive systems aspects of social phenomena. These include determining appropriate context, understanding both linear and non-linear causality, representing differing time scales, uncertainty about what constitutes entities that affect the system, and issues with agency or agent identification [5]. These can be overcome by viewing the social problem of interest as a system then conceptualizing both the problem system and response system as a set of conceptual and then dynamic models. Research related to enterprise systems of systems and sociotechnical systems analysis introduces a methodology to address these issues.

Shared experimentation implies agreement on paradigms that reflect the problem definition and contexts of interest, as well as the semantic descriptions of the sociotechnical system of interest, and the conceptual model of the current systems' behaviors and future states. The concept of an experimentation platform implies a set of methods and tools to define and address these agreements, which we discuss prior to descriptions of the tool framework.

In Section II, we introduce the concept of an experimentation platform, using references from a United States Air Force concept as an appropriate framework for this application. We describe emerging computer platforms that make this concept a viable approach, and a methodology for building community-wide models in these platforms. In Section III, we describe the characteristics of a tool platform for experimentation, and the technological approaches that might be used to build it. We do not at this point describe a complete toolset, but a call for research to create these tools.

II. EXPERIMENTATION PLATFORM CONCEPT

In this section, we discuss a set of methods and tools that can be applied to social situations in support of a system level experimentation platform.

A. *System Level Experimentation*

Alberts et al. [6][7] captured a useful vision for information age transformation of social theories and related analytics in pursuit of a set of methods we refer to as "System Level Experimentation." The authors define this as a "campaign of experimentation," or a "set of related activities that explore and mature knowledge about a concept of interest." Although developed as an approach for transforming military command and control, the general model of such a campaign provides a framework for joint experimentation in any social decision making domain. The framework is a scientific method for experimentation, which includes theory development, conceptualization or conceptual modeling, formulation of questions and hypotheses, collection of evidence, and analysis. The approach views system transformation as a campaign of multiple experiments that produces a body of knowledge that creates a foundation for future experiments. Such campaigns have leaders and goals, research cohorts who use and create knowledge aligned with the goals, and a shared knowledge capture framework that allows federated cohorts and experiments against a common knowledge model.

With respect to reproducibility, repeatability, and generalization of experiments, the idea of a campaign focuses the research process on aligned goals with deliberate urgency and resource allocation. Alberts and Hayes note, "*reuse here applies to ideas, information about investigations conducted, data collected, analyses performed, and tools developed and applied. In terms of experiments, it implies replication. Reuse, and hence progress, is maximized when attention is paid to the principles of science that prescribe how these activities should be conducted, how peer reviews should be executed, and when attention should be paid to the widespread dissemination of findings and conclusions.*"

The authors stress the importance of a shared conceptual model as a key to generalization, reproducibility, and replicability. Although in many scientific studies there exists a shared paradigm of study and generally shared conceptualization, this is difficult to achieve in social situations where stakeholder perspectives, even those of research communities, are difficult to align. For example the community measurement paradigm for "standard of living" is moving from a Gross-Domestic Product (GDP)-based measure of production to more representative consumption-based representations. However, the GDP measure was conceptually simple, and consumption measures are conceptually complex. Although the community is accepting the paradigm shift, there do not exist common agreed upon conceptual models of standard of living that can drive shared and replicable experimentation. Thus an effective shared experimentation platform must address common conceptualization artifacts as well as data and potentially dynamic models.

B. *Emerging Data Analytics Platforms*

What we can do much more easily these days is collect the data. Public datasets that report social variables in both broad and localized contexts are becoming widespread. Shared community data warehouses and models for experimentation purposes are becoming more widely used in complex health and medical studies, leading one to believe that such approaches may also have use in social research and analysis. Notable examples of medical research platforms include the Global Alzheimer's Association Interactive Network (GAAIN) [8] and the Medical Informatics Platform (MIP) of the European Union's Human Brain Project [9]. Common features of these projects include a federated data model, shared schemas or data codings, machine learning tools for extraction and matching of data, and web-based interfaces to data, research cohorts, and visualizations. In all such projects, a shared database is created where an entity-relationship model defines the schema of the resultant "data warehouse," and agreed upon data codings provide a map between the larger sets of data and the phenomena of interest. We will further explore the possibility of designing similar projects for social data experimentation.

To reach this point, the community must develop not just common data, but also methods for agreement on research paradigms, related stakeholder perspectives of problem and solution spaces, associated viewpoints, and shared conceptualizations. Thus long-term success in social analytics must address the capture of both the data and conceptual relationship models that make the data meaningful. These conceptual relationships are often determined using soft systems approaches, which is appropriate, but existing methods and tools do not adequately connect the conceptual artifacts with the data-driven analytics. In the social analytics field, there is a need for research that connects the resulting collected data to its conceptual model artifacts. Without these problems with abstraction, generalization, reproducibility, and replicability cannot be resolved. Research from the systems engineering community centered on management of enterprise systems-of-systems provides a set of useful methods and tools.

C. Enterprise Systems of Systems Methodology

Sociotechnical systems analysis is a specific methodology that supports assessment of multiple factors across all layers of a complex enterprise or societal construct using sets of tools derived from system science and system modeling. The methods recognize that factors arise from the interaction of many and diverse enterprises that can be defined by their entities, relationships, established processes, pursued strategies, and emergent phenomena. The sociotechnical systems analysis attempts to capture the combined conceptual, data, and analytical modeling artifacts necessary to completely describe the problem [10][11].

With respect to social situations, the method produces a set of artifacts that describe the system context and boundaries, system entities and relationships, primary construct variables, potential causal variables, and phenomena of interest. The process is conducted such that insight can be fed into dynamic computer models. Hypotheses that intervene in lower level causal factors can then be viewed as they aggregate up into larger population behaviors. The sociotechnical systems analysis produces artifacts that communicate the abstractions and aggregation of behaviors across different scales, helping to explicitly document both the assumed and modeled variables.

At the core of a sociotechnical systems model are entities and their relationships, which can be organized into associated databases and warehouses. The entity-relationship model can be created, modified, and refined over periods of short and long term study. Standardized codings of the data entities then make relevant data elements accessible to researchers and analysts. One use of this is for data collection and analysis, but the sociotechnical systems analysis methods are focused on development of experimentation platforms. Experimentation requires that not only the data but also the underlying conceptual models context of study be updated over time.

The conceptual model representations produced by the sociotechnical systems analysis serve as a bridge between the soft systems aspects of the problem (systems thinking) and the quantitative analysis approach (design). This is an area that needs significant additional research as related to methods and tool design. However recent advances in machine learning and semantic graphs can bring the semantic model and mathematical model artifacts into the same toolsets. The bridge between the two is a conceptual model that uses semantic models to specify the analytical models. We identify these as metamodels as they should describe broader conceptual models and data, while individual experiments explore a subset of executable models and constructs related to central questions of interest. Fig. 1 describes that bridge.

We define the soft systems aspects in Figure 1 as "*System Metamodeling*" using three fundamental abstraction approaches: system metamodels, system constructs, and system architecture models. These are determined in a participative, inquiry-based process. We describe hard system aspects as "*Executable Metamodeling*" determined by a specification and design workflow using conceptual models, executable metamodels, and data visualization. It is useful to think about this as a tool framework. The tools support structuring the systems metamodel, creating the conceptual models, creating the executable metamodels, analyzing and visualizing the decision space, and managing the contained knowledge over time [12].

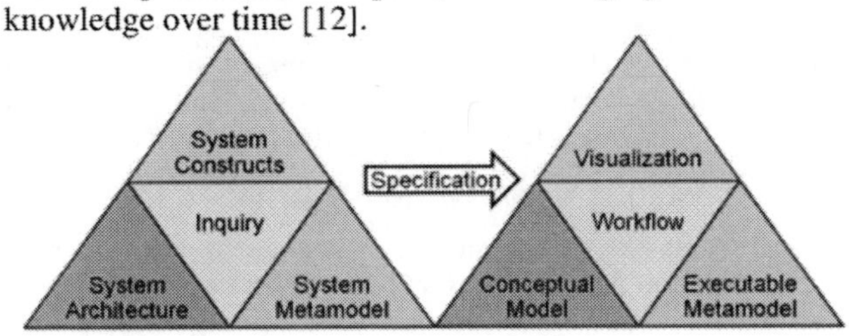

Figure 1. The bridge between soft systems analysis and social analytic model specification.

The system metamodel is described as the set of constructs and rules used to define semantic relationships across information sets, associated data sets, and methodologies or processes [13]. The metamodel definition on the semantic side is an architectural description of the system using modeling views and stakeholder viewpoints. The executable metamodel is the dataset design and any associated computational models.

D. Metamodels and Federated Data Models

The emerging medical community models link together research cohorts by providing a common data model for integrating federated datasets. As experimentation platforms they provide a cohort discovery tool to link research communities, a federated data model integration architecture, and a common data visualization toolset that allows data exploration across multiple cohort data. The federated approach to data model integration allows individual cohorts to maintain their own working datasets while sharing and using data from other cohorts via a common data model representation. State of the art tools for data discovery, transformation, and integration automate most of the source data integration into the common data model. The common data model is implemented as a schema in a relational database using agreed upon codings for data tables and variables.

In a federated data model design, metadata or data descriptions are essential to data harmonization – integrating data from different sets and integrating experimental data back into the common data warehouse. Emerging data mining and machine learning tools can automate data harmonization assuming the metadata has a rich enough natural language description of the data elements to link multiple sets. Mapping variables between federated datasets and the common data model is accomplished by extracting and matching the data entities via descriptive data mapped from element descriptions in data dictionaries, a component of metadata. Adequate metadata provides a path to harmonizing the often cryptic tags placed on data elements in databases. Transformation tools are provided to map data between the common model representation and federated datasets [14].

The conceptualization of most existing common data model examples were developed initially from manual coding and integration of existing datasets [15][16]. In the social analytics area, a common conceptual definition of the data tables and entities would be a huge undertaking due to the tremendous differences in terminology, conceptual data relationships, and assumptions made around data generalizations across societal scales. Emerging approaches for graph representation of data entities and relationships should be explored in the social sciences arena as a tool for amassing large volumes of linked data and knowledge supporting both generalized and contextual research results.

III. Social Experimentation Tool Framework

We present a generalized concept for social experimentation and analytics using both bottoms-up software environment and top-down conceptual architecture descriptions. The purpose of this discussion is not to present the design of an existing tool (none exist), but to describe the characteristics and architectural constructs of future frameworks for social experimentation and analysis. Fig. 2 presents our high level system and process architecture.

Alberts et al. note that "*For purposes of building knowledge, the most important elements are (1) consistent language (clear and operational definitions and measures), (2) explicit use of metatags (meta-data) on data, and (3) clear and complete descriptions of assumptions. These are part and parcel of an explicit conceptual model.*"

A *consistent language* and *use of metatags* relate to the semantic model of the system of interest. This is often described as an ontology, but the term "System Metamodel" is more appropriate. The *description of assumptions* refers to appropriate documentation of construct variables and associated contextual assumptions of lower level abstractions.

The use of inconsistent language to name the data elements in the resulting database is the major limitation of a common data model, it can take years to agree on data element definitions and a static data schema can make the data model difficult to modify. Data element names are often useless to infer meaning. These issues can be abated by consistent mapping generated from data element descriptions in data dictionaries, a primary component of metadata. Data providers that create rich metadata and share this across the data federation will aid in effective model and data sharing. Metadata has additional benefit as it can hide the actual data if it is restricted, without impacting the federation [15]. Data value ranges and units must also be consistent or readable from the metadata.

Three general developments emerging from modern web standards aid in linking different data collections from different domains. The first is the Web Ontology Language (OWL) and widely used Resource Description Framework (RDF) stores such as Google's FreeBase. The standard subject-predicate-object or object-attribute-value framework and semantic linking ease in the standardization of semantic terms and relationships. Various domains are rapidly creating large RDF stores or web ontologies describing their domain. To date relatively little development and standardization of common web ontologies have been undertaken across the social sciences domain. However as researchers opt to use existing ontologies and create domain specific ones, conditions will improve. A consistent language representation is the foundation of a good system metamodel.

A second development is extensive use of web linked data standards. Most database schemas remain defined in eXtensible Markup Language (XML) form but the web community is transitioning to JavaScript Object Notation (JSON) format for standard document annotation and linking of data to research. JSON is a computer language independent format for sharing objects and attribute-value relationships across different datasets, documents, etc. in addition, the use of annotated Hyper-Text Markup Language (HTML) documents to describe research experiments and link input data and results will aid in broader community sharing.

A third area of exploration is the evolution of linked graphs of semantic and mathematical information, an area that

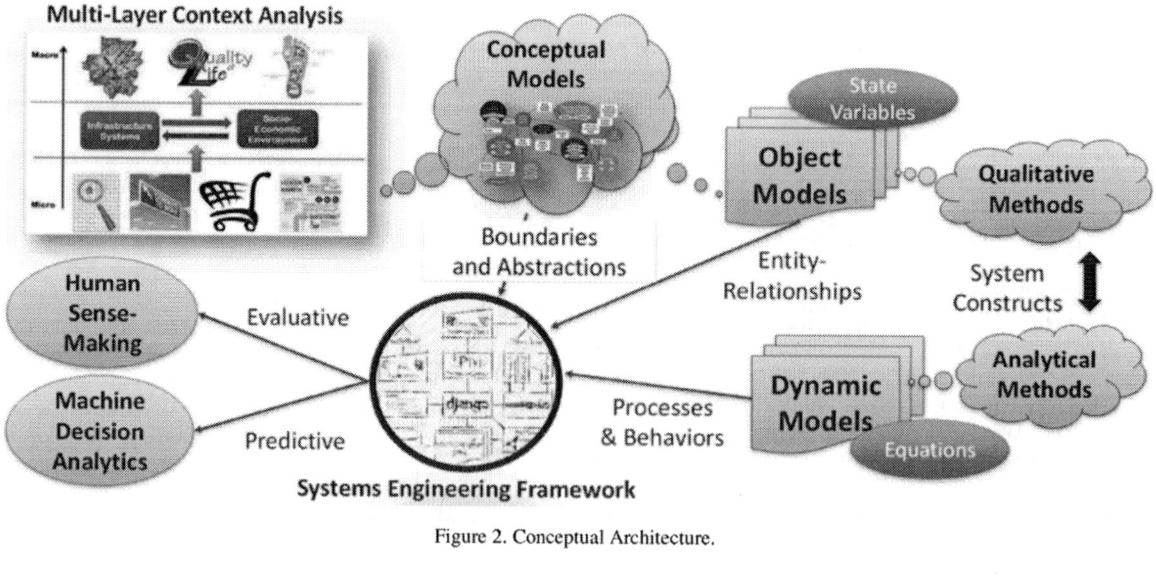

Figure 2. Conceptual Architecture.

is rapidly developing due to Google's introduction of Knowledge Graph and similar entity-driven stores of large information sets. Graph structures support semantic integration and structuring of linked data by compiling text into linked nodes and then relating these to concepts that provide shared meaning to the text. In the graph structure the metadata of our data federation could be linked into a semantic network that can be grown over time with new data. This is an area of needed research; the ability to create large curated sets of community shared and agreed upon causal data and linked experimental results could transform social science research.

A significant hurdle in social science use of these tools is reconciling the linking of different actors' viewpoints to the standard object-attribute-value ontologies. Different actors assign different meaning to social entities and relationships, making contextual features of language by the actor an important variable. The specific meaning associated with the language used by different actors requires a different structuring of shared ontologies than used in most of these applications today. This is an area for further research.

Finally, the use of these new technologies does not inherently capture the conceptualizations that defined that data to be important in the first case, and it does not capture assumptions made about missing data elements in the graph. Discerning real causality from experimental measurement of a social construct often requires a qualitative analysis of the underlying causal variables that cannot be measured directly. This is an underlying conceptual model that is often not fully documented in the research results, particularly those potentially causal variables that were purposefully not assessed in the research. This is where context becomes critical – discussions of why these variables are assumed to be causal in this context versus different variables in another context – becomes a key component of the knowledge base. Existing computer-based data models and analytical models are not linked to their conceptual parent models, primarily because the available modeling tools have not been built. A related area of research is specific to this problem, which is how to formally link more freeform conceptual diagramming or facilitation artifacts with more constrained formal modeling and simulations tools.

The "clear and operational definitions and measures" noted by Alberts et al. [7] in the military context is a difficult hurdle in less well governed social situations. Operational definitions and measures in social situations tend to be an area of great debate between different communities of interest. A GAAIN-like common data model is doomed to fail unless we can also define methods and tools to reach agreement on the conceptual models that drive entities, relationships, data definitions, and assumptions. Much of this disagreement involves data conceptualization, definition, and abstraction/aggregation at different scales (for example macroscale measures like "GDP per capita" versus microscale measures like "owning a dishwasher" – both used to describe standard of living). Emerging computer approaches to semantic integration offer hope for much richer microscale measurement sets, as long as the community can clearly see the need for research in this area.

IV. CONCLUSIONS

We discussed a concept for a social experimentation and data analytics platform based on emerging data and model federations that are emerging in medical and other research areas. This type of platform has not been explored for use in social science research, although the type of tools and technologies that can be applied are finding broad use in other disciplines.

The differences between social science research and other domains of research make a platform of this type much more difficult to envision and build. Problems of data abstraction and aggregation, differing actor viewpoints, and differing conceptualizations of system models make traditional data federations too expensive and time consuming to maintain. However emerging technologies associated with linked data, knowledge graphs, machine learning, and conceptual design tools provide a research base to explore implementation of social data experimentation platforms. This summary paper describes the concept as a means to encourage such exploration.

REFERENCES

[1] S.A. Umpleby, "Second-order science: logic, strategies, methods," Constructivist Foundations 2014, vol. 10, no. 1, pp. 16-23, 15 November 2014.

[2] K. Bollen, J Cacioppo, R.M. Kaplan, J.A. Krosnick, and J.L. Olds, Social, Behavioral, and Economic Science Perspectives on Robust and Reliable Science, Report of the Subcommittee on Replicability in Science, Advisory Committee to the National Science Foundation Directorate for Social, Behavioral, and Economic Science, May 2015.

[3] J. Rotmans, R. Kemp, and M. van Asselt, "More evolution than revolution: transition management in public policy", Foresight, vol. 3, no. 1, pp. 15-31, February 2001. ISSN 1463-6689.

[4] F.W. Geels, "Technological transitions as evolutionary reconfiguration processes: A multi-level perspective and a case-study." Research Policy, vol. 31, pp. 1257–1274, 2002.

[5] R. Wagner-Pacifici, J.W. Mohr, and R.L. Breiger, "Ontologies, methodologies, and new uses of Big Data in the social and cultural sciences," Big Data & Society, vol. 2 iss. 2, pp. 1-11, December 2015. DOI: 10.1177/2053951715613810.

[6] D.S. Alberts, R.E. Hayes, D.K. Leedom, J.E. Kirzl, and D.T. Maxwell, Code of Best Practice for Experimentation, Washington DC: CCRP Publication Series, 2002.

[7] D.S. Alberts and R.E. Hayes, Code of Best Practice for Campaigns of Experimentation: Pathways to Innovation and Transformation, Washington DC: CCRP Publication Series, 2002.

[8] www.gaain.org, retrieved: July 2016.

[9] www.humanbrainproject.eu/mip, retrieved: July 2015.

[10] W. B. Rouse and D. Bodner, Multi-level modeling of complex socio-technical systems – phase 1, A013 - final technical report, SERC-2013-TR-020-2, Systems Engineering Research Center, 2013.

[11] W. B. Rouse and M. Pennock, Multi-level modeling of socio-technical systems a013 - final technical report, SERC-2013-TR-020-3, Systems Engineering Research Center, 2013.

[12] T. McDermott and D. Freeman, Systems thinking in the systems engineering process: new methods and tools, in Systems Thinking: Foundation, Uses and Challenges, Eds. Frank, Shaked, Kordova, Nova Publications, 2016.

[13] J. Ernst, "What is metamodeling, and what is it good for," http://infogrid.org/trac/wiki/Reference/WhatIsMetaModeling, retrieved: November 2015.

[14] N. Ashish and A.W. Toga, "Medical data transformation using rewriting," Frontiers in Neuroinformatics, vol. 9, no. 2, pp. 1-8, 20 February 2015. doi: 10.3389/fninf.2015.00001

[15] N. Ashish, P. Dewan, JL Ambite, and A.W. Toga, GEM: The GAAIN Entity Mapper, in Data Integration in the Life Sciences, 11th International Conference, DILS 2015, Eds. Ashish, N. and Ambite, J., Springer 2015.

The Lightweight Smart City and Biases in Repurposed Big Data

Christian Voigt
Technology & Knowledge
Centre for Social Innovation
Vienna, Austria
voigt@zsi.at

Jonathan Bright
Oxford Internet Institute
University of Oxford
Oxford, UK
jonathan.bright@oii.ox.ac.uk

***Abstract*— This paper addresses the implications of 'big data' on the smart city paradigm. In addition to grids of sensors to track traffic flows or monitor service delivery, urban governments around the world are starting to experiment with repurposing stores of data collected by third parties: using mobile phone data to track movement or social media to identify failing services. The use of this type of data has considerable potential to both augment the existing smart city vision and to spread it out to small and medium sized cities that are unable to afford investment in sensor grids, creating what we call a "lightweight" version of the smart city. However, it also implies a number of problems which previously smart cities were less prone to. After defining the lightweight smart city this paper reviews these challenges, mainly in the area of interpretation biases, before offering pointers to potential remedies and solutions.**

Keywords- ***Smart City; Big Data; Interpretation Biases.***

I. INTRODUCTION

Urban policymakers and planners are increasingly challenged by the scarcity of relevant and intelligible data, available in the policymaking contexts, particularly with the increased interest in accountability and transparency. The movement towards "smart cities" has often been presented as a way of fixing these problems. The smart city vision sees, as Kitchin puts it, "pervasive and ubiquitous computing and digitally instrumented devices built into the very fabric of urban environments" [1]. These devices promise a step change in the amount of data available to policymakers, and their corresponding ability to both create policy and respond to changing situations.

However, the smart city movement has been recently attracting more skepticism, for a variety of reasons. Some reports have highlighted the high up-front costs of installing large sensor grids, which in many cases seem to have been allied to relatively low returns [2]. These costs have also meant that, rather than spreading throughout the world, smart city technology is largely limited to a few urban megacities and one off projects, such as Songdo in South Korea and Masdar in Abu Dhabi. Furthermore, smart cities have been strongly criticized for promoting technological lock-in, by encouraging cities to sign large scale contracts with the IT services firms providing the infrastructure [1] [3], another factor which discourages investment on the part of governments. Finally, a variety of reports have critiqued the underlying focus of smart cities on business and enterprise, at the expense of other more progressive goals [4]. In this context, it is interesting to note the growing enthusiasm for "big data" within the smart cities movement. Big data is a concept which has attracted a variety of definitions [5], but for our purposes the key characteristic is that at least part of the definition involves a move to *creatively repurpose large stores of data which have been created as a by-product of another social activity*; for example, the use of Google query patterns to detect flu outbreaks [6], or Wikipedia search data to predict electoral outcomes [7] [8]. Big data are being drawn into a huge variety of fields and being used for a wide variety of different purposes. However, their use in the field of smart cities is particularly interesting: by offering the promise of relatively cheap, already collected data, they seem to provide a possibility for the smart city vision to break through some of the financial and technological barriers which currently impede it, and start being implemented around the world.

Our paper assumes a distinct social science perspective, as we focus on the societal implications that come with such a fundamental change in urban governance as the use of big data. Big data is effectively hailed as a game changer, turning classic hypothetico-deductive research into inductive analyses of big data [9]. Such grandiose statements try to establish a market for big data technologies from public, private-sector companies, such as IBM, Google, Facebook or Twitter. What is needed though, and increasingly delivered [10] [11], is a critical reflection on the inclusiveness of 'smart city' benefits, as well as a discussion of possible unintended effects, such as future dependencies in terms of data or technology lock-ins. It is useful to remember that cities have been trying to be 'data smart' before, e.g., using predictive computational models to address complex problems including city safety and public health in the 1960s [12]. But, as pointed out by Shelton et al. [11], "the fact that similar discourses are uncritically recycled by contemporary proponents of the smart city is troubling". The main aim of this article is to remedy this deficit, by discussing the potential implications of using *repurposed* big data in terms of information quality and potential interpretation biases. Its structure is guided by the following questions and thoughts:

- What difference could big data make in addressing some of the barriers to smart city adoption? We select prominent examples of smart city technologies and examine their potential from a social science perspective. On the basis of this discussion, we develop the concept of the "lightweight" smart city.

- What challenges might come with repurposed 'big data'? To avoid the trap of replacing old problems with new ones, we discuss some of the inherent challenges of governing cities by 'big data'.
- We conclude by opening up the discussion, suggesting a number of supportive activities, which make smart city services more accessible to an increasing number of cities and citizens.

The paper is organized as follows: section 2 introduces possible application scenarios for big data in smart cities. Then, section 3 gives an overview of known interpretation biases and their implications for lightweight smart cities. Finally, section 4 concludes with a discussion of measures to remedy distorting effects of interpretation biases and additional research needed.

II. How Repurposed Big Data Affects the Smart City Vision

As we describe above, using big data to drive smart cities involves enriching the vision (as described in [1]) of urban government using data provided by ubiquitous computing and sensor grids with the option of urban government making use of repurposed data coming from third parties, such as mobile phone companies and social media outlets [55]. In this section, we discuss the principal benefits of this move. The discussion is divided into three sections. First, we look at areas where repurposed big data can replace data generated by sensor grids. Second, we look at the use of big data to augment smart city technology (rather than replacing it), by optimizing the deployment of scarce resources and by providing new types of information. We conclude by arguing that big data offers the potential to provide a "lightweight" version of the smart city, which could potentially open up the smart city movement to a far greater range of cities, being less of a burden to already strained city budgets.

A. Sidestepping smart city sensor grids

The first way in which big data can support the smart city vision is in providing the potential for cheap data collection which does not require the installation of large scale sensor grids. Co-opting data from companies with stores of big data, such as mobile phone operators and social media providers is of course not cost free: license fees may need to be purchased, computing infrastructure may need to be set up to host the data, and skilled staff may be required to collect and process it. An example of this is provided by a recently completed collaborative study between Google and tw Netherlands Organisation for Applied Scientific Researchin Amsterdam [13]. They analyzed the extent to which anonymized urban mobility data from their Android mobile phone platform could be used to replace traffic sensor data on a 10 kilometer long stretch of highway. The results showed that the mobile phone data could duplicate the data provided by the sensors with high accuracy, "potentially saving €50,000 Euro per year [on that 10 km stretch of road alone] if the redundant sensors were removed". The potentially cheaper nature of data collection is allied to a second benefit, which is potential ease of implementation. To give an example of this, consider two different approaches to automatic failure detection in street lights, one found in Los Angeles and the other in the small town of Jun in Spain (which has just a few thousand inhabitants). Los Angeles has recently started rolling out smart LED street lighting along 4,500 miles of roads [14]. These lights communicate automatically with the bureau of street lighting, letting them know in particular if they are broken. This could be considered a classic implementation of part of the "smart city" vision: elements of the city themselves are able to communicate with government. The town of Jun, by contrast, has no such smart street lighting. However, what they have instead is a centralized effort to place the entire town on Twitter: everyone in city government and the vast majority of the residents have a Twitter account, and citizens are encouraged to interact with the government through this platform. The Huffington post gives an example of the way this works in practice [15], highlighting a case where a citizen noticed a streetlight had gone out, and sent a tweet to the mayor about the issue. The mayor responded that it will be fixed, with the Twitter handle of the engineer responsible also included, who himself tweeted the day after to notify that the streetlight had been fixed. Jun, in other words, have a kind of crowdsourced "smart" streetlight system [16] [17], with very rapid notification coming from citizens themselves.

B. Augmenting smart cities by optimizing resources and providing new data

Of course, there are many areas where repurposed big data will not be complete enough or accurate enough to fully replace smart city technology (or indeed parts of already existing government). However, in these cases, big data might still have a role to play in terms of optimising resources. For example, TomTom has recently started cooperating with Dutch police authorities, selling information about driver velocity from its Global Positioning System (GPS) tracking devices [18]. This information could not be used to directly convict people of speeding, both because it likely does not have the required degree of accuracy and also because of the concern TomTom itself would have to protect the privacy of its consumers. However, the authorities made use of the aggregate data to find the areas where speeding was most likely to occur, and then placed their mobile traffic cameras at these locations. In this case, big data does not replace the sensor grid, but rather augments it. Another example of this comes from the Mayor's Office of Data Analytics in New York [19]. One of the early successful projects this office worked on was a way to target restaurants which were illegally disposing of cooking oil into the city's sewers, something which was responsible for a considerable amount of blockages in the sewer system. The office compared data on restaurants which did not have an official oil disposal system with geographic information on sewer locations and blockages, in order to identify likely suspects of illegal dumping. These suspects were then visited by inspectors. Again, what this example shows is that this kind of big data technique does not replace existing information capture techniques used by cities. Rather, it augments them, allowing them to be directed more accurately and efficiently. Furthermore, there are also areas where big data driven smart cities go beyond its sensor driven counterpart. To characterize broadly, automatic sensors can be roughly classified into one of two types [20]–[22]. First there are sensors, which measure and report on characteristics of the physical environment, such as heat, light, the composition of the atmosphere, or the presence of physical objects. These types of sensors could, in a smart city context, provide real time indications of pollution, or measure water levels to check for flooding risks, automatically detect faults in lighting networks, etc. Second, there are sensors which not only report on the environment but try and capture data on the characteristics or behavior of people. However, there are still a great deal of policy relevant pieces of information smart city sensors cannot collect (i.e., which fall outside of these two types of sensor). This is where repurposed big data offers a chance to go further. For example, health problems are a key area of concern for policy makers. As is by now well known, Google has shown that it is capable of characterizing the size and duration of flu outbreaks from its search data [23], a result which has recently been extended to Wikipedia [24]; as well as other types of disease, such as dengue fever [25]. Another example would be the opinions and thoughts of citizens themselves on policy relevant topics, which a number of recent reports have flagged up as a potential source of information on policy specific topics, such as changes to a city's public transport system or opening a new shopping center [26] [27]. These examples demonstrate that big data offers a potential window into types of data which sensor driven smart cities could never hope to provide.

C. *Towards a lightweight smart city?*

In the terms that we have described them above, repurposed big data offers the potential for the implementation of a kind of "lightweight" version of the smart city. A lightweight smart city, based on repurposed big data, is like lightweight software in many respects. It is relatively cheap and easy to get going, requiring little special technological infrastructure to start up. Lightweight software is developed in order to increase the potential user base of the software: by making it easier to install and use, more people may take it up. Lightweight smart cities have similar potential consequences, potentially dramatically expanding the number of cities which can engage in "smart" programs. Thus far, almost all examples of smart city work come from large and economically powerful cities: in the UAE, in Singapore, in the US, in South Korea. These cities possess an obvious advantage for smart city work, which is that they have considerable budgets which can be put in to the creation of sensor grids. Small and medium scale cities are effectively shut out of the process. However, while offering much potential promise, the lightweight city also has an inherent potential challenge: the data being used within the city is no longer created or even owned by the city itself.

III. POTENTIAL BIASES IN BIG DATA FOR LIGHTWEIGHT SMART CITIES

In this section, we will move on to consider some of the challenges that a big data driven smart city faces, framed around the concept of bias. First off, we need to acknowledge that there is no agreed canon of terms and technologies, which constitute the 'smart cities' label. Hence, many criticisms to smart cities could possibly be discarded with reference to a different understanding of 'big' or 'smart' [9]. Smart city proponents claim that being empowered by new technologies (sensor enabled cars and streets, metered energy and water supply or people always connected and always tracked), governance is revolutionized, becoming more inclusive, performative and efficient [28]. Underlying these claims is a new paradigm of data-driven transparency or as New York's mayor Bloomberg is quoted "In God we trust. Everyone else, bring data." [29]. Although big data is probably as fuzzy a concept as smart city; the five Vs including volume, variety, velocity, veracity and value commonly describe big data [30]. Initially, there were only 3 Vs (volume, variety, velocity) and when the primarily technological challenges were solved, veracity and value was needed to justify the substantial investments made by smart cities [31]. However, we will argue that interpreting big data correctly and extracting value might be less straightforward than what we think. Biasing effects are a known phenomenon in information systems research, see [32] for a systematic overview. In general cognitive biases are not inherently detrimental to human judgment and decision making. Information filters, i.e., biasing the available information by not paying equal attention to all sources, are necessary mechanisms to deal with the constant influx of potentially useful data urban decision makers experience on a daily basis. Yet, Kahneman and Tversky showed that these filters are not always applied on a consistent and rational basis [33]. Depending on its presentation, the same data is perceived important or not (framing bias); similarly, data that is linked to recent events is more likely to influence people's decision making than data which is known to be important but has not had any recent appearance (recency bias). Hence, even though big data applications are meant to process vast amounts of heterogeneous data, this does not mean that biasing effects in designing and interpreting big data analyses would disappear. Jagadish [30] addresses a number of myths about big data including the misconception that big data automatically produces deep insights, without a need for theories. Multiple decisions are made, before big data analyses produce results. Following the big data life-cycle [30], these decisions concern *acquisition, cleaning, aggregation, modeling* and *interpretation* of data, decisions which in turn influence content, consistency and comprehensiveness of big data. However, the degree of comprehensiveness or consistency that can be realistically expected, depends on the problems big data analyses are applied to [34]. The following sections explore some examples of interpretation biases of mostly social media related big data.

A. *Selection bias: How inclusive are the data sources?*

Even though big data is generally said to be on the raise, access to big data might still hamper widespread analysis and research. Hence, the type of data cities might repurpose for their own uses can be limited. For example, control over the use of available data from most social media websites is restricted by service providers' business models, wherefore accessing large quantities tends to be either impossible or costly. An exception is Twitter, which allows users to access large parts of their historical data. Depending on the Twitter API (e.g., Twitter's freely available search or streaming APIs, or Twitter's commercial Firehose service) and the type of information requested, different amounts of Tweets can be acquired, ranging from tenth of thousand to several millions of tweets [35]. The availability of Twitter data has led to a number of studies investigating the use of Twitter as proxy for urban life or events impacting urban life. Nonetheless, prominent examples of Twitter's influence, such as the Arab Spring, the Obama elections or the Occupy Wall-street Movement, are often criticized due to a lack of systematic and more nuanced research [36]. Being aware of selection biases, we need to ask what a given set of big data is representing or suppressing, and whether our inferential claims are justified. For example, Arribas-Bel et al. [37] monitored geo-located Twitter activities (on average 1% of all tweets are geo-tagged) in order to understand activity levels in specific neighborhoods. The authors could show that activities in the virtual world of Tweets reflected expected behaviors as suggested by land use specifications (office space, residential area, tourism and leisure). In this instance, non-probabilistic sampling had been applied without drawing mistaken conclusions. However, there are questions about the inclusiveness of smart city data and their ability to represent elderly and economically isolated citizens [38]. Offenhuber reminds us that what citizens expect from smart cities is likely to be different depending on citizens' socio-economic status [39]. Citing the example of Boston where less affluent neighborhoods reported significantly less city maintenance issues through digital channels than areas that were better off. Offenhuber showed that there was not a lack of needs that prevented citizens from reporting more maintenance issues, but a mix of digital divide effect as well as a discomfort with calling on those who are accountable for city maintenance.

B. *Attentional bias: Are causations claimed where there are none?*

Whereas the neighborhoods analysis above discussed the issue of social media's representativeness of groups and activities in the physical city, Tufekci [40] highlights another issue which concerns the validity of conclusions drawn. Tufekci was observing social media used around Turkey's Gezi Park protests, exemplified by the use of the #jan25 hashtag. A frequency count over time showed a significant decline of the hashtag's use during June 2013. Concluding that the actual protest was declining in June, however, would have been far from correct, the topic became just so dominant that the hashtag was almost superfluous and was used less. This example is to illustrate that any data driven analysis might have blind spots, wherefore a theory is still needed, even though some big data proponents predict the end of theory as correlation supersedes causation [41]. The issue is magnified since with ever larger data sets, the likelihood of getting statistically significant results increases, leading to a proliferation of claims based on data patterns unrelated to the real world [42], also known as clustering illusion or the Texas sharpshooter fallacy [43].

C. *Framing bias: Does data interpretation reflect data collection?*

There is often an unstated assumption that 'hard' data is objective. Yet the matter of data is a matter of interpretation. Wilson [44] differentiates between the factual, representative side of data and its imaginative, urban-political side. In fact, as shown by the author, data can be used for diametrically opposed purposes. For example, citizens geo-mapped urban aspects, such as potholes or graffiti, which were simultaneously used to inform city officials about needed repairs as well as feeding into a 'desirable cities ranking' [44]. Clearly, whereas very active mapping would potentially lead to improvements of the build environment, it could also negatively impact the city's ranking and consequently the city's attractiveness for investors or a neighborhood's development prospects. Framing biases are also closely related to our assumptions about the nature of urban governance problems and the role scientific management and smart technologies can play. Criticism of prevalent 'Command-and-control' structures of IT-aided urban management in the 60s, highlighted already the inadequacy of cybernetic feedback loops, based on sensors, change actuators and controllers [45]. Goodspeed provides the example of urban renewal and freeway constructions and describes the situation as a wicked problem, one that has multiple, competing descriptions and where the solution requires value judgment and taking sides (i.e., land use decisions might create jobs and displace people at the same time) [45]. Clearly, there is no overriding single value that can be evoked in order to consent on the best decision. Hence, in such situations hard collective decisions need to precede the use of big data. The consideration of complex second and third order consequences cannot be delegated to big data if transparent decision making is a firm objective of smart cities.

D. *Information bias: Are some data more convenient than others?*

Information bias refers to the unwarranted over-interpretation of data; either through the way we classify, match and display data [46] or through including irrelevant data into their decision making and gain confidence where caution might be in order [33]. The classic example for the latter is Tversky and Kahneman's experiment of people ascribing jobs or study results to descriptions of people, containing little or no relevant information with regards to the question. The authors found that stereotypes, such as the clothing of librarians or a high degree of internal consistency of an in other ways completely irrelevant description of a person influenced people's confidence in their judgment considerably. Information bias can become a serious issue, when we think about predictive policing and the use of big data in law enforcement. New York City alone has 3,000 public surveillance cameras, 200 automatic license plate readers, 2,000 belt-mounted radiation sensors and diverse police databases [47]. This sensor driven city is then analyzed to identify high risk areas based on past crimes, but also circumstantial factors, such as text-mined tweets or Facebook postings related to specific areas [47]. As a consequence, these areas receive more police attention. Could big crime data replace human judgment in determining situations of reasonable suspicion, which would then lead to further investigations? Predicting citizens' behavior based on big data might represent a new privacy challenge, but as commented in [42], observational data are mostly generated and analyzed without citizens' knowledge and in public or open online spaces, where there is no right to be let alone. While privacy advocates call for a proper due process that ensures the right to be informed about how big data adjudicated a given course of action (police, land use permission, etc.) [48], others demand a more equitable distribution of riches made from user-generated content [42].

IV. Discussion

The smart city debate used to be about performance and competitiveness. Now we can arguably see a more inclusive debate emerge, addressing the reality of many small and medium-sized cities not being able to offer broadband in all city areas (let alone installing expensive sensor networks monitoring street lightening). Repurposed big data provides the potential for these cities to also innovate in the smart city debate. However, as shown in the previous section on biases, the lightweight smart city does not become automatically more inclusive by relying on smartphones and social media, mainly because these technologies are not equally distributed or used across all social groups. Still we think the benefits of the lightweight smart city outweigh the risks of biased interpretations. Being aware of the difference between data purposefully collected for urban management and repurposed, often social media-driven 'big data' is a first step to mitigate harmful effects of interpretation biases. Possibly biased data were also used prior to the raise of 'big data'. Simplified models of complex socio-economic systems can be as misguiding as uncritically following big data analyses. What is needed are dynamic interpretation and sense-making processes, that can supplement - rather than replace - urban management relying on traditional data sources, such as surveys, neighborhood meetings or purposeful observations. For repurposed 'big data' to be integrated successfully, urban management processes need to adhere to the proven principles of transparency and stakeholder participation.

Transparency. Early examples of master-planned cities have mostly reflected normative assumptions about 'good citizenship' [49], when in fact a substantial body of literature suggests that cities thrive on spontaneous encounters between people from all walks of life generating a collective creativity, which might get lost if people feel trapped in a virtual panopticon. Hence, cities need to be transparent about the data they collect and in what sense this data is repurposed. Even though reducing the opaqueness big data analytics (e.g., through required consultation and approval steps) can undo the efficiency gains also pursued by big data analytics [50]. Yet, more important than efficiency is the fairness of decisions - with or without the use of 'big data' -, wherefore citizens need a due process to question big data logic and, if necessary, police any unfair discrimination [51].

Participation. Greenfield smart city projects have shown that cities cannot be designed with technologies alone, smart cities understood as socio-technical challenges need socially rich innovation system, that enable learning, iterative experimentation and progressive social embedding of new technologies with existing stakeholders [49].

Limitations and future work. So far the paper has not covered a number of trends, such as the decreasing cost of sensors and wireless networking which avoids costly cabling [52]. Also, the emerging 'maker movement' might well enable cities to crowdsource data from citizens' sensors. Future research needs to explore the extend to which social media can support smaller cities if they do not have such a strong usage pattern as the Italian city of Jun or if privacy concerns motivate citizens to disable location tracking on their smart devices, so that it becomes increasingly difficult to geo-locate social media data. In the end, the question will be whether the lightweight smart city is better equipped than current variations of smart cities to address issues of economic growth as well as social inequalities.

Acknowledgment

The UrbanData2Decide project is funded under the Joint Programming Initiative Urban Europe (2014 -2016).

References

[1] R. Kitchin, "The real-time city? Big data and smart urbanism", GeoJournal, vol. 79, no. 1, pp. 1–14, 2014.

[2] T. Saunders and P. Baeck, "Rethinking Smart Cities From The Ground Up | Nesta", 2015.

[3] G. Graham, "Too-smart cities? Why these visions of utopia need an urgent reality check", The Guardian, 13-Mar-2014.

[4] R. G. Hollands, "Will the real smart city please stand up?", City, vol.12, no.3, pp. 303-320, 2008.

[5] V. Mayer-Schönberger and K. Cukier, Big Data: A Revolution that Will Transform how We Live, Work, and Think. Houghton Mifflin Harcourt, 2013.

[6] D. Lazer, R. Kennedy, G. King, and A. Vespignani, "The Parable of Google Flu: Traps in Big Data Analysis", Science, vol. 343, no. 6167, pp. 1203–1205, 2014.

[7] T. Yasseri and J. Bright, "Predicting elections from online information flows: towards theoretically informed models", [Available from: http://arxiv.org/abs/1505.01818]

[8] T. Yasseri and J. Bright, "Can electoral popularity be predicted using socially generated big data?", it - Information Technology, vol. 56, no. 5, pp. 246–253, 2014.

[9] C. Rabari and M. Storper, "The digital skin of cities: urban theory and research in the age of the sensored and metered city, ubiquitous computing and big data", Cambridge Journal of Regions, Economy and Society, vol. 8, pp.27-42, 2014.

[10] S. Abiteboul et al., "The elephant in the room: getting value from Big Data", in Proceedings of the 18th International Workshop on Web and Databases, pp. 1–5, 2015.

[11] T. Shelton, M. Zook, and A. Wiig, "The 'actually existing smart city'", Cambridge Journal of Regions, Economy and Society, vol.8, pp. 13-25, 2014.

[12] A. Townsend, "Cities of Data: Examining the New Urban Science", Public Culture, vol. 27, no. 2 76, pp. 201–212, 2015.

[13] A. Eland, "Google Europe Blog: Tackling Urban Mobility with Technology", 2015. [Online]. Available: http://googlepolicyeurope.blogspot.co.uk/2015/11/tackling-

urban-mobility-with-technology.html?m=1. [Accessed: 15-Mar-2016].
[14] A. Rogers, "8 Cities That Show You What the Future Will Look Like", Wired Magazine, Available from: https://www.wired.com/2015/09/design-issue-future-of-cities/, [Accessed: 15-Mar-2016].
[15] W. Powers and D. Roy, "The Incredible Jun: A Town that Runs on Social Media", Huffington Post, 20-Apr-2015.
[16] D. C. Brabham, Crowdsourcing, London: MIT Press, 2013.
[17] V. Lehdonvirta and J. Bright, "Crowdsourcing for Public Policy and Government", Policy & Internet, vol. 7, no. 3, pp. 263–267, Sep. 2015.
[18] B. Waterfield, "Tom Tom sold driver"s GPS details to be used by police for speed traps", The Telegraph, 28-Apr-2011.
[19] E. Copeland, "Big Data in the Big Apple: The lessons London can learn from New York's data-driven approach to smart cities", Available from: http://capitalcityfoundation.london/wp-content/uploads/2015/06/Big-Data-in-the-Big-Apple.pdf, [Accessed: 15-Mar-2016].
[20] S. Tilak, N. B. Abu-Ghazaleh, and W. Heinzelman, "A taxonomy of wireless micro-sensor network models", ACM SIGMOBILE Mobile Computing and Communications Review, vol. 6, no. 2, pp. 28–36, Apr. 2002.
[21] I. F. Akyildiz, Y. Sankarasubramaniam, and E. Cayirci, "A survey on sensor networks", IEEE Communications Magazine, vol. 40, no. 8, pp. 102–114, Aug. 2002.
[22] N. Xu, "A Survey of Sensor Network Applications", IEEE Communications Magazine, pp.1-9, 2002
[23] J. Ginsberg et al., "Detecting influenza epidemics using search engine query data", Nature, vol. 457, no. 7232, pp. 1012–1014, Feb. 2009.
[24] K. S. Hickmann et al., "Forecasting the 2013-2014 Influenza Season using Wikipedia", vol.5, no.2, pp.1-15, 2015.
[25] N. Generous, G. Fairchild, A. Deshpande, S. Y. Del Valle, and R. Priedhorsky, "Global disease monitoring and forecasting with Wikipedia", PLOS Computational Biology, vol.10, no.11, pp.1-16, 2014.
[26] "Social Media and Public Policy, September 2013 | The Alliance for Useful Evidence". [Online]. Available: http://www.alliance4usefulevidence.org/publication/social-media/. [Accessed: 29-Feb-2016].
[27] "Use of social media for research and analysis - Publications - GOV.UK". [Online]. Available: https://www.gov.uk/government/publications/use-of-social-media-for-research-and-analysis. [Accessed: 29-Feb-2016].
[28] C. Harrison et al., "Foundations for smarter cities", IBM Journal of Research and Development, vol. 54, no. 4, pp. 1–16, 2010.
[29] L. Hoffmann, "Data mining meets city hall", Communications of the ACM, vol. 55, no. 6, pp. 19–21, 2012.
[30] H. V. Jagadish, "Big data and science: Myths and reality", Big Data Research, vol. 2, no. 2, pp. 49–52, 2015.
[31] E. Pinkerton and D. N. Edwards, "The elephant in the room: the hidden costs of leasing individual transferable fishing quotas", Marine Policy, vol. 33, no. 4, pp. 707–713, 2009.
[32] P. J. Kirs, K. Pflughoeft, and G. Kroeck, "A process model cognitive biasing effects in information systems development and usage", Information & Management, vol. 38, no. 3, pp. 153–165, 2001.
[33] A. Tversky and D. Kahneman, "Judgment under Uncertainty: Heuristics and Biases", Science, vol. 185, no. 4157, pp. 1124–1131, 1974.
[34] R. Clarke, "Big data, big risks", Information Systems Journal, vol. 26, no. 1, pp. 77–90, 2016.
[35] F. Morstatter, J. Pfeffer, H. Liu, and K. M. Carley, "Is the sample good enough? comparing data from Twitter"s streaming api with Twitter"s firehose", arXiv preprint arXiv:1306.5204, 2013.
[36] Z. Tufekci and D. Freelon, "Introduction to the special issue on new media and social unrest", American Behavioral Scientist, vol. 57, no.7, pp. 843-847, 2013.
[37] D. Arribas-Bel, K. Kourtit, P. Nijkamp, and J. Steenbruggen, "Cyber Cities: Social Media as a Tool for Understanding Cities", Applied Spatial Analysis and Policy, vol. 8, no. 3, pp. 231–247, 2015.
[38] A. Glasmeier and S. Christopherson, "Thinking about smart cities", Cambridge Journal of Regions, Economy and Society, vol. 8, no. 1, pp. 3–12, 2015.
[39] D. Offenhuber, "Infrastructure legibility—a comparative analysis of open311-based citizen feedback systems", Cambridge Journal of Regions, Economy and Society, vol.8, no.1, pp. 93-112, 2015.
[40] Z. Tufekci, "Big questions for social media big data: Representativeness, validity and other methodological pitfalls", arXiv preprint arXiv:1403.7400, 2014.
[41] C. Anderson, The end of theory: The data deluge makes the scientific method obsolete. Available: https://www.wired.com/2008/06/pb-theory/, 2008 [Accessed: Sept. 2016].
[42] H. Ekbia et al., "Big data, bigger dilemmas: A critical review", Journal of the Association for Information Science and Technology, vol. 66, no. 8, pp. 1523–1545, 2015.
[43] H. D. Shane, Standard Deviations: Flawed Assumptions, Tortured Data, and Other Ways To Lie with Statistics, The Overlook Press: London, 2014.
[44] M. W. Wilson, "Data matter (s): legitimacy, coding, and qualifications-of-life", Environment and Planning D: Society and Space, vol. 29, no. 5, pp. 857–872, 2011.
[45] R. Goodspeed, "Smart cities: moving beyond urban cybernetics to tackle wicked problems", Cambridge Journal of Regions, Economy and Society, vol.8, pp. 79-92, 2014.
[46] P. Brey, "Values in Technology and Disclosive Computer Ethics", in The Cambridge Handbook of Information and Computer Ethics, pp. 41–58, 2010.
[47] E. E. Joh, "Policing by Numbers: Big Data and the Fourth Amendment", Washing. Law Review, vol.89, pp.35-68. 2014.
[48] K. Crawford and J. Schultz, "Big data and due process: Toward a framework to redress predictive privacy harms", BCL Rev., vol. 55, p. 93, 2014.
[49] L. Carvalho, "Smart cities from scratch? A socio-technical perspective", Cambridge Journal of Regions, Economy and Society, vol.8, no.1, pp. 43-60, 2014.
[50] T. Zarsky, "The Trouble with Algorithmic Decisions An Analytic Road Map to Examine Efficiency and Fairness in Automated and Opaque Decision Making", Science, Technology & Human Values, vol. 41, no. 1, pp. 118–132, 2016.
[51] D. K. Citron and F. A. Pasquale, "The scored society: due process for automated predictions", Washington Law Review, vol. 89, no.1, pp.1-33, 2014.
[52] G. P. Hancke and G. P. Hancke Jr, "The role of advanced sensing in smart cities", Sensors, vol.13, no.1, pp. 393–425, 2012.

SEA-SF : Design of Self-Evolving Agent based Simulation Framework for Social Issue Prediction

Joonyoung Jung, Euihyun Paik, Jang Won Bae, Dongoh Kang, Chunhee Lee, and Kiho Kim
Data Analysis Software Research Section
Electronics and Telecommunications Research Institute
Deajeon, Korea
e-mail: jyjung21@etri.re.kr

***Abstract*— Simulation is the imitation of the operation of a real-world process or system over time. Actual real world expectation is expensive and impossible because the modern society is complex and various. Therefore, simulation can be carried out to take proper measures for the problem which may be happened in the future. Agent based model (ABM) models each individuals and interactions among them. ABM mostly defines behaviors based on rule. However, ABM simulation has the weak point that simulation error is accumulated. If long term simulation is conducted, the simulation result will be highly inaccurate because of error accumulation. To overcome error accumulation, the model should be reconfigured using the real data recursively. In this paper, we propose the self-evolving agent based simulation framework (SEA-SF). The SEA-SF is consisted of data management, change recognition, model evolvement, ABM reconfiguration, user interface and ABM simulation environment. The SEA-SF should mitigate the long-term simulation error. Therefore, the SEA-SF performs change recognition between real data and simulation result. And then autonomously, it updates model parameters or the model configuration to increase accuracy of simulation. The proposed framework can be applied to solve the social issue problems because the social issue problems are happened through a long period. Therefore, the social issue simulation, such as the house policy and supply, can be performed using the proposed SEA-SF.**

Keywords-Simulation; Agent Based Model; Self-Evolvement.

I. INTRODUCTION

Simulation is the imitation of the operation of a real-world process or system over time [1]. Simulation is used for predicting future in various fields. Simulation can be carried out to take proper measures for the problem which may be happened in the future. For example, the birthrate, the rearing of children, income, employment and education may be simulated in the field of society. So, various features of social members can be predicted. The policy of social security service can be established using the result of simulation which predicts socio-demographic characteristic. Therefore, the social problem, such as low birthrate and aging, can be prevented.

Social issue prediction has been accomplished both macrosimulations and microsimulations. The macro simulation predicts the overall tendency of the social issue using the stochastic approach of entire social structures and characteristics. However, the microsimulation could predict the behavior and characteristic of each member related with the social issue. Therefore, the cause of social phenomena could be analyzed variously by the microsimulation. Therefore, population dynamics is simulated by microsimulation to analyze various social features recently.

Actual population expectation is expensive and impossible because the modern society is complex and various. Therefore, microsimulation modeling (MSM) and agent based modeling (ABM) are used for modeling and simulation. Microsimulation models the individuals with real data and defines behaviors based on transition probabilities derived from micro data. ABM models individuals and interaction between the individuals. ABM mostly defines behaviors based on rule. However, these technologies have the weak point that simulation error is accumulated. If long-term simulation is conducted using these technologies, the simulation result is highly inaccurate because of error accumulation.

To overcome error accumulation, the model should be evolved using the real world data recursively. In this paper, we propose the self-evolving agent based simulation framework.

The rest of the paper is organized as follows. Section II describes related work. In Section III, we describe the architecture of self-evolving agent based simulation framework. In Section IV, we describe the proposed framework for social issue prediction, and some concluding remarks are finally given in Section V.

II. RELATED WORK

Most social issues, such as a lower birthrate problem and an aging phenomenon, relate with population dynamics. Therefore, the microsimulations of population dynamics have been performed for a long time. A MSM describes a system at the micro-level and the system is consisted of micro units. G. H. Orchtt [2] proposed a new type of model, MSM, of a socio-economic system in 1957. He described the model which was consisted of various sorts of interacting units. The outputs of each unit were related to prior events and were the result of a series of random drawings from discrete probability distributions. The appropriate probability distributions were determined by inputs into the unit and the operating characteristics of the unit. The units of this new type of model might be large aggregates, such as markets or industries, but they were elemental decision-making entities, such as individuals, families, firms, labor unions, and governmental units. He represented individual units in the socio-economic system and analyzed the units' behaviors. MSM could facilitate and improve prediction about socio-economic aggregates and could be used either for short-run or long-run forecasting by appropriate selection of initial conditions and by altering the number of periods the model is run. A. Harding [3] described that dynamic population MSM provided one of the most useful available modelling tools for projecting the future distributional consequences of possible policy changes. He contended that the construction of a reliable dynamic population MSM for use in social policy formulation is a very demanding multi-year project. Nowadays, a lot of countries have implemented the dynamic population microsimulation models for predicting the future population and preparing a countermeasure. For example, the dynamic simulation of income model (DYNASIM3) was developed by USA for designing to analyze the long-term distributional consequences of retirement and ageing issues [4]. The dynamic microsimulation model (DYNAMOD 1 & 2) was developed by Australia for modeling economic and demographic change in the Australian population over time, such as superannuation, age, education, health, and housing policy [5][6].

An agent is a micro unit that can decide its own behaviors based on environment, its own state, and interaction with other agents. Therefore, each agent independently acts according the rules of the simulation and their own preprogrammed behaviors. And more, each agent is free for activity with the ability to make independent decisions [7]. ABM means that individuals have characteristic of the agent. T. C. Schelling [8] proposed the segregation model using ABM in 1971. He described a model that individual members of two recognizable groups distribute themselves in neighborhoods defined by reference to their own locations. The most previous works in the field of ABM have been proposed on dynamic demography, such as household demography [9] and population dynamics [10]. However, the previous ABMs are not able to evolve the structure and parameters of model autonomously. Therefore, when long-term simulation is performed, the simulation error is accumulated, according as times go on. In this reason, we propose the self-evolving agent based simulation framework (SEA-SF) to reduce the long-term simulation error.

III. SEA-SF ARCHTECTURE

The SEA-SF is an agent based simulation framework in order to reduce long-term simulation error. Therefore, the SEA-SF should perform change recognition between real data and ABM simulation result. And then autonomously, it should change model parameters or the model configuration to increase accuracy of simulation using the change recognition result. In the SEA-SF, there are some component modules as shown in Fig 1. First of all, the data management module (DMM) collects domain data and saves the data in database (DB). So, the domain data digitization and DB management are required in this module. Second, the change recognition module (CRM) estimates the difference between real world data and simulation result. So, data trace and change recognition is required in this module. Third, the model evolvement module (MEM) defines the strategy how to evolve the present model autonomously. The machine learning is required to micro-level and macro-level model evolvement. Forth, the ABM reconfiguration module (ARM) changes the model parameters or structure according to the evolving strategy. So, the agent should be consisted of the components. And the ARM also includes the ABM simulation engine to execute ABM simulation. Fifth, the user interface module designs the initial model and visualizes a simulation result. And more, simulation is conducted in distribution and parallel computing environment to improve simulation performance.

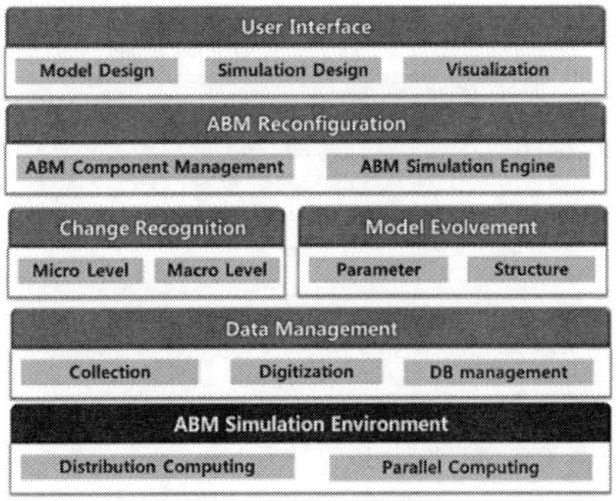

Figure 1. SEA-SF Architercure.

In these modules, the essential modules are CRM, MEM, and ARM. Therefore, these important modules are described more detail below.

A. *Change recognition*

Change recognition detects the difference between the real world data and the simulation result as shown in Fig. 2. The CRM is consisted of the data trend analysis (DTA), feature point extraction (FPE), error estimation (EE) and change recognition (CR) function.

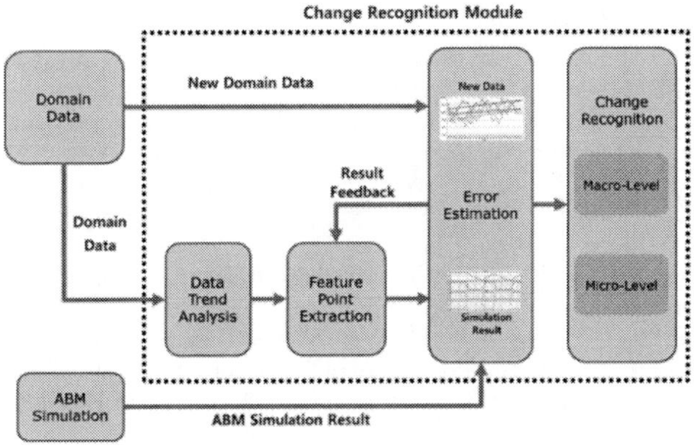

Figure 2. Change recognition.

The domain data are received from DMM, and then the DTA analyzes these data for detecting data trend using machine learning, such as Hidden Markov Model. The FPE extracts the comparison point for EE using the results of DTA and the feedback from EE. The EE estimates error between the ABM simulation result and new domain data, and then the result of EE is sent to the FPE and CR. The CR estimates whether the change is detected or not. Whenever the change is recognized either micro-level or macro-level, the CRM informs the MEM of the result of CR.

B. Model evolvement

MEM performs micro-level and macro-level evolvements to make agent evolvement strategy and environment transition strategy as shown in Fig. 3.

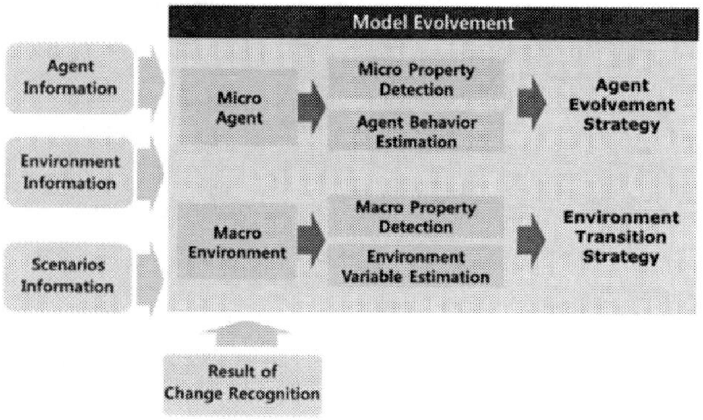

Figure 3. Model Evolvement.

The MEM receives data, such as agent information, environment information, scenarios information and the result of CR, from the DMM and CRM to perform model evolvement. The MEM is consisted of micro agent and macro environment function. The micro agent's property and the agent's behavior are estimated to make the agent evolvement strategy. The macro property of environment is detected and the environment variable is estimated to set out the change recognition direction of environment. This module informs ARM of the agent evolvement and environment transition strategies.

C. ABM reconfiguration

The ARM reconfigures ABM using component, previous ABM, and model evolvement strategy as shown in Fig. 4.

ABM is consisted of agents, environments and interaction among these. The component of ABM means the behavior of agent, property of environment and interaction among agents and environment. For ABM reconfiguration, ABM should be componentized because structure and parameter of ABM are reconfigured using these components autonomously. The previous ABM is the ABM before reconfiguration is performed. ABM based simulation is conducted using this model and produces the simulation result in CRM. The model evolvement strategy (MES) is the result of MEM to reconfigure the ABM.

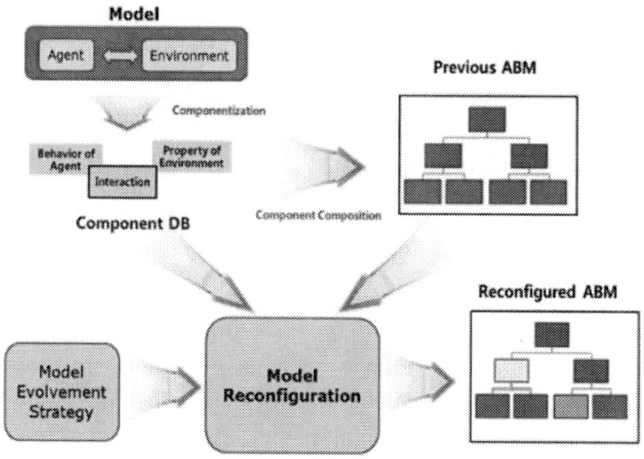

Figure 4. ABM reconfiguration.

Whenever the ARM receives the MES from the MEM, it reconfigures model using the component information, its own present ABM and MES. According to the request of MES, the model is reconfigured at parameter level or structure level.

IV. SEA-SF FOR SOCIAL ISSUE PREDICTION

The proposed framework can be applied to solve the social issue problems because the social issue problems are happened through a long period. Among the social issue problems, this framework can be applied to the house policy and supply. That is, the effect of government policy, such as house policy, is analyzed macro-level and micro-level on socio-economics, such as house supply, as shown in Fig. 5.

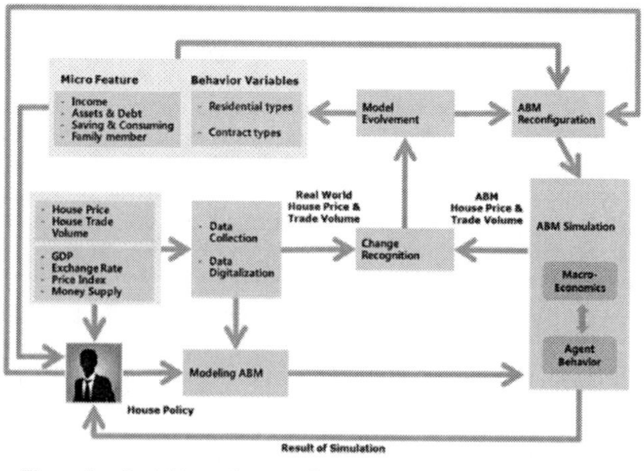

Figure 5. Social issue, house policy and supply, simulation using the SEA-SF.

The leading economic indicators related to the house price and trade volume are gross domestic product (GDP), exchange rate, price index and money supply. These economic data, such as GDP and house price, are collected and digitalized. The ABM is designed using these data and the policy decision factors, such as interest rate, rebuilding and rental house. The ABM simulation is performed using economic data, agent behavior and interaction. The CRM receives real world data and ABM simulation result about the house price and trade volume. Whenever this module recognizes the difference between these data, it notifies the result to MEM. The MEM evolves the present ABM using machine learning approach. It changes the micro features of agent, such as income, assets, debt, family member, saving and consuming, and agent behavior variables, such as residential types and contract types. The ARM reconfigures previous ABM using the changed ABM parameters and structure autonomously. The decision maker can also change the present policy to reconfigure the ABM. The result of evolved ABM simulation is compared with real world data at the CRM. These processes are repeated recursively. Therefore, the long-term simulation error can be reduced by SEA-SF.

V. Conclusion And Future Work

This paper addressed the design of SEA-SF for social issue prediction. The simulation result may be inaccurate in a long-term simulation because the simulation error is accumulated. In this reason, the model of simulation should be evolved using change recognition method. We describe the architecture of the SEA-SF. It is consisted of DMM, CRM, MEM, ARM, user interface and ABM simulation environment. Among these modules, CRM, MEM and ARM conduct essential role of the self-evolving ABM. CRM detects the difference between the real world data and the simulation result and informs MEM of it. The MEM performs micro-level and macro-level agent based model evolvement. The ARM reconfigures ABM using component, previous ABM, and MES. The proposed framework can be applied to solve the social issue problems, such as house policy and supply, because the social issue problems are happened through a long period.

We will implement the proposed framework to simulate a social issue problem, such as house price of South Korea.

Acknowledgment

This work was supported by the IT R&D program of MKE/IITP, [R-20160224-002790, Development of Predictive Analysis Technology on Socio-Economics using Self-Evolving Agent-Based Simulation embedded with incremental Machine Learning].

References

[1] J. Banks, J. Carson, B. Nelson and B. Nicol, "Discrete-event system simulation," Prentice Hall, 1984.

[2] G. H. Orchtt, "A new type of socio-economic system," The review of economics and statistics, vol. 39, no. 2, pp. 116-123, May 1957.

[3] A. Harding, "Challenges and opportunities of dynamic microsimulation modelling," Plenary paper presented to the 1st General Conference of the International Microsimulation Association, Vienna, Aug. 2007.

[4] M. Favreault, and K. Smith, "A primer on the dynamic simulation of income model (DYNASIM3)," Urban Institute, Feb. 2004.

[5] S. Antcliff, "Introduction to DYNAMOD: a dynamic population microsimulation model," Technical Paper No 1, National Centre for Social and Economic Modelling (NATSEM), University of Canberra, 1993.

[6] A. King, M. Robinson, and H. Baekgaard, "DYNAMOD-2: An overview," Techincal Paper No. 19, National Centre for Social and Economic Modelling (NATSEM), University of Canberra, Dec. 1999.

[7] A. Getchell, "Agent-based modeling," Physics, pp. 757-767, Jun. 2008.

[8] T. C. Schelling, "Dynamic models of segregation," Journal of mathematical sociology, vol. 1, pp. 143-186, 1971.

[9] N. Geard, J. M. McCaw, A. Dorin, K. B. Korb, and J. McVernon, "Synthetic population dynamics: A model of household demography," Journal of Articial Societies and Social Simulation, 16(1) 8, Jan. 2013.

[10] K. Singh, M. Sajjad, and C. W. Ahn, "Towards full scale population dynamics modelling with an agent based and micro-simulation based framework," International Conference on Advanced Communication Technology (ICACT), pp. 495-501, Jul. 2015.